Preface

Computing audit requires a thorough understanding of three areas, namely:

(1) audit methodology, tools and techniques;
(2) the specific controls relevant to the area of data processing;
(3) information and computing technology.

This book covers all three parts, each part in four chapters. Part I, on audit and controls, attempts to establish in chapter 1 the meaning of controls and why they are necessary. It further examines, in chapter 2, the role of audit and the nature of its role in data processing. Chapters 3 and 4 then examine the essential controls, and control objectives, in application computing systems and the systems development process.

Part II, on systems development, is devoted to the system development process and chapter 5 covers the particular methodology known as the systems development cycle (SDC). Chapter 6 looks in detail at the different aspects of project management and chapter 7 tackles particular methods that may be applied within the framework of the SDC such as constraint identification, problem analysis, data analysis, functional analysis, etc. Chapter 8 looks at one particular strategy, prototyping, that has become favoured in recent years with the evolution of fourth generation software.

Part III, on systems development auditing, deals with the specific role of the auditor in the systems development process. Chapter 9 looks at the general audit methodology, tools and techniques which form part of the auditor's essential trademark. Chapter 10 discusses a methodology for the selection and evaluation of the framework of controls in the systems development process. This is followed by chapter 11, which describes a methodology by which the computing auditor may practically assist in designing the application framework of controls for a computing system. Finally, chapter 12 deals with the methodology for the review of a system following implementation and further to a period of practical operational experience.

There is much excellent literature available in all of these areas, some of which the author has listed in the references. However, there does not appear to be anything available in the area of systems development auditing that brings all the strands together, between two covers, and written in a form that is easily and quickly digestible.

The objective of this book is not an attempt to re-invent the wheel but to bring together material, which is now widely dispersed, to serve as a reference book for those involved in the audit of the systems development process as well as other persons who may be involved in the systems development area. Finally, the author does claim some originality within this book especially in the application of risk and exposure analysis in the area of selecting and evaluating system development controls.

B J T

September, 1987

AUDITING THE DEVELOPMENT OF COMPUTING SYSTEMS

AUDITING THE DEVELOPMENT OF COMPUTING SYSTEMS

B J TRAVIS, BSc, BSc(Econ), DIP Marketing, FCMA
Senior Computing Auditor, Shell UK Exploration and Production

London
Butterworths
1987

United Kingdom	Butterworth & Co (Publishers) Ltd, 88 Kingsway, LONDON WC2B 6AB and 61A North Castle Street, EDINBURGH EH2 3LJ
Australia	Butterworths Pty Ltd, SYDNEY, MELBOURNE, BRISBANE, ADELAIDE, PERTH, CANBERRA and HOBART
Canada	Butterworths. A division of Reed Inc., TORONTO and VANCOUVER
New Zealand	Butterworths of New Zealand Ltd, WELLINGTON and AUCKLAND
Singapore	Butterworth & Co (Asia) Pte Ltd, SINGAPORE
South Africa	Butterworth Publishers (Pty) Ltd, DURBAN and PRETORIA
USA	Butterworths Legal Publishers, ST PAUL, Minnesota, SEATTLE, Washington, BOSTON, Massachusetts, AUSTIN, Texas and D & S Publishers, CLEARWATER, Florida

© Butterworth & Co (Publishers) Ltd 1987

British Library Cataloguing in Publication Data

Travis, B.J.
    Auditing the development of computing systems.
    1. Electronic digital computers
    2. Electronic data processing departments —— Auditing
    I. Title
    004   QA76.5
    ISBN 0 406 50093 2

Printed in Great Britain by Billing & Sons Ltd, Worcester

To Els, Andrew, Elizabeth, Richard, Stephanie

Contents

PART 1

Audit and controls

1 Risk, exposure and controls

This chapter discusses the meaning, and relationship, of the terms risk, exposure and control, as they apply in the business context, and particularly with regard to computing systems. It also attempts to explain why controls are necessary and emphasizes that controls have both a cost and a hindrance factor and must, therefore, be used with discretion.

Risk is defined as the possible occurrence of some form of adverse event that results from an action taken by an individual, a private, corporate or public enterprise, etc as a result of which, they become vulnerable. The risk is a penalty which is exacted against the decision maker. Business enterprises are concerned principally with financial risk and they become vulnerable through the acquisition of resources. The wider the range of resources, under their control, the wider the range of adverse factors—'threats'—which may operate against those resources.

A business enterprise may obtain an overall picture of the risk situation by constructing a risk matrix in which the resources are shown on the vertical axis and the threats to those resources, along the horizontal axis. An exposure may be defined as the product of the value of a particular resource and the probability of occurrence of the adverse factor or threat. The risk matrix may be converted into an exposure matrix by inserting the monetary value of the exposures calculated in this way. Thus, the exposure is a quantitative assessment of the risk.

Controls are defined as any means by which a business enterprise seeks to minimise or prevent an exposure by acting against the threats that cause the exposure. The objectives of controls in computing systems are to ensure:

(1) security;
(2) privacy;
(3) accuracy;
(4) completeness;
(5) effectiveness;
(6) efficiency.

The controls which satisfy these objectives may be preventive, detective or corrective.

1. RISK AND VULNERABILITY

Risk arises, in the first instance, because of vulnerability which is due to an action taken by an individual, a private business, a corporate or a public enterprise, etc and which may result in the occurrence of some form of adverse event. There are different types of risk, of greater or lesser seriousness, which result in a penalty being exacted against the decision maker. Thus, if I, as a private individual, decide to drive my car upon the road I become vulnerable to the limitations of other road users as well as my own, possibly inept, capabilities of handling my vehicle. These factors, which create the risk, may be referred to as threats.

The consequences which may arise, should I be involved in an accident, are some form of penalty which may range from minor damage to my vehicle and to myself, to more serious consequences such as the loss of my right to be a road user, ie to the loss of my licence. These may also include a financial penalty such as a fine being imposed, the cost of repairing my own and possibly a third party's vehicle, and even a loss of my employment. Thus, the risk which the private individual faces, in these circumstances, may or may not be financial in nature. He may face the risk either of physical injury or of financial loss.

In a similar way, a private business, a corporate or public enterprise may become vulnerable by some action which it takes and which results in a penalty being exacted. This penalty is usually of a financial nature although, in the case of a public enterprise, it could be the loss of goodwill which may or may not have financial consequences. In a private or corporate enterprise, the penalties will always have financial implications since the ultimate test of any action is its effect on the profit/loss account and balance sheet—whatever may be said otherwise. Thus, the risk which is faced, in this case, is one of financial loss and not of physical injury.

A private, corporate or public enterprise, or even an individual becomes vulnerable—incurs a risk—by the employment of resources at its command. The risk may be described under the following headings, namely:

—liquidity;
—motivation;
—uncertainty;
—time.

These factors, and their implication for risk, are discussed in the following sections.

2. RISK AND LIQUIDITY

A private citizen, whose income exceeds his expenditure, will generally seek some means of deploying his surplus funds in order to earn a return, which is referred to as interest. He may, however, simply leave his funds lying idle in a current account, in a bank, which will yield him nothing but has the advantage that he has immediate access to his money.

If he decides to employ his surplus funds gainfully, there are numerous opportunities available to the individual with widely varying rates of return. Some examples of these are shown in **Figure 1**.

At one end of the scale are investments which yield a minimum return as, for example, a deposit account in a bank; at the other are those which yield a

Figure 1 Risk and liquidity

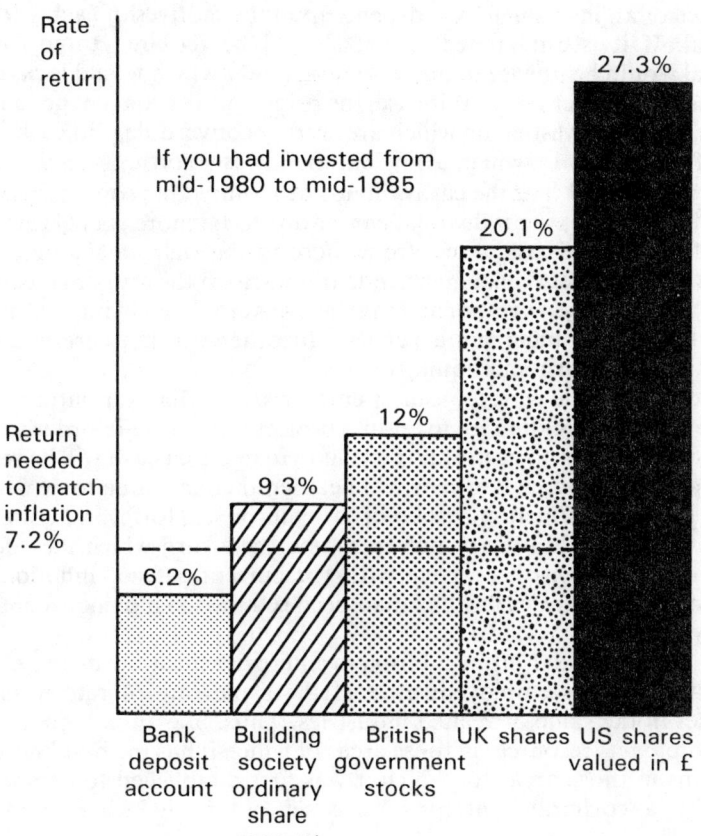

Rate
of
return

If you had invested from
mid-1980 to mid-1985

27.3%

20.1%

12%

Return
needed
to match
inflation
7.2%

9.3%

6.2%

Bank
deposit
account

Building
society
ordinary
share
account

British
government
stocks

UK shares

US shares
valued in £

substantially higher return such as shares in an industrial enterprise.These differ essentially in the ease with which they can be converted back again into cash, ie their liquidity. Liquidity then is the convenience of holding cash as opposed to some form of pseudo-cash like a bank deposit or industrial shares.

Money invested in a deposit account in a bank or building society may be retrieved with no prior notice being given but there may be a limit on the total withdrawal at any one time. To retrieve money invested in industrial shares depends upon someone being willing to purchase those shares and the price they are prepared to pay, which may be substantially lower than the seller's original purchase price. In the former case, there is a high degree of liquidity, or ease of conversion back to cash, and in the second case liquidity could be much more restricted if no-one wishes to purchase the shares.

3.   RISK AND MOTIVATION

The choice of an investment will depend upon the motives of each particular individual. If it is anticipated that cash will be required tomorrow, the individual would be unwise to make an investment which would lock up cash for a considerable period. In this case, the prime motivation will be to remain liquid, ie acquire investments which are readily convertible into cash—those to the left in **Figure 1**—which also yield the lowest return.

If it is anticipated that the cash will not be required for some considerable period in the future, the individual can afford to be more speculative in the choice of investments and select from those to the right in Figure 1. Thus, there is a trade off between a higher rate of return on the investments and the ease with which the investment may be converted back into cash again without the risk of incurring a penalty. In other words, there is a choice between rate of return and liquidity.

In exactly the same way, a business enterprise, of whatever nature, has the choice to make in deciding to invest in a project or venture in order to earn a return which we refer to as profit. If it is anticipated that cash will be required in the near future, which it always will be, then there must be some degree of liquidity in the investment portfolio of the enterprise. However, liquid assets, as we have seen, yield little or no return and the return which they do yield may be inadequate to keep pace with the current rate of inflation; as is shown, in **Figure 1**, for cash which had been retained in a bank account over the five-year period.

If it is to survive and grow, a business enterprise must be able to earn, on its capital resources employed, at least the same rate of return as other enterprises in the same or related industries. Thus, like an individual, it will seek to employ its resources in those areas of which it has the best knowledge. This means in those areas for which it was first established to compete and which, for a corporate enterprise, are set out in its Memorandum of Association.

4.   RISK AND UNCERTAINTY

In the two cases discussed in **3.**, there is a considerable difference in the degree of certainty with which the investments may be converted back again into cash. This ranges from almost complete certainty with the bank deposit—not totally complete because banks have been known to fail—to considerable uncertainty with the industrial shares.

In other words, in the one case there is almost no risk and in the other, there may be a high degree of risk. Thus, the risk arises, in this situation, from uncertainty of the future—in the above case, the future retrieval of the cash— and the further ahead, in terms of time, the greater the degree of risk involved. In making an investment for a long period of time, we are attempting to forecast the future conditions that will prevail when we attempt to retrieve our money.

The uncertainty is due to the possibility of change which may take place between the time we first invest our money and the time at which we expect to convert our investment back again into cash. If the time period is short between these two events occurring, then the possibility of change is more restricted than if the interval is a long one.We are more confident of predicting changes which may take place between today and next week, than of forecasting the events which might take place over the next few years.

5. RISK AND TIME

Business investments are generally of a long-term nature which implies that there is a high degree of illiquidity, as well as uncertainty and, therefore, a high degree of associated risk, ie that some form of adverse event will occur during the investment period which will result in a penalty. The payback period ie number of time periods before the enterprise recovers its original investment, and starts to earn a profit, may be several years, if ever. During this period, there may be violent changes in the market conditions which substantially affect the viability of the venture.

In the early 1970s, under the influence of OPEC, there occurred a sharp escalation in the price of crude oil from around $1.5-2 per barrel (at which level it had been priced for more than a decade) to a peak of around $35 per barrel by the early 1980s, as shown in **Figure 2.**

This rapid change in market conditions encouraged the major independent oil companies to seek alternative sources of supply for the raw material on which their business was based. One particular area that appeared promising was the UK sector of the North Sea, for gas had already been discovered in the North of Holland where the geological formations were similar.

Exploration soon met with success and gas was found for the first time in the southern North Sea in late 1965. By the end of 1984, oil and gas were being produced from 35 North Sea fields and taken ashore through 2,300 miles of underwater pipelines or by tanker. To achieve this has, so far, entailed £46 billion in investment (in 1984 money terms) and must be considered to be one of the technological miracles of the twentieth century.

However, the remarkable success of the oil independents in finding oil placed increasing strain on the OPEC producers, as their share of world markets began to decline, with the rising glut of crude oil supply. In mid-1985, with increasing disarray amongst the OPEC producers, the price of crude oil crashed on the world markets and, at one time, came down under the $10 per barrel figure for the first time in over 10 years.

This has left the oil companies with massive hardware investments in the North Sea, in platforms and pipelines, which are totally illiquid. It is not easy to convert pipelines on the floor of the sea bed back into ready cash, even should this be desirable.

6. RISK AND EXPOSURE

The acquisition of investments, as we have seen, is accompanied by a risk which arises from uncertainty with regard to the future. This risk may be expressed in financial terms as the value to the enterprise of the particular resource and the probability of the occurrence of an event (threat) acting

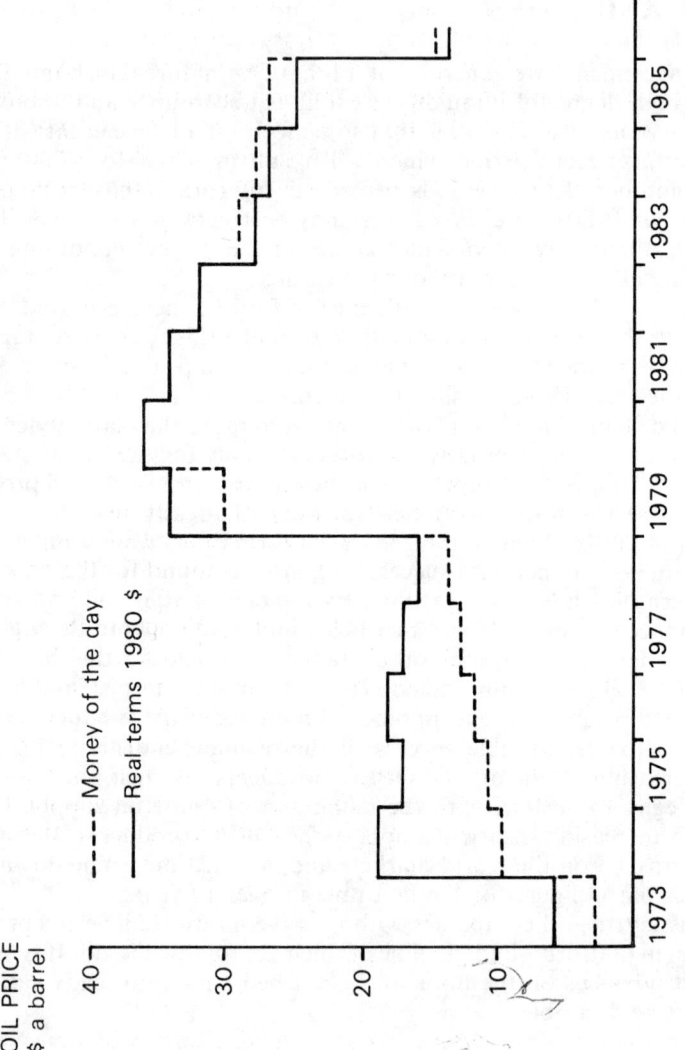

Figure 2   Risk, uncertainty and time

OIL PRICE
$ a barrel

----- Money of the day

——— Real terms 1980 $

Based on the price of Arabian light crude on the Rotterdam Spot Market

adversely against that resource. The resulting monetary value of the risk is referred to as the exposure which the enterprise faces. The exposure is created by an act, such as the purchase of property, plant or equipment, which makes the enterprise vulnerable, or more vulnerable, to forces which are detrimental to those assets which we have already referred to as threats.

The exposure is greater the higher the level of investment, and the less liquid the investments, ie the longer the period before the recovery of the cash outlay, and the greater the volatility of outside forces which act on the resources of the enterprise. One of the objectives, in any investment decision, must be to reduce the level of exposure to an acceptable level for that enterprise. The investment of £20K to some enterprises may require the same degree of consideration as the investment of £20,000K to another. The message is essentially that, in a gambling situation, it depends upon how much you can afford to lose and, we must never forget, that an investment decision is essentially a gambling situation.

7. RESOURCES AND THREATS

It should be clear, at this stage, that there are two factors that operate to create an exposure, namely a resource and a threat which operates adversely against that resource. In this context, resources are not only balance sheet resources such as cash and pseudo-cash, property, plant and equipment,etc but also non-balance sheet assets such as people, systems and procedures by which the balance sheet assets are operated and, most important for computer systems, data—especially data on how effectively those other resources are being used. This is illustrated in **Figure 3.**

In simplistic terms, a business enterprise commences operation with people and cash. At this stage, the threats to the enterprise are minimal since the range of resources is strictly limited and so is the complexity of the enterprise. However, as the business develops, and the cash is expended in a variety of ways, the range of resources grows and, at the same time, so does the vulnerability with the range of threats which may act adversely upon those resources. We have already seen that the acquisition of fixed assets, of any kind, reduces the liquidity of the enterprise and so creates a potential cause of exposure.

8. RISK MATRIX

If it is to survive and develop, a business enterprise must seek some means to minimise or prevent the potential exposures with which it is faced. As part of the corporate planning process and/or in the planning of any new project, eg computing project, or venture, the business would be wise to construct a customised risk matrix along the lines of **Figure 4.**

The risk matrix simply shows the resources employed by the business, project or venture on the vertical axis with a list of potential threats against those resources along the horizontal axis. The process of actually construct-ing the risk matrix is a valuable exercise in its own right, because it helps to

Figure 3   Resources and threats to an enterprise

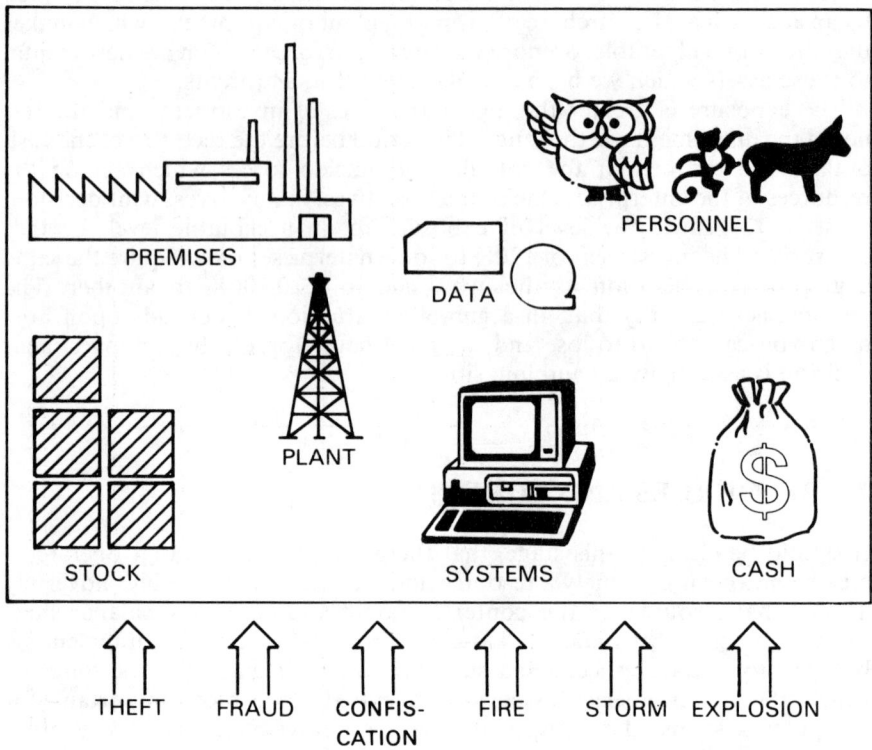

focus the mind on areas of potential danger to the enterprise even, perhaps, before any threats actually arise. This helps the enterprise to produce contingency plans to combat exposures before the actual occurrence of the threats which cause them.

A simple example may be used to illustrate the concept of the risk matrix in contingency planning. If a business purchases property, plant and equipment it becomes vulnerable to risk by reducing its liquidity and by committing its resources for a long time period. The acquisition of fixed resources of this nature exposes the enterprise to threats such as fire, storm, wilful damage, etc which may result in a destruction of these resources and to an interruption of the business of the enterprise. Thus, the business enterprise would be well advised to make contingency plans for the occupation of temporary premises in the event of some disaster, as mentioned above, as well as to have a spare set of accounting records retained in an alternative location so that the business may continue to operate. This we refer to as providing fallback facilities and it is an important issue in the use of computing systems.

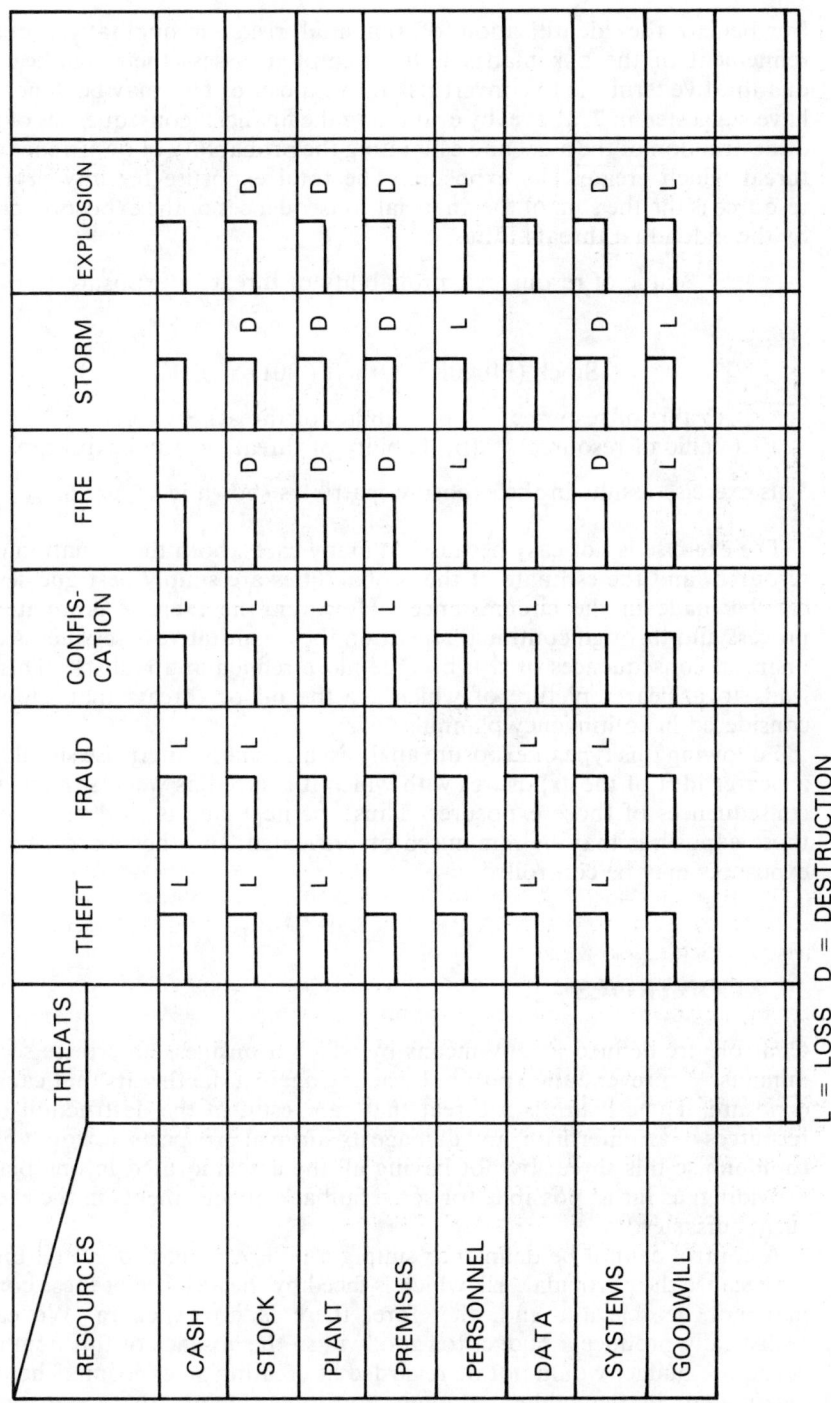

Figure 4   A company risk matrix

9.   EXPOSURE MATRIX

Further to the identification of potential risks in qualitative terms, a refinement of the risk matrix is to attempt to assess their significance in quantitative terms, ie to convert risk into exposure. This may be done, as we have suggested in **7.** above, by evaluating the financial consequences of a loss or destruction of the asset and estimating the probability of occurrence of the threat which creates the exposure. The total exposure for any particular resource is the the sum of the financial consequences of the exposures created by the individual threats. Thus,

Value of resource * probability of threat = exposure

eg,

Stock (£1000K) * theft (.001) = £1K

(Value of resource) * (probability of threat) + ...
(Value of resource) * (probability of threat) = total exposure

This exercise results in the exposure matrix as shown in **Figure 5.**

The exercise is not easy because, in many cases, both the valuation of the resources and the estimate of the probabilities are simply best guesses that can be made in the circumstances. However, the exercise is an iterative process and through continual repetition the quantitative assessments of the financial consequences of risk become more refined and realistic. This then leads to a clearer picture of which are the major threats that should be considered in contingency planning.

Following this type of exposure analysis, a business enterprise should have a clearer idea of the exposures with which it is faced as well as the financial consequences of those exposures. Thus, the next step is to determine how those exposures may be minimised or prevented. In other words, how the exposures may be controlled.

10.   CONTROLS

Controls are defined as any means by which a business enterprise seeks to minimise or prevent an exposure by acting against the threats that cause the exposure. Thus, if fire is a threat that can result in the destruction of the resources of an enterprise, and damage its survival prospects, it would be well to minimise this threat by not having all the assets located in one place or providing, as far as possible, for some fallback arrangements in the event of such a disaster.

A control cannot be defined as simply a policy, plan, procedure, budget, etc because the particular risk which is faced by the absence of these controls may not be relevant and, therefore, there is no exposure. We cannot realistically produce a budget for goodwill so the absence of this item in the corporate budget would not be regarded as creating an exposure.There may be an item in the budget, though, for other factors that contribute to goodwill, eg safety.

Figure 5 A company exposure matrix

RESOURCES	VALUE £K	THEFT	FRAUD	CONFIS-CATION	FIRE	STORM	EXPLOSION	TOTAL EXPOSURE £K
CASH	500	.001 L <1	.001 L <1	.001 L <1				1.5
STOCK	1000	.001 L 1	.001 L 1	.001 L 1	.001 D 1	.001 D 1	.001 D 1	6
PLANT	5000	.001 L 5		.001 L 5	.001 D 5	.001 D 5	.001 D 5	25
PREMISES	5000			.001 L 5	.001 D 5	.001 D 5	.001 D 5	20
PERSONNEL	1000				.001 L 1	.001 L 1	.001 L 1	3
DATA	10,000	.001 L 10	.001 L 10	.001 D 10				30
SYSTEMS	1000	.001 L 1	.001 L 1	.001 L 1	.001 D 1	.001 D 1	.001 D 1	6
GOODWILL	10,000				.001 L 10	.001 L 10	.001 L 10	30
	33,500	17.5	12.5	22.5	23	23	23	121.5

L = LOSS   D = DESTRUCTION

Since the same controls will not be relevant in every circumstance, a control should not be regarded as something which is fixed and immutable. Some controls will have wide applicability such as policies, plans, budgets, procedures, authority levels, etc while other controls have narrow applicability such as double keying in the entry of data into a computing system. The art of the auditor, whether a computing auditor or any other kind of auditor, is to identify the threats which are relevant and the potential exposures with which the company is faced—some auditors prefer to refer to the 'significance of the findings' rather than to potential exposures. This accomplished, the task of the auditor is to make recommendations on the controls which should be applied bearing in mind that controls have both a cost factor and a hindrance factor.

For example, the introduction of procedures incurs a cost in their initial production as well as a cost in their maintenance. Procedures that are several years out-of-date are worse than useless because they may be misleading. The creation of new systems very frequently makes existing procedures and practices obsolete and requires that new procedures should be written.

The author was involved in the implementation of a replacement materials management system in which, in the new system, the purchase orders were produced automatically by the system once a materials requisition had been raised. In the system being replaced, the purchase orders had been produced by a 'typing pool' from a pro-forma purchase order prepared from the materials requisition. With the older system there were procedures for the preparation of pro-forma purchase orders as well as for the paper handling between different sections in the buying organisation which were no longer required with the new system. At the date of changeover, therefore, it was required that the old procedures should be withdrawn and that new procedures be available covering the changed mode of operation.

We have all no doubt heard line management complaining about the bureaucracy in a corporate enterprise and how little freedom there is for individual initiative with all the form filling that is required before decisions are made. The author is well aware of the complaints made by line management that auditors are very good at recommending the introduction of new procedures but not very good at recommending the cancellation of existing procedures which appear to be no longer relevant or are unnecessarily obstructive.

An illustration of over-control and unnecessary hindrance is provided by an example drawn from a company in which the following situation arose a number of years ago. In order to spend money on capital items—the specific case referred to was the painting of a fence at one of the company plants which had been included in the budget as a capital item—an authorisation for expenditure (AFE) had to be raised. This was undertaken by the head of the maintenance department at the plant site, and then countersigned by the plant manager. However, there the matter did not rest for the AFE then had to be signed by the technical director. This also was considered to be insufficient control and the AFE had to be further countersigned by the finance director and then, penultimately, by the company general manager. The final step in the process was that the AFE was returned to the finance director who signed it for the second time. The impression given was that the Board of Directors spent most of their time countersigning each other's documents. This true story is an excellent example of how controls may be allowed to run riot if not used with common sense and discretion.

11.   CONTROLS IN COMPUTING SYSTEMS

The objectives of the controls framework of a computing system are to ensure:

(1) security;
(2) privacy;
(3) accuracy;
(4) completeness;
(5) effectiveness;
(6) efficiency.

Security refers to the protection of data held within the system against accidental or intentional disclosure to unauthorised persons, or unauthorised modification or destruction. Privacy refers to the rights of individuals and organisations to determine for themselves when, how, and to what extent, information about them is to be transmitted to others. Accuracy means that the data must be correct and up-to-date and completeness that all the data which should be processed has been included in the processing operation.

The effectiveness of a computing system refers to the way that the system satisfies the user's requirements from the system. For example, when the user receives hard copy output from the system there is no further laborious manual transcribing caused by the original listings not being in the format required.

Efficiency refers to the operational performance of the system: for on-line users, logging-on is a simple and rapid process, response times—even at peak periods—are fast (within seconds) and hard copy listings are easy to read and quickly available; the machine is not over/under-sized for the processing required and there is a high level of availability time to the users, eg daily back-ups are not made at times of peak demand, there are suitable backup/recovery and fallback arrangements available, at a cost which is realistic for the system criticality and company resources.

12.   TYPES OF CONTROLS

Controls, whatever the objectives for which they are employed, may be one of three types, namely:

(1) preventive;
(2) detective;
(3) corrective.

Examples of each of these different types are shown in **Table 1** against each of the control objectives discussed in **11.**, above.

Preventive controls are the front line of defence for an enterprise and are intended, as the name suggests, to prevent the occurrence of a threat.They are designed to maintain the security and privacy of the system, reduce the threat of innaccurate and incomplete data entering and being processed by the system as well as to ensure that the system is used effectively and efficiently.

The second type are designed to reduce the threat of inaccurate data, that

Table 1   Examples of controls by objectives

Control Types / Objectives	Security	Privacy	Accuracy	Completeness	Effectiveness	Efficiency
(1) *Preventive*	Procedures Authorities User ID's Passwords	Procedures Authorities User ID's Passwords	Input forms Double Keying Field checks Range checks	Procedures Batch input Control slip Source input	Requirements analysis Development methodologies User participation Project management	Development methodology Performance appraised User participation Project management
(2) *Detective*	Console log Security check System anomaly Information leak	Information leak Legal sanction	Error message Error listing Control totals	Batch totals Transaction listing	User dissatisfaction Response delays Down time User difficulties	Downtime Under-utilisation Excessive costs Schedule difficulties
(3) *Corrective*	Revise procedures Revise authorities ID change Password change	Revise procedures Revise authorities ID change Password change	Procedures Re-input Control totals Focal point	Procedures Re-input Control totals Focal point	Function re-design Procedure/User manual Training Equipment upgrade	System re-design New equipment Training Re-scheduling

has bypassed the preventive controls, remaining undetected in the system as well as any breaches of security or any ineffective and inefficient use of the system passing unnoticed. Finally, corrective controls are meant to ensure that data which is rejected by the preventive and detective controls, for some reason of inaccuracy, is returned to the system in a corrected format, and that any breaches of security or privacy, lack of effectiveness and efficiency are quickly rectified.

References

1 The *Which* Magazine, January 1986.
2 Mair W C, Wood D R, Davis K W *Computer Control and Audit* (1978) Institute of Internal Auditors Inc.
3 Martin J *Security, Accuracy and Privacy in Computer Systems* (1973) Prentice-Hall Inc.

2 The role of internal audit

This chapter describes the role of internal audit and, especially, the role of the auditor in computing audit. Audit is defined by the Institute of Internal Auditors as 'a control which functions by examining and evaluating the effectiveness of other controls'. An important aspect of the audit objective is to promote effective control at reasonable cost. The responsibility for internal control properly resides with the line management in the functional area who are responsible for carrying out the business processes.

The prime characteristic which distinguishes internal audit from any other function in the organisation and which makes the internal auditor uniquely qualified to make judgements on internal controls, is independence or objectivity.

Internal audit also differs from external audit in two principal ways, namely, in the:

(1) reporting relationships;
(2) control objectives.

Internal audit report essentially to the Internal Audit Committee and external audit to the Board of Directors and shareholders. The control objectives of internal audit cover security, privacy, accuracy, completeness, efficiency and effectiveness while the principal control objectives of external audit are security, accuracy and completeness.

As a result of their investigations, internal audit may make recommendations. However, these recommendations do not have the force of commands and whether they are accepted and enforced, depends upon the auditor's reporting status in the organisation and his own credibility.

There are five principal areas of control in computing audit, namely:

(1) Application computing system controls.
(2) Application computing system development controls.
(3) Computer operations centre controls.
(4) DP department organisation controls.
(5) Information and strategic planning controls.

The objectives for an audit of the controls in each of these five areas are described in **5.** to **9.** of this chapter, below.

The responsibilities of internal audit and external audit, with regard to systems under development, are described in **11.** The differences are due to the control objectives that each is required to satisfy. Internal audit is concerned very much with effectiveness and efficiency while external audit is primarily concerned with security, accuracy and completeness. However, a harmonious working relationship can be established by the adoption of common methodologies and practices.

The computing auditor should not be regarded as a completely separate breed from his brethren auditors. Instead, he shoud be regarded as a sub-species of the same generic type. The main reasons that computing audit has been singled out for special attention are:

(1) few persons can now work effectively without some knowledge of computers;
(2) companies spend large amounts of money on their computing systems;
(3) sensitive and important data is highly concentrated.

1. OBJECTIVES AND SCOPE

The following statement of objective and scope is included in the Statement of Responsibility issued by the Institute of Internal Auditors in the UK, to its members.

STATEMENT OF RESPONSIBILITIES OF INTERNAL AUDITORS

The purpose of this statement is to provide in summary form a general understanding of the role and responsibilities of internal auditing. For more specific guidance, readers should refer to the 'Standards for the Professional Practice of Internal Auditing'.

NATURE

Internal auditing is an independent appraisal activity established within an organisation as a service to the organisation. It is a control which functions by examining and evaluating the adequacy of other controls.

OBJECTIVE AND SCOPE

The objective of internal auditing is to assist members of the organisation in the effective discharge of their responsibilities. To this end, internal auditing furnishes them with analyses, appraisals, recommendations, counsel, and information concerning the activities reviewed. The audit objective includes promoting effective control at reasonable cost.

The scope of internal auditing encompasses the examination and evaluation of the adequacy and effectiveness of the organisation's system of internal control and the quality of performance in carrying out assigned responsibilities. The scope of internal auditing includes:

● Reviewing the reliability and integrity of financial and operating information and the means used to identify, measure, classify, and report such information.

● Reviewing the systems established to ensure compliance with those policies, plans, procedures, laws, and regulations which could have significant impact on the operations and reports, and determining whether the organisation is in compliance.

● Reviewing the means of safeguarding assets and, as appropriate, verifying the existence of such assets.

● Appraising the economy and efficiency with which resources are employed.

● Reviewing operations or programmes to ascertain whether results are consistent with established objectives and goals and whether the operations or programmes are being carried out as planned.

It is clear that the scope of audit activities goes beyond the more conventional areas of ensuring that there is compliance with company policy, plans and procedures and extends into the area of ensuring that the company activities are both effective and efficient.

2.   RESPONSIBILITY FOR CONTROL

The internal auditor is quite clearly concerned with controls although he is not responsible for the controls. The responsibility for internal control properly resides with line management and the role of the internal auditor is to judge the adequacy of controls and to recommend control improvements.

The strength of the auditor's position in influencing the line management to accept his recommendations on controls, will depend upon the audit mandate within the company and the personal capability of the auditor. If the senior management have accepted that internal audit has a positive and valuable role to play in maintaining and improving the framework of internal control, and have established an appropriate organisation structure, then the auditor's position will be a strong one.

However, this is insufficient, in itself, and the internal auditor must establish his credibility by demonstrating to line management that he is an ally in assisting to maintain a strong framework of control. The internal auditor must not be seen as an individual whose function is to criticise and find evidence of failure. Rather he should be seen as someone whose role is to assist line management in identifying potential control weaknesses and to provide a service by making recommendations to strengthen the framework of control.

The credibility of the internal auditor will be built upon his understanding of the business processes in the functional areas to which he is assigned, as well as his specific expertise as a controls 'expert'. The latter is acquired through the synergistic effect of assignments, in different functional areas, whereby he is able to identify controls that have worked effectively in one situation and may be equally relevant in another.

The internal auditor must also be conscious that controls incur a cost and that over-controlling is as debilitating to an enterprise as under-controlling. Too many controls may reduce the flexibility of the enterprise to respond rapidly to changing market forces and may stifle the spirit of entrepreneurship on which the enterprise was originally based. Thus, the internal auditor has a delicate and sensitive responsibility to both line and senior corporate management to ensure that recommendations are both sensible and practical. The role is challenging and demanding but can be extremely rewarding if properly exercised.

3.   AUDIT INDEPENDENCE

The prime characteristic which distinguishes internal audit from any other function within an organisation and, therefore, makes it uniquely qualified to make judgements on controls, is independence or objectivity. In this context, attention is drawn to the final part of the Statement of Responsibilities issued by the Institute of Internal Auditors of the UK.

INDEPENDENCE

Internal auditors should be independent of the activities they audit. Internal auditors are independent when they can carry out their work freely and objectively. Independence permits internal auditors to render the impartial and unbiased judgements essential to the proper conduct of audits. It is achieved through organisational status and objectivity.

Organisational status should be sufficient to assure a broad range of audit coverage, and adequate consideration of and effective action on audit findings and recommendations.

Objectivity requires that internal auditors have an independent mental attitude, and an honest belief in their work product. Drafting procedures, designing, installing, and operating systems are not audit functions. Performing such activities is presumed to impair audit objectivity.

It is not easy to achieve true independence in a line organisation, of which internal audit is a functional part, unless there is a sound understanding and commitment to the role that internal audit is expected to play. The effectiveness of the function will depend very much upon its organisational status and the established reporting relationships, as well as recognition of its objectivity.

In the first instance, internal audit should not be seen as reporting through any other function within the organisation to the corporate management. This makes it difficult to provide objective appraisals in the functional area, of which it is part, as well as making the internal auditor less acceptable to other line functions.

For historical reasons, internal audit has been lodged—in some organisations—for its accomodation and daily 'bread and butter' with the finance function from which its origins were spawned. Although the auditor has survived in this environment, his work has sometimes been prejudiced by the jaundiced eye with which he is viewed by his colleagues in other functional areas. He has frequently been viewed as the company 'policeman' whose role is to ensure that greedy fingers are kept out of the corporate 'till' in place of a friendly 'consultant' helping line management to maintain the effectiveness and efficiency of company operations.

The effective placement of the internal audit function depends upon a proper appreciation of the audit role and accordance of the proper organisational status. In companies where the internal audit role has been successfully exploited, the function reports either to the chief executive or to an audit committee which is chaired by the chief executive. The reporting relationships are then clearly seen as different from other functions, such as quality assurance—discussed in chapter 6, **8.**, below—which have a direct line management reporting relationship.

In the second instance, the success of an internal audit function will depend upon that function not being required to exercise line management responsibilities. There have been instances of unscrupulous line managers seeking audit 'advice' before making a decision on the basis that a second opinion is always valuable. This places internal audit in the invidious position of participating in line management decisions with the result that audit can be blamed should the decision prove incorrect. There is a danger that audit may simply concur with the line management proposals, for the sake of a 'quiet life', with a consequent loss of objectivity.

In the third instance, the internal audit function must have the rights of access to all company records, sites and persons in order to be able to form an effective judgement on the controls framework that is being evaluated. If the auditor is debarred from reviewing any company records which are relevant to his investigation, he is being unfairly required to make a judgement without the full facts.

In the fourth instance, internal audit must be given the freedom to review any area of the company operations that present a potential exposure. This even extends into the area of company policy making, although not into challenging company policy per se. This deserves some explanation for it is still an area of confusion even amongst internal auditors themselves.

The right to challenge the company policy–making process must clearly be distinguished from the right to challenge company policies. By challenging company policies the auditor is undertaking a line management role and suggesting that he can make better policies.

An analogy may be drawn from the area of budgeting and cost control. If at the end of an accounting period the budget and actuals are widely at variance the auditor could conclude that the budget was a bad one. However, this is a line manager's prerogative and the auditor's correct conclusion should be that there may have been something remiss with the budget-making process. After analysing the budget foundations, however, he may conclude that the premises on which the budget was based were sound and sensible. There have occurred, in the meantime, some violent changes in the market circumstances which no reasonable man could have foreseen (see chapter 1, **5.**, above).

In the same way, if company policies are unsound there may be something remiss with the processes by which those policies were arrived at. Thus, if policies were formulated when the company was first founded but no formal mechanism exists for a regular review with changing environmental, political and social forces then there is clearly a control weakness which the auditor should highlight.

Finally, attention is drawn to the remark that the 'internal auditors should be independent of the activities they audit'. This is a particularly important point in the area of systems development auditing, for the auditor may be expected to offer recommendations on the standards of control to be incorporated in the new system. Indeed, if he is to gain acceptance and enhance his credibility he should welcome the opportunity to do so.

However, this could appear to prejudice his objectivity and independence, as an auditor, which is discussed further in **5.**, below. Suffice it to say at this stage that:

● If the auditor has maturity, integrity and candour he is more likely to be objective. It goes without saying that the better his technical grasp of data processing the less likely it is that he will make ill-judged recommendations in the first place, and the more likely it is that he, and therefore his recommendations, will be acceptable to data processing management.[1]

4.   INTERNAL AND EXTERNAL AUDIT—A COMPARISON

It is worth, at this stage, comparing the role and responsibilities of the

[1] Andrew Chambers *Computer Auditing* (2nd edn, 1986) Pitman.

internal auditor with those of the external auditor. The essential differences between internal audit and external audit are in the:

(1) reporting relationships;
(2) control objectives.

The reporting relationship of internal audit, discussed more fully in **3.** above, is to the Internal Audit Committee which usually consists of the company chief executive and his senior line management. The reporting relationship of external audit is the company Board of Directors, who have ultimate responsibility for the custody of the assets in their charge, and the shareholders of the company.

This distinction affects the types of written reports that are produced and their distribution. The reports of internal audit are confidential in nature and circulate, within the company, to the Internal Audit Committee and other, involved, senior line management, to the external auditors and, perhaps, joint parties. The reports of external audit are non-confidential and are circulated, outside the company, to the shareholders and to other parties who may have an interest in the company's affairs, eg Companies House, bankers, stockbrokers, external auditors, etc.

The control objectives of the internal auditor are discussed in **6.–10.** of this chapter, and described in detail in Part 3 of this book. We briefly summarise latter material, by saying that the internal auditor is concerned with controls on the effectiveness and efficiency of systems development and security, privacy, accuracy, completeness, effectiveness and efficiency of systems operation.

The external auditor has statutory obligations and requirements to fulfill in his reporting responsibility to the Board of Directors and shareholders. He is, therefore, concerned with assessing the financial statements for a period, ie balance sheet, profit and loss account, source and disposition of funds, so as to form an opinion on whether they represent a true and fair statement of the company's financial situation. He is also concerned with ensuring that there is an adequate audit trail, adequacy of data retention for recovery and interrogation purposes, system integrity and reliablity of controls to support a compliance or substantive audit approach.

The essential control objectives, therefore, of the external auditor are to ensure:

(1) security;
(2) accuracy;
(3) completeness.

He is not concerned directly with privacy, effectiveness and efficiency, although he may regard these as peripheral control objectives. He is concerned with security because he must assure himself that the company's assets, of whatever kind, are being adequately protected and with accuracy and completeness in order to fulfill his statutory obligations with regard to expressing an opinion on the company financial situation.

5. AREAS OF CONTROL

The majority of writers on computing audit divide the subject into three principal areas, namely the auditing of:

(1) application computing systems;

(2) application computing systems development;
(3) computer operations centres.

However, there are two other areas which deserve to be included in this list, namely the auditing of:

(4) DP department organisations;
(5) information and strategic planning.

These last two, especially the latter, have received scant attention in the literature on computing audit to date, although organisation auditing, it must be fair to say, has been included in audits carried out in the areas originally listed, but not as a totally separate audit activity. In conducting an audit in one of these areas, there will inevitably be some overlapping with the others because they should be conceived of as intersecting sets, as shown in **Figure 6**, and not as discrete, totally independent, packages of controls.

The six essential control objectives which are relevant to the conduct of an audit, in any of these key control areas have been described in chapter 1, **11.** The objectives and scope for the audit—discussed in chapter 9, **3.**—should, therefore, contain a reference to one or more of these control objectives. If this is not so the auditor should question whether he is on the right track with his proposed audit.

6.   AUDITING APPLICATION COMPUTING SYSTEMS

The audit of an application computing system is concerned with the review and evaluation of the controls to:

(1) maintain the SECURITY and PRIVACY of the data being processed by that system;
(2) ensure that the data is ACCURATE and COMPLETE;
(3) ensure that the data is being processed EFFECTIVELY and EFFICIENTLY.

These controls are discussed in detail in chapter 3.

This is an important area for the auditor who is concerned with the development of systems for he may well be called upon to play an active role in assisting the system project group in the actual design of the system controls. There has been much discussion on the justification of placing the internal auditor in the invidious position of actually designing the controls which he may subsequently be called upon to audit. The essential argument is that, by contributing to the design of the system controls, the auditor is prejudicing his objectivity and cannot later be called upon to review and evaluate his own work.

There is indeed some substance of truth in this reasoning. However, there is a strong counter-argument against it along the lines that, since the internal auditor is the acknowledged 'controls' expert in the organisation, who should be in a better position to advise the project group. Further, by playing a pro-active role in the system development process the internal auditor is more likely to enhance his credibility and prestige than if he simply appears on the scene afterwards to criticise and search for the imperfections of failure.

The undertaking of the responsibility for designing the framework of controls, in an application system, is no matter to be approached lightly. The internal auditor must have as much knowledge about the system objectives and functionality as the most involved member of the project group.

Figure 6   Intersecting sets of data processing controls

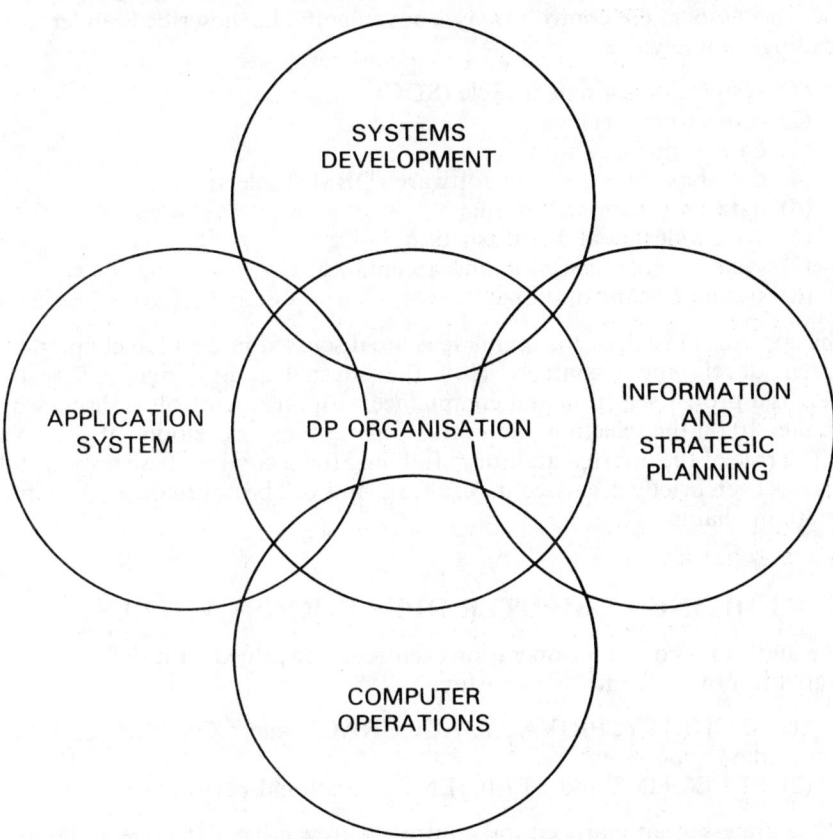

However, it must be appreciated, as discussed in **2.**, above, that the responsibility for internal controls properly resides with line management in the data processing department, and the user groups responsible for the preparation and processing of transactions, record keeping and resulting reports. The internal auditor can make recommendations but he cannot insist, at this stage, that his recommendations should be accepted. Responsibility to implement and maintain appropriate controls resides with data processing functions and user organisations.

7.   AUDITING THE DEVELOPMENT OF COMPUTING SYSTEMS

The responsibility of the internal auditor with regard to systems under development is twofold, namely to:

(1) ensure that there are adequate controls on the EFFECTIVENESS and EFFICIENCY of the systems development process;

(2) give reasonable assurance to management that critical systems are implemented with adequate built-in controls for SECURITY and PRIVACY of data, ACCURACY and COMPLETENESS of processing and EFFECTIVENESS and EFFICIENCY of operation.

The effectiveness and the efficiency of the systems development process and the associated controls may conveniently be described under eight headings, namely:

(1) systems development cycle (SDC);
(2) project management;
(3) data administration;
(4) data base management software (DBMS) selection;
(5) data base administration;
(6) system design and construction;
(7) system implementation and acceptance;
(8) system documentation.

The controls in each of the main areas are discussed in detail in chapter 4 on system development controls. How the internal auditor may ensure that there is a proper selection and compliance with these controls is discussed in chapter 10 on the selection and evaluation of system development controls.

The role of the internal auditor in fulfilling the second of these responsibilities has been briefly discussed in **5.**, above, and will be covered again, in more detail, in chapter 11.

8.   AUDITING COMPUTER OPERATIONS CENTRES

The audit of a computer operations centre is concerned with the review and evaluation of the controls to ensure:

(1) SECURITY, PRIVACY, ACCURACY and COMPLETENESS of data processing,
(2) EFFECTIVE and EFFICIENT operational performance.

These are essentially procedural controls—preventive, detective and corrective—covering the acquisition or deployment, use and maintenance and temporary/permanent modification of the hardware, software, personnel and data within the management responsibility of that operations centre.

The operations centre is, in essence, an information processing factory and, like any production environment, it is essential that there should be clearly understood standards, practices and procedures which are rigidly complied with. These may be grouped into the following control areas:

(1) input/output scheduling;
(2) media library maintenance;
(3) malfunction reporting/preventive hardware maintenance;
(4) environmental controls/physical security;
(5) backup/recovery and fallback;
(6) separation of duties;
(7) cost allocation/recovery;
(8) resources planning.

It is not proposed, in this work, to discuss in further detail the controls which are applicable in the area of computer operations centres. However, some specific examples of these types of controls are shown in **Table 2**.

The sub-division of computing audit into discrete areas is somewhat artificial and, as shown in **Figure 6**, the controls should be conceived of as intersecting sets with certain controls being relevant in several areas. This is discussed again in chapter 3, where we describe, in more detail, the specific types of controls relevant in computing systems. However, as mentioned in **3.**, of that chapter, we specifically exclude the general operational controls, like those in **Table 2**, from the controls for a specific application system.

9. AUDITING THE DATA PROCESSING (DP) DEPARTMENT ORGANISATION

The audit of the computer department organisation is concerned with the review and evaluation of the controls to ensure:

> (1) that there is an EFFECTIVE and EFFICIENT acquisition and deployment of the manpower resources being used by that organisation.

These controls cover the following areas:

- (1) remuneration policy;
- (2) permanent/contract staff;
- (3) segregation of duties;
- (4) balance of skills;
- (5) acquisition policy;
- (6) job rotation;
- (7) career planning;
- (8) training;
- (9) job descriptions;
- (10) division of labour;
- (11) departmental procedures;
- (12) standards/guidelines.

The organisation of the computer department in one large UK company is shown in **Figure 7**. This company is sufficiently large to have developed the principle of the division of labour to the degree where all recognised job functions in the computing world can find a place.

It is not the intention in this book to review in detail the controls in this particular area of computing audit. However, it is important to emphasise that the computer department organisation controls will also be relevant to the other four areas of computing audit as shown in **Figure 6**. Indeed, the organisation controls will be the central hub around which the other intersecting sets of controls revolve.

Thus, to take an example, the balance of skills in the organisation will clearly have an influence on the way the special activities in the spheres of information and strategic planning, systems development, operations and application system control are carried out. Each specific area will require a certain detailed know-how but will be more effective if those performing these duties also have some knowledge of the way other duties are conducted. This know-how can be most effectively acquired by job rotation combined with structured career planning taking cognisance of an individual's own expressed interests.

10. AUDITING INFORMATION AND STRATEGIC PLANNING

The audit of the information and strategic planning process is concerned

Table 2   Computer operations centre controls

Control reference	Key control area	Control details
1.	Input/output scheduling	
1.1		There is an input/output control group responsible for logging all jobs received for processing.
1.2		There are established and written job handling procedures.
1.3		There are established processing schedules, with cut-off times/dates, for daily and monthly batch processing.
1.4		All jobs submitted for processing require to be properly authorised.
2.	Media library maintenance	
2.1		The data storage media are held in a fireproof room which is normally kept locked.
2.2		The data storage media are clearly labelled as to their contents and retention period.
2.3		There is a log which records the serial number and contents of all data storage media.
2.4		The issue/return of all data storage media is recorded in the log.
3.	Malfunction reporting, etc	
3.1		There is a person, or group, to whom all faults should be reported.
3.2		There are established procedures for the reporting and correction of all faults.
3.3		There is a preventative maintenance agreement with the supplier(s) of all equipment.
3.4		There is a schedule of preventative maintenance drawn up for all equipment in the operations centre.
4.	Environment/ physical security	
4.1		The computer operations area/room is installed, and functioning, air conditioning, temperature and humidity control equipment.
4.2		There are adequate fire fighting provisions including automatic smoke detectors, fire detection and gas extinguishing systems (HALON) and appropriate instructions for personnel.
4.3		There is a clean, uninterruptable power supply and all electric/telecommunications cables are hidden under false flooring.
4.4		There are clearly documented procedures for allowing personnel access to the computer operations area.
5.	Back-up/ recovery/ fallback	
5.1		There is a daily backup carried out on the system using an established cycle of backup tapes.
5.2		There is at least one recent generation of backup tapes stored at another location in order to provide for recovery in the event of a disaster.

Control reference	Key control area	Control details
5.3		There is a written, and up-to-date, disaster plan, to provide for recovery in the event of a catastrophe.
5.4		There are fallback arrangements covering the provision of alternative equipment included in the disaster plan.
6.	Separation of duties	
6.1		The DP department is separate from any other function in the organisation.
6.2		There is a clearly established company policy on the segregation of duties in the DP department.
6.3		Persons who write programs are not allowed to input data to the system.
6.4		Persons who have charge of negotiable instruments should not be allowed to authorise those documents.
7.	Cost allocation/ recovery	
7.1		There are appropriate service contracts in existence between the DP department and its users to provide for the recovery of services.
7.2		There is a clearly established schedule of charges which is understood, and agreed, by the users.
7.3		The users are charged on a regular basis, eg monthly, in order that they may monitor their costs.
7.4		The statement of charges provides a clear breakdown of the services for which the users are being charged.
8.	Resources planning	
8.1		There is a long term plan for the acquisition and deployment of hardware/software.
8.2		There is an annual expenditure budget for the acquisition of hardware/software.
8.3		There is a regular reporting and review by line management of actual expenditure against budget.
8.4		There is a manpower plan for the development and deployment of personnel in the DP department.

with the review and evaluation of the controls which are designed to achieve two objectives, namely, to ensure there is:

(1) an EFFECTIVE and EFFICIENT mechanism for information planning to support the company policies and objectives;
(2) an EFFECTIVE and EFFICIENT computing strategy to support the information requirements of functional users.

The controls in the area of information and strategic planning have been explored only scantily in the literature which is available on computing audit. However, this is a very large subject in its own right, and it is not the intention in this book to discuss the subject in any depth.

The controls in the area of information planning may be considered under four headings, as follows:

(1) information management;
(2) information resources planning;

Figure 7 Information and computing services organisation of a large UK company

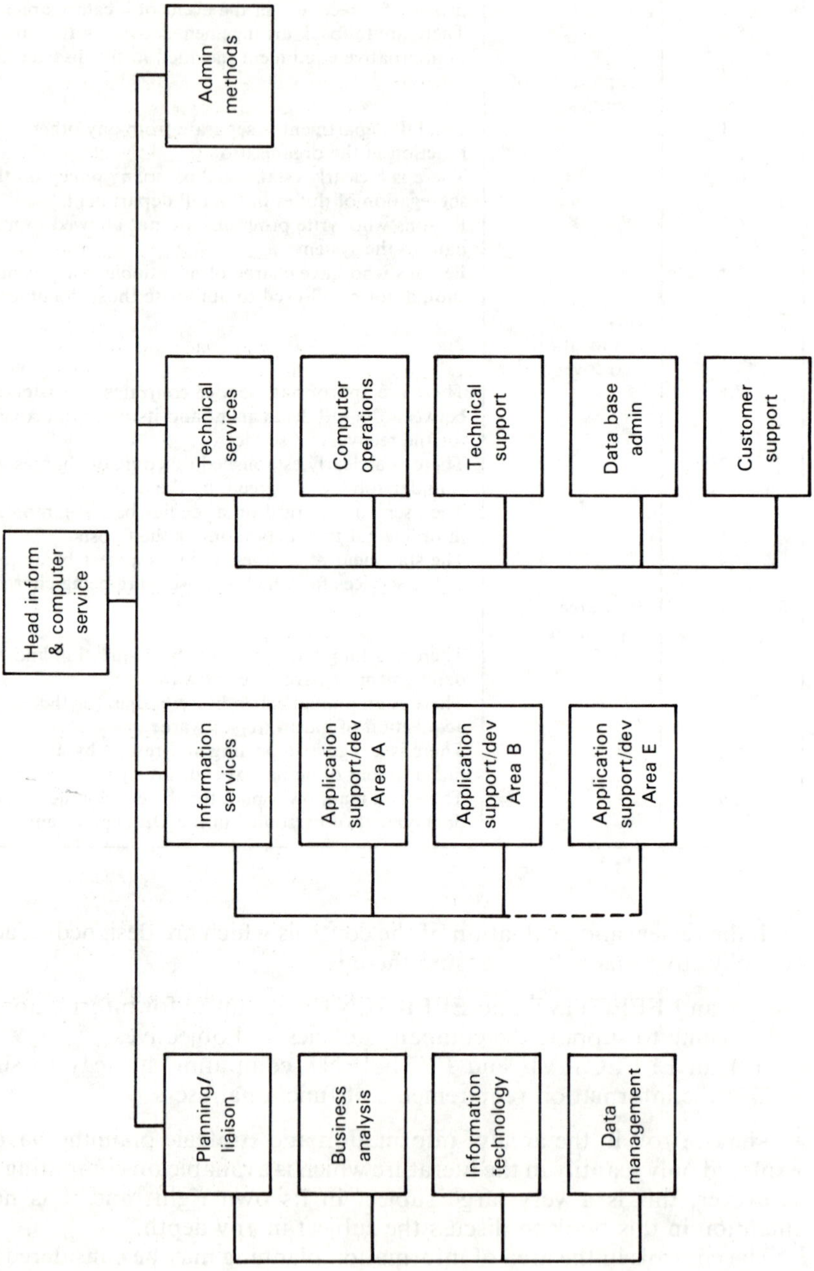

Table 3 Information planning controls

Control reference	Key control area	Control details
1.	Information management	
1.1		There is an executive steering committee (ESC) responsible for the overall co-ordination of company policy, planning and strategy.
1.2		The chairman of the ESC is the chief officer of the company.
1.3		The members of the ESC represent all the main functional areas of the company.
1.4		There is a clear written statement of the Terms of Reference of the ESC.
2.	Information planning	
2.1		There is a specifically designated information planning study team which reports to the ESC.
2.2		There is a top down planning of data combined with the localised design of systems.
2.3		There are formal study techniques —preferably automated, where applicable, —for strategic data planning, eg
		—informal subject data base planning
		—mapping subject data bases into systems
		—entity-activity matrices
		—entity affinity analysis
2.4		There is an overall enterprise model showing the functions necessary for running the enterprise.
3.	Information systems planning	
3.1		There is an annual planning process resulting in the production of a five year plan.
3.2		There is a written development, maintenance, enhancement and support plan broken down by function, by cost and by manyears of effort.
3.3		The annual plan is presented to, and approved by, the ESC.
3.4		There are established procedures and practices for the regular review and reporting of progress against plan.
4.	Management information reporting	
4.1		There is a management information package (MIP) presented to members of the ESC, and other approved parties, eg internal audit, at regular intervals.
4.2		There is an established focal point responsible for the preparation of the MIP to which all queries can be addressed.
4.3		There are procedures and practices by which all queries from the ESC, resulting from the MIP, can be quickly followed up and a written reply provided.
4.4		There are established procedures and practices by which the MIP is evaluated for accuracy, timeliness and usefulness and for making changes where necessary.

(3) information systems planning;
(4) management information reporting.

Some examples of the detailed types of controls applicable in this area are
shown in **Table 3**. This is not intended to form a comprehensive list.

The areas to be included in strategic planning are less easy to define than
those of information planning and will depend, inter alia, on company size,
state of technology, company policies and committment to systems development. Some areas which might be covered in any consideration of Strategic
Planning are as follows:

(1) hardware;
(2) software;
(3) communications;
(4) systems development;
(5) data base design and development, etc.

Some examples of the types of controls which are applicable in this area
are shown in **Table 4**. This is not intended to form a comprehensive list.

Table 4   Strategic planning controls

Control reference	Key control area	Control details
1.	Hardware	
1.1		There is an overall company policy on the purchase and use of computer equipment.
1.2		There is a technical support group responsible for advising on all aspects of computing equipment to assist management in the selection and purchase of the most appropriate hardware.
1.3		There are written standards and guidelines on the evaluation of equipment from different suppliers.
1.4		There is a written company policy on security provisions to be adopted for different items of the company's computer equipment.
2.	Software	
2.1		There are written procedures for the authorisation and acquisition of different types of software.
2.2		There is a selection strategy on the purchase of different types of software as, for example, operating systems, application packages, database management systems.
2.3		There is a process for evaluating the reliability of different types of the company's software.
2.4		There is a user focal point responsible for the co-ordination of software training requirements in each functional area.
3.	Communications	
3.1		There is a well considered, and written, expansion policy and plan which is periodically reviewed and revised where necessary.

Control reference	Key control area	Control details
3.2		There are guidelines on the selection, installation, use and security of local area networks (LANS).
3.3		There is a well defined organisational structure within the company with responsibility for all aspects of the data communications network.
3.4		There are user focal points with specific responsibilities for co-ordinating the communications requirements within functional areas.
4.	Systems development	
4.1		There is an appropriate organisation structure within the DP department to support the development of computing systems.
4.2		There is a proper system of planning, including the production of an annual written information plan to support the development of computing systems.
4.3		There is an appropriate segregation of duties within the DP department in order to provide the expertise required for the development of computing systems.
4.4		There is an accepted and well understood methodology being used by the DP department for the development of computing systems.
5.	Data base design and development	
5.1		The design of data bases relates to broadly shared data rather than being narrowly focussed on one application.
5.2		The logical structures of the data models are designed using third-normal-form and canonical synthesis.
5.3		There is a thorough data analysis with end-user participation including a formal procedure for collecting the end-user views of data and reviewing the logical data model with the end-users and systems analysts before implementation.
5.4		There is an appropriate data base management software (DBMS) selection procedure with the choice of DBMS being related to high productivity application generation languages and a distinction between heavy-duty DBMS and decision support software.

Control reference	Key control area	Control details
6.	Data distribution	
6.1		There is a company policy with regard to the distribution of data on central or local systems.
6.2		There is a company data administrator responsible for the overall planning of data distribution.
6.3		A regular review is made of data distribution to determine whether the original decision criteria are still valid.
6.4		There is a synchronous update of distributed data to ensure that the same data at different locations are consistent.
7.	Security and privacy	
7.1		There is a company policy guideline for both security and privacy for the entire organisation and, where appropriate, for the separate organisational functions.
7.2		There is a specific written policy regarding who within the organisation has right of access to specific information and any limitations on the use of this information by those approved for access.
7.3		There is a clear written statement as to who owns the data bases and the information contained therein as well as the authority to originate, modify, or delete existing data within a specific database.
7.4		All systems containing information which falls within the scope of the Data Protection Act have been registered with the Registrar.
8.	Outside data centre	
8.1		There are procedures and practices for establishing that a requirement exists for outside computer processing facilities.
8.2		The benefits to be gained from using outside data centre facilities can be clearly demonstrated.
8.3		There are appropriate selection criteria used to evaluate, and rank, available data centres.
8.4		There is a formal written contract available with the outside data centre specifying level of services and the charges.

11. INTERNAL AUDIT AND EXTERNAL AUDIT IN SYSTEMS DEVELOPMENT

We have discussed the responsibility of the internal computing auditor, with regard to systems under development, in **7.**, above, and describe in detail, in Part 3 of this book, how he may fulfill his responsibility. This responsibility differs from that of the external auditor because the control objectives are different. However, there is an overlap since both internal audit and external audit are concerned with controls for security, accuracy and completeness.

The internal auditor is very much concerned with controls on the effectiveness and efficiency of the company's operations, as we have pointed out in **1.**, above. This area is of minor concern to the external auditor since he is not required to give a statement on how well the company is managed. This the shareholders, and other interested parties, must judge for themselves, from the company's annual report and other information, which may be available, about the company, eg share price, performance compared with other companies in the same business area, etc.

If the external auditor were required to give a statement on management performance controls, he would need to be involved full time in the company's activities in order to assess the controls on effectiveness and efficiency of operation. This would be beyond the current resources of firms in the practice of external auditing—one large UK company has around 30 full-time internal audit staff for a working population of around 4000.

The first conclusion to be drawn from the control objectives of the internal and external auditor, is that controls on the system development process, which are essentially concerned with effectiveness and efficiency, are primarily the responsibility of the internal auditor and the company line management. This is not to suggest that the external auditor should not reassure himself that controls which have an effect on the future integrity of the system, eg data conversion controls, are being, or have been, used in converting data from an older generation system to a new. The selection, evaluation and reporting of the system development controls forms the substance of chapter 10 of this book, and the external auditor should be sufficiently familiar with the methodology and reporting formats so that he can quickly assess the internal auditor's work, should he consider this necessary.

The second conclusion to be drawn from the control objectives of the internal and external auditor, is that controls for application computing systems are the responsibility of both parties since they are equally concerned with security, accuracy and completeness of data and processing. The external auditor must satisfy himself that there are adequate controls on security, accuracy and completeness in order to provide a statement as to whether the financial statements represent a true and fair view of the company's financial position. The internal auditor must satisfy himself on the adequacy of security, accuracy and completeness controls in order to give reasonable assurance to management that critical systems are implemented with adequate built-in controls. Thus, although the reporting relationships are different, it is clear that both internal and external audit have a common interest.

Since there clearly is a common interest, the question arises as to how the task of ensuring adequate controls on security, accuracy and completeness are built into systems during their development. If we accept, as argued previously in this chapter, that designing the system controls framework is an important part of the computing auditor's work, then there are three ways in which this may be approached;

(1) both internal audit and external audit can independently design the controls framework for the system and compare their work upon completion;
(2) internal audit and external audit may work together on designing the system controls framework;
(3) internal audit may design the framework of controls for latter review and evaluation by the external auditor.

The first approach is least favoured, because it involves a complete duplication of effort, although the author has had the experience of external auditors repeating his work under the name of compliance testing. A further disadvantage is that it tends to antagonise development staff, who see no reason why their time should be taken up by two separate sets of persons working towards the same goal.

The second approach is, therefore, more to be favoured. However, it is doubtful whether major firms carrying out external auditing work could afford to have their staff involved for protracted periods in the design of system controls.

Thus, the third approach would appear to be most realistic but may not be practical. It will only be possible if there are committed, trained and experienced computing audit staff available within the company.

There is, as with quality assurance, discussed in chapter 6, **8.**, no clear-cut black and white solution to application computing system controls design. There are only shades of grey whose intensity depends upon the company situation. If there is no committed, trained and experienced internal computing audit staff the work on application computing system controls design will have to be undertaken either by the external auditor or by the systems development staff.

If there is an internal computing audit function, they may opt for the third approach and insist that all application system controls should be designed by them, for subsequent review by external audit. Alternatively, they may agree that a joint approach may be profitable, for some systems, where development is not seen as a protracted process.

Whatever approach is adopted, makes no difference to the fundamental requirement that there should be an established methodology, such as that described in Part 3 of this book, which is thoroughly understood by internal and external audit alike. Thus, if internal audit are responsible for drawing up the type of audit programme shown in **Table 27**, in chapter 11, it is essential that the external auditor understands the methodology, by which it was derived, and the significance of the controls details in the programme. Further, if the internal auditor carries out a post-implementation review (PIR), such as that described in chapter 12, as the final stage of his involvement in a project, it is essential that the external auditor is able to follow his methodology and accept his conclusions.

It is clear that, if the methodologies which are described herein, are understood and followed by both internal and external auditors, the design of application system controls will be more effectively and completely carried out. The external auditor should be quickly able to assess the internal auditors work, without having to repeat that work and, one hopes, be able to offer useful suggestions for controls design at the system development stage, which are necessary to satisfy statutory requirements.

12.   COMPUTING AUDIT—A PERSPECTIVE

There appears to be a widespread view that computing audit is a specialist subject and there are numerous works in the audit literature which are specifically devoted to this area. However, we believe it would be more realistic to regard computing audit, not so much as a separate generic type, but rather as a species in the same generic type much as an alsatian and a bulldog are species of the same generic type Canis (dog). This is illustrated in **Figure 8** which shows internal audit as a main generic type which may be divided into a number of different specific types, one of which is computing audit.

The methodology of audit, which is discussed further in chapter 9, is equally applicable to computing audit as to any other form of audit. The use of audit tools and techniques such as questionnaires, flowcharts, sampling, audit programmes, etc are likewise equally applicable to computing audit. There are, however, certain tools and techniques, specifically applicable in the computing audit area which make use of the unique capabilities of the computer itself.

The actual process of auditing also requires an understanding of controls and what types of controls are most effective and efficient for particular business processes. Further, during the course of an audit, the auditor must acquire a thorough understanding of the business processes that he is reviewing and how the controls are, or should be, applied. This is fundamentally no different from auditing any other area.

Therefore, if there is any difference between computing audit and auditing other processes, in the business environment, this must be due to the technology involved. The technology involved—hardware, software, communications, systems analysis, design and contruction—make the area of data processing a specialist engineering discipline with its own terminology, knowledge and know-how, just as aeronautical, marine or petroleum engineering are unique disciplines each with a terminology and body of knowledge and know-how of its own.

In the early days of auditing, the internal auditor was essentially a finance specialist and his interests were largely concerned with reviewing and evaluating controls in the finance function. This he was well qualified to do because he was usually someone with the specific expertise in this area, acquired through working in a line management role in finance. The role of internal audit has now expanded into other areas and, as a result, the internal auditor is no longer a finance specialist, but an engineer, a personnel officer, a marketing expert, etc recruited to carry out assignments in the areas in which he has specialist know-how.

In like manner, computing audit is the review and evaluation of controls in the specialist area of electronic data processing, which includes the evaluation of corporate information requirements as well as processing by

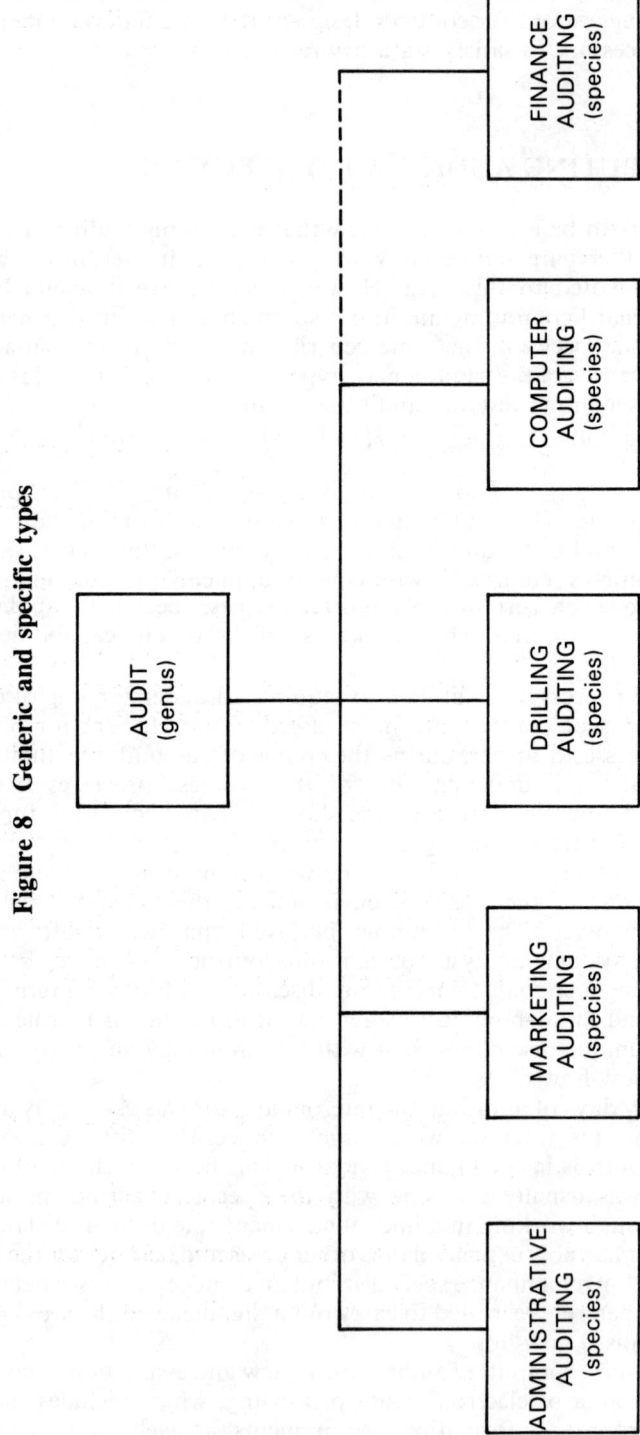

Figure 8 Generic and specific types

electronic means. The ideal computing auditor would, therefore, be someone with an in-depth understanding of the terminology, knowledge and know-how of the information and computing services world. Thus, the require ments demanded of the computing auditor would include an understanding of:

(1) audit methodology;
(2) specific EDP controls;
(3) electronic data processing technology:

—hardware;
—software;
—communications;
—systems analysis;
—systems design;
—systems construction;
—systems operation.

In conclusion, the computing auditor is one of the new generation of technical auditors (who are part of the generic type 'auditor'), who has specialised in the review and evaluation of controls in the area of electronic data processing.

But why has the computing auditor been singled out for special attention? We believe there are three reasons for this, namely:

(1) the computer has infiltrated our working lives to such an extent that very few of us, in this age of electronic data processing, can function effectively without some knowledge and understanding of comput-ing—even if this is limited to understanding how to work with a visual display unit (VDU);
(2) companies spend large amounts of money on their computing hardware, software, data, communications and systems develop-ment;
(3) sensitive and important data is now highly concentrated in single locations. This makes organisations which own that data more vulnerable than they have ever been to threats to that data from outside, or even within, the organisational environment.

References

1   Sawyer L B *The Practice of Modern Internal Auditing* (1981) Institute of Internal Auditors Inc.
2   Chambers A D *Computer Auditing* (1981) Pitman.
3   Mair W C, Wood D R, Davis K W *Computer Control and Audit* (1978) American Institute of Internal Auditors.
4   Davis G B, Adams D L, Schaller C A *Auditing and EDP* (1983) American Institute of Certified Public Accountants.
5   Martin J *Strategic Data-Planning Methodologies* (1982) Prentice-Hall Inc.

3 Application computing system controls

This chapter describes the controls framework of a typical application computing system and the objectives for the controls. The controls framework is viewed as being composed of a number of concentric layers, namely:

(1) the legal and societal controls of the business and economic environment applicable to all companies working in that environment;
(2) the general framework of company controls represented by the company policies, plans, procedures, etc which are applicable to all functions within the company environment;
(3) the specific framework of functional controls represented by plans, procedures, practices, etc of that particular business function;
(4) the framework of specific controls on the computing processes.

The framework of specific controls on the computing processes is described under eight headings, namely the controls on:

(1) system management;
(2) application management;
(3) transaction origination;
(4) data entry;
(5) data communications;
(6) computer processing;
(7) data storage and retrieval;
(8) output processing.

The principal objectives for the controls in each of the main control areas is discussed in **3.-10.**, below and a list of main controls under these headings is given in **Table 6** at the end of the chapter.

1.   A CONTROLS FRAMEWORK

The controls framework for a computing system consists of several concentric layers surrounding the 'black box' environment as shown in **Figure 9**.

The outermost layer is represented by the legal and societal controls which determine the broad framework within which the company has chosen to operate. These controls are represented by the generally accepted codes of business practice of the economic society as well as the formal legal framework of controls determined by various legislative provisions such as

Figure 9   An application system controls framework

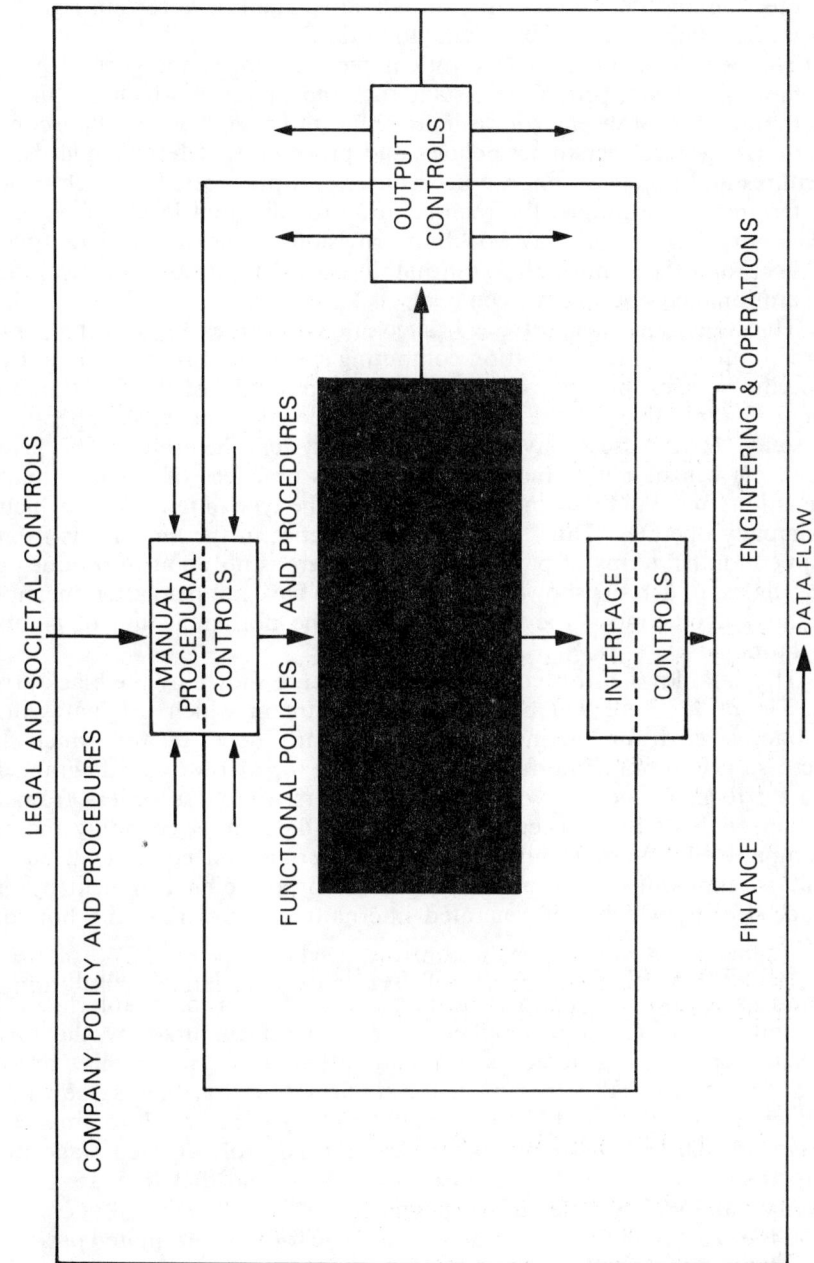

the Factory Acts, Finance Acts, Data Protection Act, etc. The latter Act, which was introduced in 1985, provides that all computing systems which hold data about persons should be registered with a Registrar of Data Protection and determines that an individual shall have certain rights with regard to data which is being held about him.

The next layer of the framework is represented by the general body of company policies, procedures, standards and practices which all functions within the corporate environment are obliged to comply with. These controls comprise general personnel policies and procedures, safety standards, procedures and practices, finance procedures and practices, etc. Such controls determine, for example, the remuneration for different levels of personnel, the hours that persons may work, the provisions for heating and lighting and a host of other considerations that have an important bearing on the operational computing environment.

The innermost layer of the framework constitutes the direct operating environment of the application computing system and is represented by the specific policies, procedures, standards and practices of the functional user and, if applicable, of the data processing department which operates the system—for the users may well operate the system themselves. This layer of controls will be determined by the business practices of the user and DP functions and will be strongly influenced by the type of industry in which the company operates. Thus, if the normal practice in the industry is to grant three months' terms of payment on sales there is no point in producing an ageing list of debtors showing customers who have not paid after one month; although, of course, they will appear in the normal listing of company debtors.

The data flows in this controls framework are shown by the black arrows in **Figure 9**. There will be a major data stream which originates in the economic environment in which the company operates and which flows across the corporate interface as shown in the top arrow in the diagram. This data stream includes invoices from suppliers, purchase orders from customers, data on the market situation, finance data on the economy and other company situations, technical data on materials and equipment, etc This data stream will be reinforced within the corporate environment by other data streams which are generated internally as shown by the horizontal arrows.

Within the company environment, there will be manual procedural controls to regulate the flow of data across the corporate interfaces. For example, invoices from suppliers may be received, first, by the finance department and registered as outstanding liabilites. The invoices are then sent to the materials department for confirmation that they agree with the materials ordered, and delivered, and are then returned to finance for payment. There will be manual procedural controls at each stage of the process to ensure that the invoices are not lost and that they are properly verified and swiftly returned for payment.

If the heart of the corporate activity is some form of automated processing, the data stream will eventually be fed into this part of the system. At the interface, there will be invoked the types of controls which we discuss in **4.-10.** of this chapter, below, and examples of which are listed in **Table 6**. The processes that take place in this part of the system are discussed in more detail in **2.**

The data stream which emerges from the 'black box' environment may pass in one of two directions. First, the data may pass directly into another computing system by a distributed communications link or indirectly via a file produced on magnetic tape or disc. There will be interface controls between the systems to ensure that the data transfer is carried out accurately, completely and efficiently as well as to ensure that there is adequate data security.

The second data stream emerges in the form of hard copy output into the functional user environment, the corporate environment and even perhaps into the broader economic and societal environment outside the corporate boundaries. For example, the output from a finance system may be month end accounting figures of the profit and loss account, source and disposition of funds and balance sheet which are distributed to the finance and other company directors. This enables the senior corporate management to monitor the company affairs on a sufficiently short term basis to make the necessary steering decisions.

At the end of each company accounting period, there will be produced from the finance system the year end accounting figures of the profit and loss account—showing essentially the trading movements that have taken place since the previous accounts—a source and disposition of funds—showing movements in the company liquid resources—and a balance sheet—showing the company assets and the ownership of those assets as at the date the accounts were closed. These accounts are distributed to a number of different persons or institutions depending on the type of ownership of the company.

If the company is private, that is the shareholding in the company is not publicly quoted on a stock exchange, the accounts will only be distributed internally and to Companies House. If the company is public, that is the shares are quoted on a stock exchange and held by the wider general public, the accounts will be distributed both inside and outside the company, eg to the shareholders, to the company statutory auditors, to investment institutions, to Companies House, etc.

The output controls which regulate the stream of data flowing in this second channel are essentially manual procedural controls similar in nature to the manual procedural controls regulating the flow of data in the main input channel. The objectives of these controls are described in **3.**, below.

2. APPLICATION SYSTEM CONTROLS

There are two important individuals, or possibly groups, who are necessary in the operation of an application computing system. The first of these, the system manager, has the most extensive capabilities of any user on the system. This is a demanding technical role which we do not propose to discuss in detail in this book. Suffice it to say that the system manager controls the configuration and operation of the hardware and, to accomplish this, he must have a thorough understanding of the operating system software—although he need have no knowledge of the application software.

The system manager has all the system capabilities of a standard user as well as those that are unique to the system management function, such as:

(1) system configuration;
(2) system 'tuning' to optimise performance;
(3) creation of accounts (authorised users) and account managers;
(4) modification of account capabilities and status;
(5) deletion of entire accounts with associated groups, users and files;
(6) listing of any or all files on the system;
(7) obtaining account reports of system usage and resources;
(8) storing/restoring on magnetic tape, or serial disc, any or all files on the system;
(9) defining private disc volume sets and classes;
(10) altering/deleting private disc volume sets and classes.

Although the system manager has very powerful capabilities with regard to the system, he does not actually 'own' the system. An application computing system rightfully belongs to the users who own the data it processes—even if these users do not own the equipment on which the data is stored and manipulated. To make effective and efficient use of the system, and to preserve security and privacy, it is essential that one of these users should be responsible for the tasks necessary to achieve these objectives. This particular person we refer to as the application manager and s/he should have a comprehensive understanding of the processing performed by the application software and the particular business functions it is designed to satisfy.

For some systems, the tasks of application management may be too much for one person and the work is undertaken by a team. These tasks would include:

(1) maintaining system documentation, eg user guide(s), training manual(s), procedure manual(s), etc;
(2) issuing passwords to new users;
(3) changing user access profiles;
(4) planning the introduction of new programs;
(5) providing 'front-line' user help;
(6) organising training for new users;
(7) liaising with the system manager to set up account structures;
(8) liaising with operations to determine back-up scheduling;
(9) liaising with the data base administrator on data base maintenance;
(10) planning fallback arrangements.

To the majority of users, the computer is simply a 'black box' which provides cetain output from certain input. However, if we were to open up the 'black box' and peer inside, we should observe a number of distinct operations taking place as shown in **Figure 10**.

These operations are controlled by an executive program which we refer to as the 'task scheduler' whose function is to optimise the processing capacity of the machine by allocating the central processing unit (CPU) time to the various jobs which are queuing for attention. This is necessary because the different machine components function at different speeds. For example, an input/output operation performed by 'data management' is slow compared with reading from main memory. If the CPU were to be kept waiting for new input or for output to be sent to storage then it would spend a great deal of

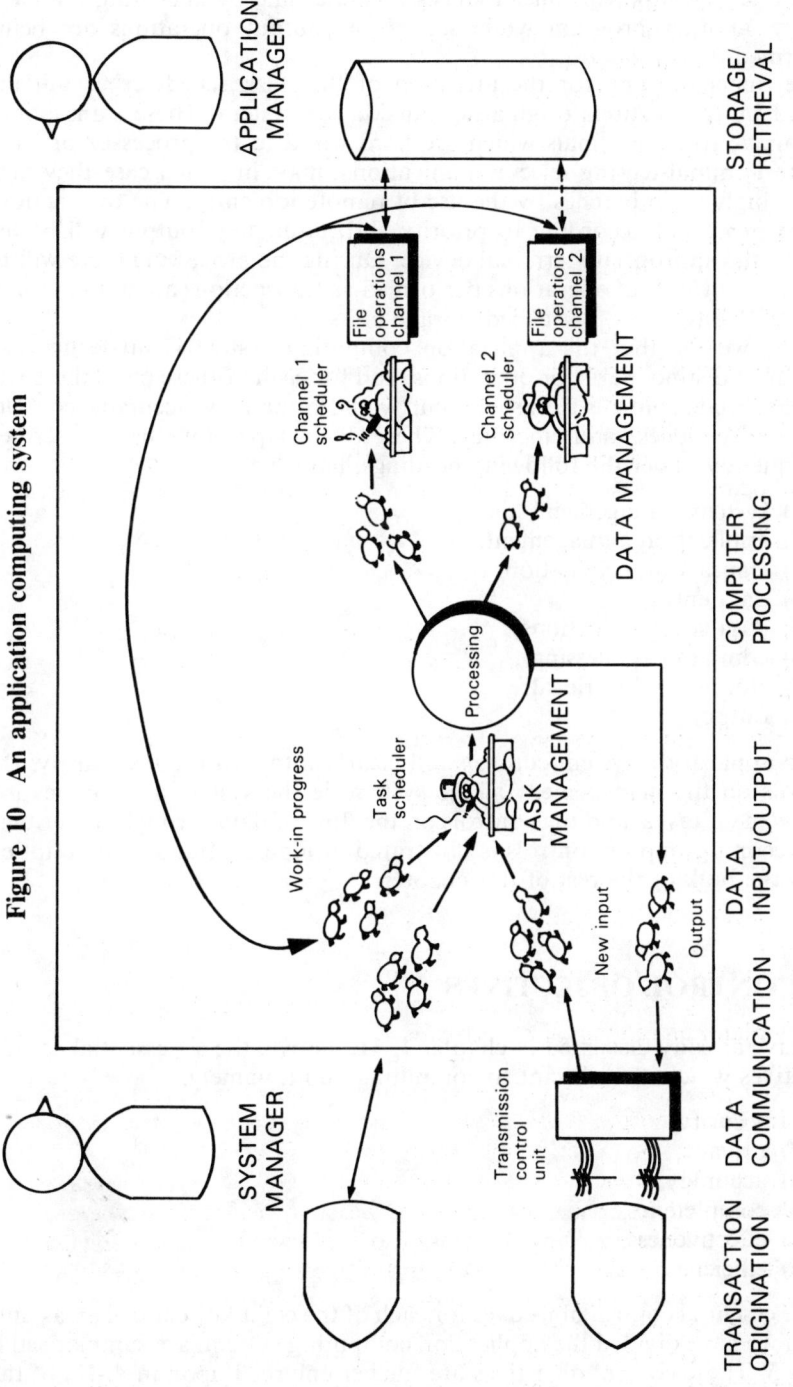

Figure 10 An application computing system

time doing nothing. This is a very inefficient use of expensive computing resources. The task scheduler reduces this idle time by allocating the CPU time to another program while slow input/output operations are being performed.

The queue waiting for the attention of the 'task scheduler' is initially formed by transactions originating outside the system. These transactions may arrive from terminals which are hard wired to the processor or from remote terminals, using telecommunications links, in which case they may arrive singly or in batches by the use of remote job entry. The transactions will be processed according to priority and, ultimately, output will be fed back to the appropriate terminal device. During the processing there will be various input/output operations performed as transactions are written to, or retrieved from, files on attached storage units.

Thus, we see that the application computing system is made up of a number of distinct parts, or operations, and for each of these parts there will be appropriate controls to ensure security and/or privacy, accuracy, completeness, effectiveness and efficiency. These distinct parts we have described subsequently under the following headings, namely:

(1) system management;
(2) application management;
(3) transaction origination;
(4) data entry;
(5) data communications;
(6) computer processing;
(7) storage and retrieval;
(8) output.

The application system controls fall clearly into two groups namely, the controls on the management of the system, ie the system and application management tasks, and the controls on the flow of data through the system. This second group of controls is illustrated in **Figure 11** and its description forms the bulk of the rest of this chapter.

3.   CONTROL OBJECTIVES

We have already discussed in chapter 1, **11.**, above, the six essential control objectives which are relevant to computing audit, namely:

(1) security;
(2) privacy;
(3) accuracy;
(4) completeness;
(5) effectiveness;
(6) efficiency.

The essential control objectives for each of the eight key control areas, into which we have divided the application computing system, are summarised in **Table 5**. These control objectives are further enlarged upon in **4.-10.** of this chapter, below, and a selection of controls, which are relevant in each of the key control areas is given in **Table 6** at the end of the chapter.

Figure 11 The application system data flow controls

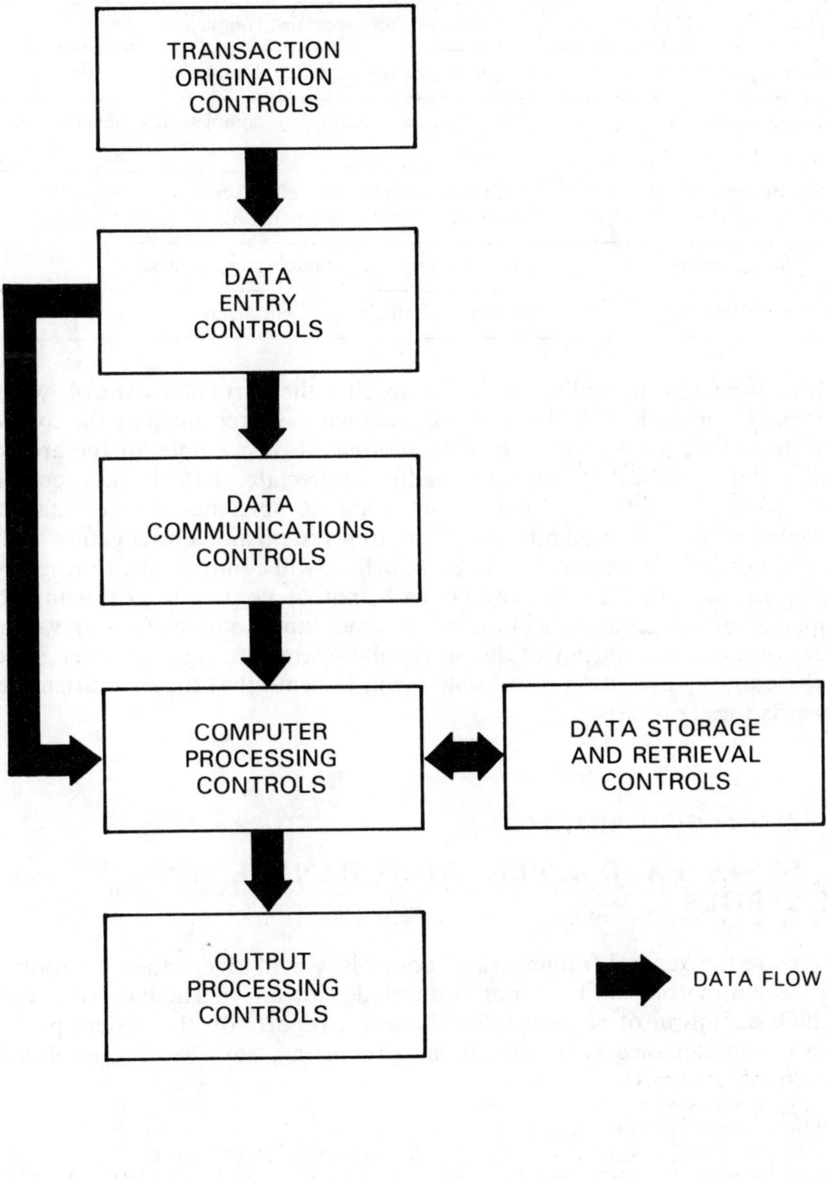

Table 5   Control objectives

Control area	Principal control objectives
System management	Security, privacy, effectiveness, efficiency
Application management	Security, privacy, effectiveness, efficiency
Transaction origination	Security, privacy, accuracy, completeness
Data entry	Security, privacy, accuracy, completeness
Data communications	Security, privacy, accuracy, completeness, effectiveness, efficiency
Computer processing	accuracy, completeness, effectiveness, efficiency
Data storage/retrieval	Security, privacy, accuracy, completeness
Output processing	Accuracy, completeness, effectiveness

It is important to realise, at this stage, that the particular controls which are relevant in each of the key control areas will be determined by the control objectives that we set for each of these areas. For example, in the area of transaction origination, we can readily appreciate that the key control objectives are security, privacy, accuracy and completeness of the data that will eventually be entered into the computing system and a brief glance at the type of controls in section 3 of **Table 6**, below, will confirm this. Further, we can appreciate that in the key control area of computer processing the emphasis of the controls will be on accuracy and completeness as well as effectiveness and efficiency of the processing operation. Again, a brief glance at the controls in section 6 of **Table 6** will indicate that they are orientated towards these objectives.

4.   SYSTEM AND APPLICATION MANAGEMENT CONTROLS

These are the general framework of controls which govern the operation of the system in total and are not connected with any particular part. They include definition of responsibilities, control reports on the system performance, maintenance arrangements and reporting, etc They are essentially preventive controls.

The control objectives are to:

(1) ensure that there is adequate system SECURITY and PRIVACY by appropriate authorisation and access procedures;
(2) support EFFECTIVE management control over organisational and procedural aspects of the system;

(3) ensure that the system operates EFFICIENTLY with regard to availability and performance.

A sample list of essential controls in these two areas is given in sections 1 and 2 of **Table 6**, at the end of this chapter. These controls do not include the general operational controls—examples of which have been given in **Table 2**—which are applicable to all systems operated in a specific operations centre. Such controls would be audited in a computer operations audit, as we have suggested in chapter 2, **7.**, above. However, if the application system is operated on a 'stand-alone' basis, by the users, then these operations controls would be included in an application computing system audit.

5. TRANSACTION ORIGINATION CONTROLS

These are controls governing the origination, approval and processing of source documents, the preparation of data processing input transactions and associated error prevention, detection and correction procedures.

The control objectives are to maintain:

(1) SECURITY and PRIVACY by ensuring that transaction origination is only performed by authorised user personnel;
(2) ACCURACY and COMPLETENESS by ensuring that there are written procedures governing the preparation of all source documents.

A sample list of the essential controls in this area is given in section 3 of **Table 6**.

6. DATA ENTRY CONTROLS

These are application controls governing both remote terminal and batch data entry, data validation, transaction or batch proofing and balancing, error identification and reporting and error correction and re-entry. They include prevention, detection and correction controls.

The control objectives are to maintain:

(1) SECURITY and PRIVACY by ensuring that data entry is only performed by authorised user personnel;
(2) ACCURACY and COMPLETENESS by procedures to ensure that all data is submitted, that there is proper validation of source data and all errors are detected, corrected and resubmitted quickly for further processing.

A sample list of the essential controls in this area is given in section 4 of **Table 6**.

7. DATA COMMUNICATION CONTROLS

These are controls governing data communications including message accountability, data protection, hardware and software, security and privacy, error identification and reporting. They include prevention, detection and correction controls.
The control objectives are to:

(1) ensure the SECURITY and PRIVACY of data sent over the transmission networks;
(2) maintain the ACCURACY and COMPLETENESS of data sent over the transmission networks;
(3) ensure that the data transmission networks are operated EFFECTIVELY and EFFICIENTLY with appropriate backup and fallback facilities and that the rates of data transfer are adequate for operational requirements.

A sample list of the essential controls in this area is given in section 5 of **Table 6**.

8. COMPUTER PROCESSING CONTROLS

These are application controls governing the processing of transactions including error identification and reporting. They are essentially detective and corrective controls.
The control objectives are to ensure:

(1) the ACCURACY and COMPLETENESS of data generated by computer processing;
(2) the EFFECTIVENESS and EFFICIENCY of the computer processing operation.

A sample list of the essential controls in this area is given in section 6 of **Table 6**.

9. DATA STORAGE AND RETRIEVAL CONTROLS

These are application controls on masterfile data storage and handling, including transaction and masterfile cut-off dates and backup/recovery and fallback. They are essentially detection and correction controls.
The control objectives are to:

(1) ensure SECURITY and PRIVACY of all data being held on masterfiles;
(2) maintain the ACCURACY and COMPLETENESS of data held on masterfiles by ensuring the detection and correction of errors and their timely reprocessing.

A sample list of the essential controls in this area is given in section 7 of **Table 6**.

10. OUTPUT PROCESSING CONTROLS

These are application controls governing manual balancing and reconciliation of data processing input and output, distribution of data processing output, control over source documents and output data retention. They are essentially detection and correction controls.

The control objectives are to ensure:

(1) the ACCURACY and COMPLETENESS of information produced and data transfers direct to other systems;
(2) the system output is EFFECTIVE in meeting users' requirements from the system.

A sample list of the essential controls in this area is given in section 8 of **Table 6**.

Table 6 Application Computer System Controls

Control reference	Key control area	Control details
1.	System management	
1.1		There is a recognised system manager (SM) and there is a written job description describing the position.
1.2		The SM has been appropriately trained in the use of the system hardware and has a thorough comprehension of the operating system software.
1.3		The SM has copies of all the suppliers manuals on the management of the system and has—if relevant—a customised SM manual written for local operation.
1.4		The SM regularly monitors the usage and performance of the system in order to carry out 'tuning'.
1.5		There are appropriate statistics generated by the system to enable the SM to monitor usage and performance.
1.6		Any attempts at breach of security are automatically signalled at the SM's terminal and printed out on the system console.
1.7		The SM follows up all attempts at breach of security and advises the application manager of the outcome.
1.8		The SM has provided written procedures, for the system operations manual, on backup and recovery arrangements.
1.9		The SM is responsible for ensuring that the hardware is serviced in accordance with the supplier maintenance agreement.
1.10		There are written procedures, in the systems operations manual, providing for the shutdown before, and start-up after, of equipment for maintenance.
1.11		The SM is advised of all hardware faults to the central processor, discs, tape units and system console(s) and the corrective action that was taken.
1.12		The SM has created the appropriate accounts and account managers according to the instructions of the application manager.
2.	Application management	
2.1		There is a recognised application manager (AM)—or group—in the user organisation and there is a (are) written job description(s) describing the position.

Table 6—*continued*

Control reference	Key control area	Control details
2.2		The AM has been appropriately trained in the processing aspects of the application system software and the business functions it satisfies.
2.3		The AM has copies of all the relevant manuals necessary for the effective application management of the system: —functional specification(s) —user guide(s) —procedures manual(s) —training manual(s).
2.4		The AM is responsible for ensuring that the above manuals are updated, as appropriate, and up-dates are circulated to all users.
2.5		The AM is responsible for defining the password structure, eg minimum of six alphanumeric characters, and for issuing passwords to new users.
2.6		The AM is responsible for defining the user access profiles and any changes that may be required.
2.7		The AM is responsible for organising training for new users and for retraining existing users with modifications to the system.
2.8		The AM is responsible for providing 'front-line' support to users on all matters relating to the application system software.
2.9		The AM has been involved with the data base administrator in drawing up a plan for data base maintenance—including when, and how frequently.
2.10		The AM has agreed with operations the most convenient timing for the system backups to provide maximum system availability, to the users, during the working day.
2.11		The AM has agreed with the SM the most convenient time for system maintenance in order to optimise system availability, to the users, during the working day.
2.12		The AM has produced a fallback and contingency plan to provide for the operation of the business functions in the event of a complete breakdown of the computing system availability.
3.	Transaction origination	
3.1		There are written user procedures to guide the proper initiation, review and authorisation of input.
3.2		There are special purpose forms to guide the initial recording of transactions in a uniform format.
3.3		Each transaction to be entered into the system has a unique transaction identification.
3.4		The source document reference number is included in data entry to provide a cross-reference for tracing transactions.
3.5		Modifications to data on source documents are controlled by limiting access to forms during their intermediate storage and transportation.
3.6		A system of dual custody is used to maintain control over negotiable instruments, eg blank cheques.
3.7		There are written authorisation procedures for all transactions and evidence that all types of transactions have been

Control reference	Key control area	Control details
		reviewed before granting the appropriate level of authority.
3.8		A manual review of source documents is performed by user personnel in order to ensure the completeness and accuracy of data processing input.
3.9		Batches are identified by a unique serial number or sequence number.
3.10		The number of transactions in a batch is limited to simplify the reconciliation process required when batches are out of balance.
3.11		The source data are batched and balanced as close to the point of origin as possible.
3.12		The methods used to move batches of documents between departments depends upon the classification of the information but should always ensure the integrity of the batch, ie no missing forms.
3.13		Retention dates are placed on source documents, batch slips, etc which are based on legal requirements and/or management policy.
3.14		A file is maintained, in the user area, of source documents in a sequence which best fits the situation.
3.15		The source documents are destroyed, after the retention period has expired, or removed and stored as part of the company long-term records retention policy.
3.16		Records removed from storage, after the retention period has expired, are destroyed according to their classification.
3.17		There are written error handling procedures to provide user personnel with comprehensive instructions for source document error detection, error correction and corrected data resubmission.
3.18		The error correction procedures are defined in the user guide and the assignment of error correction responsibility is clearly allocated.
3.19		The user is notified immediately of all source documents that are in error.
3.20		The data fields on resubmitted source documents are subjected to the same verification procedures as the original source document.
4.	Data entry	
4.1		A predesigned screen format is used to guide terminal operators inputting data.
4.2		Each individual user group is limited to the input screens required for their work tasks.
4.3		There is a periodic review of the authority levels of all user groups.
4.4		There are editing and validation routines performed on all data fields before transactions are accepted by the system.
4.5		Transactions entered after a specific cut-off date are held in suspense and suspense listing is produced for the user.
4.6		A schedule of processing is used to ensure that all transactions are received and entered on time.
4.7		Where data are entered from source documents, the documents are retained at the input terminal until the system accepts the entire transaction.

Table 6—*continued*

Control reference	Key control area	Control details
4.8		Source documents that have been processed are cancelled to prevent double entry.
4.9		Transactions are entered from terminals in batches.
4.10		Batch control totals are used to establish controls on information to be processed.
4.11		Errors are displayed at terminals immediately upon detection.
4.12		There are meaningful error messages to assist in the correction of errors.
4.13		The re-entry of corrected data is carried out using the same rules as for processing the original transaction.
4.14		There are control totals produced for all rejected transactions.
5.	Data communications	
5.1		There is a computer table of all authorised terminal polling addresses within the communication network.
5.2		Terminal messages are identified by the sequence number of the message, date and time, transaction number or video screen number.
5.3		There is a computer table of transaction types that are authorised from specific terminal addresses which is used to control access to sensitive data.
5.4		Data communication lines are separate from the public switched network system.
5.5		Forward error correction techniques are used for the detection and reporting of data communication errors.
5.6		Parity checks and validity checks are used to detect character errors during transmission.
5.7		Echo checking is used in the detection and reporting of data communication errors.
5.8		Scrambling or encryption techniques are used in transmitting sensitive data.
5.9		Key communications lines are duplicated or there are alternative communication channels which may be readily invoked.
5.10		Detection with retransmission is used to minimise errors in transmission.
5.11		A message sequence number is automatically assigned to all messages in and out of the computer system.
5.12		A log of all input and output messages is maintained on a backup device to assist in system recovery or in tracing messages.
6.	Computer processing	
6.1		Computer generated transactions are printed out for direct feedback to users and balance controls are used for transfers between program modules.
6.2		Control totals are passed between jobs and job steps during production.
6.3		Arithmetic accuracy is ensured through the use of techniques such as double arithmetic, arithmetic overflow checks and reverse multiplication.

Control reference	Key control area	Control details
6.4		An exception report is prepared each time a program control is over-written or by-passed.
6.5		Application file control totals containing the record count and critical field amounts are balanced automatically to file control totals from the previous program run.
6.6		A file completion check is used to determine that the application file has been completely progressed including both the transaction file and the masterfile.
6.7		The number of records on the opening of a data file is balanced against changes made during the day and the closing balance.
6.8		The processing of on-line transactions is sufficiently fast to prevent operators becoming bored and losing interest.
6.9		The processing of batch transactions is carried out at off-peak periods and is suffiently fast to keep system out-time to a minimum.
6.10		All numerical manipulations are carried out by computer programs and the users do not need to make hand calculations from computer output.
6.11		Error reports indicate all data fields in error and the type of error incurred.
6.12		A production report is provided to ensure all rejects have been corrected and resubmitted.
6.13		An automated suspense file is maintained by the DP department for all rejected transactions.
6.14		The entries in the automated error suspense files have unique serial numbers.
7.	Data storage and retrieval	
7.1		There is a formal library system that indicates the content and location of all tapes, discs and documentation.
7.2		There is an account classification for regular production jobs and a separate account classification for development phase programs or modules.
7.3		Two different programs cannot simultaneously update the same application record.
7.4		Files in large systems are divided into groups for control purposes.
7.5		Application files are classified by security levels, eg standard, registered, confidential, restricted.
7.6		There are header and trailer labels on all files used for production jobs.
7.7		All transactions and messages entering the application system are retained on independent files.
7.8		All changes to security tables receive appropriate authorisation before the change is made in the computing system.
7.9		When records are changed in data base files the system records in a separate file both before and after looks.
7.10		The system reports data files that exhibit no activity for a specific period.
7.11		There is a backup copy held outside the computer operations room of all masterfiles.
7.12		There are backup procedures described in the operations manual for all files.

Table 6—*continued*

Control reference	Key control area	Control details
7.13		There are recovery procedures describing the restoration to active use of systems that have crashed.
7.14		There is a disaster plan based on specified application requirements.
7.15		There is a log of all application system processing halts and operator interruptions.
8.	Output	
8.1		The output control totals for each application are reconciled with input totals before the release of the report from data processing.
8.2		There is a report summarising the number of application reports generated, number of pages per report, cost per report and number of lines per report.
8.3		The application system output reports are delivered to authorised recipients only.
8.4		Report distribution is limited to the authorised number of report copies.
8.5		The system output reports contain the following information in the header: —date prepared; —processing period covered; —descriptive title of report contents; —processing program number.
8.6		The functional user area receives a summary report listing of all transactions produced internally by the application system.
8.7		The user department is provided with a report to compare manually maintained batch totals to the equivalent accumulated totals produced by the computer application.
8.8		There are appropriate waste disposal procedures to ensure that the confidential output reports no longer required are disposed of in the proper manner.
8.9		A periodic review is made of all application system reports received by the user.
8.10		Outstanding items on error reports are investigated regularly by the user to ensure their correction and timely re-entry into the system.
8.11		There is a means of identifying source documents in error in order to make data corrections.
8.12		The error correction procedures are defined in the user guide for the application.
8.13		The assignment of error correction responsibility is specified in the user guide.
8.14		There are error logs maintained in the user area which are used to follow up on unresolved errors and to ensure their correction and timely re-entry into the system.

References

1 The Canadian Institute of Chartered Accountants *Computer Control Guidelines* (1970).
2 The Canadian Institute of Chartered Accountants *Computer Audit Guidelines* (1975).
3 The Institute of Internal Auditors Inc *Systems Auditability and Control—Control Practices* (1977).
4 The Institute of Internal Auditors Inc *Systems Auditability and Control—Audit Practices* (1977).
5 Martin J *Security, Accuracy and Privacy in Computer Systems* (1973) Prentice-Hall Inc.
6 Martin J *Introduction to Teleprocessing* (1972) Prentice-Hall Inc.
7 Mair W C, Wood D R, Davis K W *Computer Control and Audit* (1978) Institute of Internal Auditors.
8 Fitzgerald J *Designing Controls into Computerised Systems* (1981) Jerry Fitzgerald Associates.

4　System development controls

This chapter describes the controls which are relevant to the systems development process. These controls have been divided into eight areas covering:

(1) the systems development cycle (SDC);
(2) project management;
(3) data administration;
(4) data base management software (DBMS) selection;
(5) data base administration;
(6) system design and construction;
(7) system implementation and acceptance;
(8) system documentation.

The processes involved in, and the importance of, each of these areas in systems development, are described in this chapter.

The SDC is a recognised methodology for systems development and consists of a sequence of tasks which are grouped into phases. The end of each phase is a potential checkpoint where a go/no-go decision is required.

A project is defined as a set of interrelated tasks organised to achieve a specific goal which has been recognised as desirable by management in the company. The common characteristics of computing projects are time horizons, manpower resources, machine resources and data resources.

Data administration, or data management, comprise the processes which are carried out to ensure that the data of the organisation is properly identified, described and catalogued. The person(s) responsible for these processes is usually referred to as the data administrator.

A data base is defined as an interrelated set of data items with controlled redundancy, ie duplication of data values, which may be used for a variety of applications and by a variety of users. The data in the data base is created, retrieved, updated or deleted by a collection of software modules called the data base management system (DBMS).

System design and construction are the processes by which the analysis work is converted into programs which make up a working system. This is followed by system implementation and acceptance which are the processes by which the completed system is set up and handed over for acceptance by the user and operations staff.

There are four essential types of system documentation, namely:

(1) reports on management decisions, eg steering committee minutes;

(2) reports to management on project progress, eg feasibility study reports;

(3) technical reports, eg functional specification;

(4) the 'handover package'.

A list of main controls in each of the eight important areas of the systems development process is given in **Table 9** at the end of this chapter.

1. SYSTEMS DEVELOPMENT CYCLE

The systems development cycle (SDC) is a recognised sequence of tasks, decision points and supporting documentation, leading to the successful implementation of a system. It describes what should be done in the development of systems but it does not specify how the tasks should be carried out. This is for other documentation which describes the methods and deliverables in the system development process.

The purpose of the SDC is to guide the project team along the path of minimum time, cost and risk in developing and implementing efficient and reliable systems. Its specific objectives are to:

(1) ensure that systems are developed in a controlled manner with recognised review points, in order to reduce progressively the risk involved;

(2) provide an agreed framework for the joint development of systems by users and data processing;

(3) improve communication and commitment between the project group and the end users of the system;

(4) prevent duplication of effort;

(5) minimise documentation;

(6) provide a common terminology in systems development;

(7) serve as a reference for project group staff.

The SDC is discussed in further detail in the next chapter, chapter 5, and a sample list of essential controls in this area is given in section 1 of **Table 9**.

2. PROJECT MANAGEMENT

A project may be defined as a set of interrelated tasks organised to achieve a specific goal which has been recognised as desirable by line management in the company. The common characteristics of projects are time horizons, ie beginning and ending, manpower resources, equipment resources and data resources. Since company resources are involved, and there exist potential threats to those resources, all projects present a potential exposure.

As we have seen in chapter 1, the size of the exposure will depend upon the financial value of the resources involved and the probability of occurrence of the threats to those resources. Clearly, the greater the financial commitment to a project the greater the degree of exposure. Further, the longer the time horizon between the start of the project and estimated completion date the greater is the degree of uncertainty and, therefore, the risk which is involved.

There is a very considerable degree of uncertainty at the start of a project and a broad band estimate for the final cost. As the project progresses, the degree of error which is likely in an estimate of the cost of the remainder of the project, made at a particular point, declines as the scope of the work becomes clearer. This is illustrated in **Figure 12**.

Figure 12   Project cost estimates and time

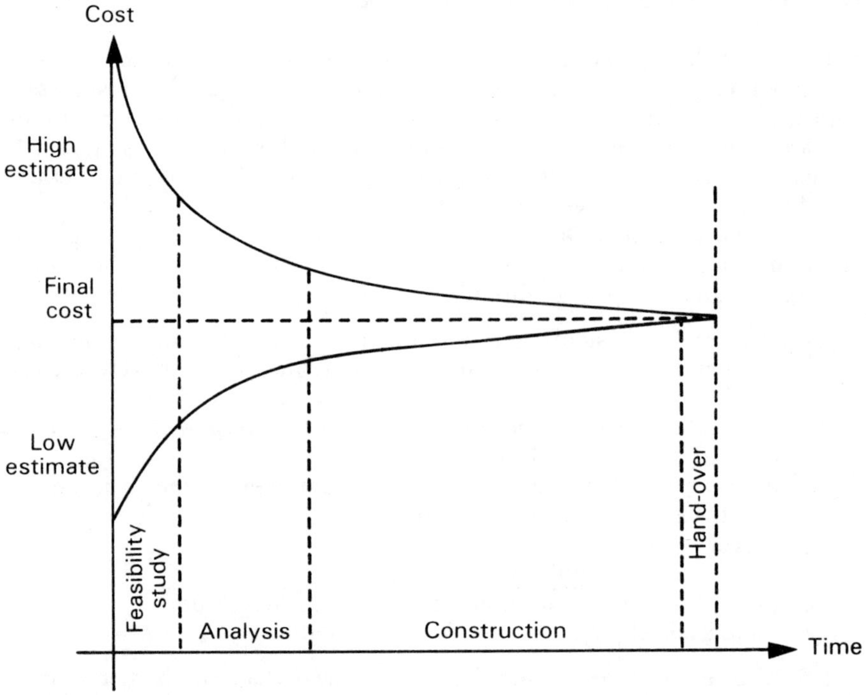

The purpose of controls in project management is to reduce the degree of exposure resulting from the commitment of company resources and the possibility that there will be no return on those resources. The chances of success with a project will evidently be higher if the project manager has a successful track record behind him of similar projects and if the line management in the user area are firmly committed to making the project a success. As shown in **Figure 13**, the total cost of a typical project rises steeply after the project initiation and feasibility study stages with the increasing commitment of resources. It is essential that, for proper control, there should be an adequate system of cost reporting as well as management checkpoints at which the continuing viability of the project is reviewed.

There must be standards and guidelines on project planning and control which are rigidly complied with. It also helps if there are automated tools available to assist in the planning process, as well as established control techniques such as critical path analysis and network analysis.

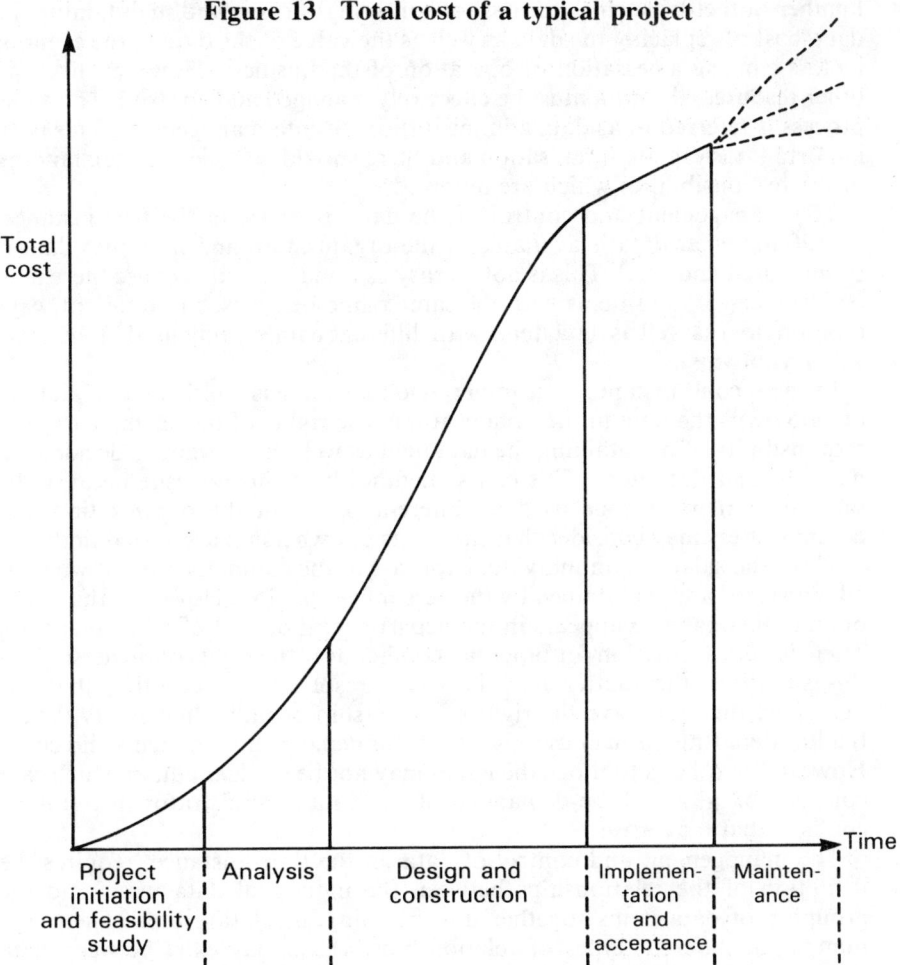

Figure 13   Total cost of a typical project

The chances of success are also greater if the project is broken down into tasks which are small enough to be effectively managed and there are established target start and completion dates set for every development phase and every task. The actual process of project management ensures that all progress, problems and delays are monitored by the project manager and by a steering committee, if applicable.

Project management is discussed in further detail in chapter 7, and a sample list of essential controls, in this area, is given in section 2 of **Table 9**.

3.   DATA ADMINISTRATION

We have already mentioned earlier in chapter 1, that data is an important resource in a business enterprise. The value of the data depends upon a number of factors such as the cost of collecting, storing and maintaining the data, cost of replacing the data as well as the value of the data in the event of its loss causing a cessation of operation of the business. However, like any other resource, the data must be effectively managed and controlled and this process is referred to as data administration or data management. This is an important task in an organisation and there should be a clear understanding of the responsibilities which are involved.

The management and control of the data involves, in the first instance, identifying what data is available in the organisation and how that data is being stored and used. This is not so easy as it may sound because there may be instances of data items with the same name being used in different ways (homonyms) as well as data items with different names being used in the same way (synonyms).

In the second instance, it is imperative that there is a clear understanding of who owns the data in the organisation. The rights of ownership carry the responsibility of maintaining the data item as well as the right to decide who may use that data item. This can sometimes be a thorny issue because the same data item may be used in different places in the organisation and different users may consider that the rights of ownership are vested in them.

Thus, the salary of an individual appears in the company payroll which is administered and maintained by the personnel function. However, the salary of an individual also appears in the departmental budget of a line manager. There is here a situation for potential conflict over the rights of ownership. In this situation, the matter may be easily resolved by accepting that the Personnel function have the right of ownership of individual salary details but line departments may use aggregates for departmental budgets and costs. However, in other situations the issues may not be so clear cut, in which case considerable skill will be demanded of the data administrator in resolving conflicts that may arise.

The management and control of data, in the third instance, requires the definition of the relationships between the individual data items and the grouping of data items together into meaningful relationships. There is a number of different types of relationships which may exist between data items and examples of these are shown in **Figure 14**. This process of defining relationships and grouping data items is referred to as data modelling.

The first step in data modelling is the identification and definition of all data items which are used in a business process and preferably the recording of those data items in an automated data dictionary which explains the nature of the data items, where those items are being used, and the relationships between them. The next step is to group those data items together into meaningful relationships to reduce the number of associations between them to comprehensible proportions.

In a system which contains N data items there are $N(N-1)$ possible relationships between those data items. Thus, the materials management system of one large company contains over 3,000 data items which means that there are 3,000 * 2999, or almost 9 million possible relationships—not all of which will be meaningful, though. The skill in data modelling is in grouping the data items together into meaningful aggregates, that will remain stable over time, and that will minimise the number of relationships in the final data model.

The grouping of data into aggregates—known as records—requires the selection of certain data items, which we call entities, against which we can

Figure 14 Some types of data relationships

(a) One-to-one (1 : 1) relationship

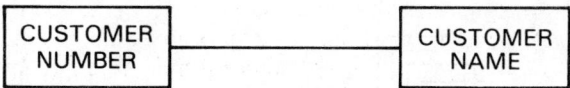

A unique customer number can have only one customer name and conversely a unique customer name can have only one customer number (in one company).

(b) One-to-many (1 : M) relationship

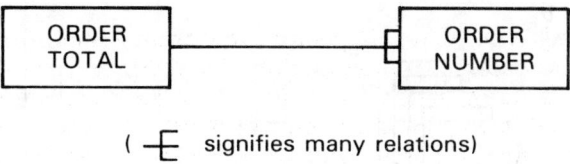

(⊣ signifies many relations)

A unique order number may have only one total but many order numbers may have the same total.

(c) Many-to-many (M : M) relationship

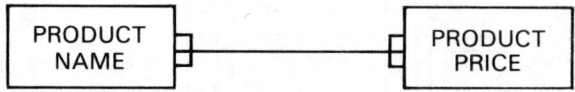

A unique product name may have many different prices, ie from different suppliers, and one unique price may apply to many different products.

usefully record other data items which we call attributes. In some cases, in order to identify uniquely a particular piece of data, the entity needs to be composed of more than one data item. This is shown in **Figure 16** where order number and product number are required to identify uniquely quantity ordered and product total.

The grouping of data items into records is illustrated in **Figure 15** in which the entity, in this case, is the order number and the attributes are the other data items which constitute the data record. If the record is accessed in the data base by the entity the latter is referred to as the primary key. However, the record may also be accessed by any one of the attributes which are then referred to as secondary keys. Where the entity is composed of two or more data items it is referred to as a compound key.

The second step in the data modelling process is to convert the first attempt data aggregates into stable associations by conversion to third-normal-form structures. The third-normal-form may be defined as simple, relatively stable groupings of data items related together in such a way as to minimise data base maintenance problems such as insert, delete and update operations. This conversion to third-normal-form is accomplished in three

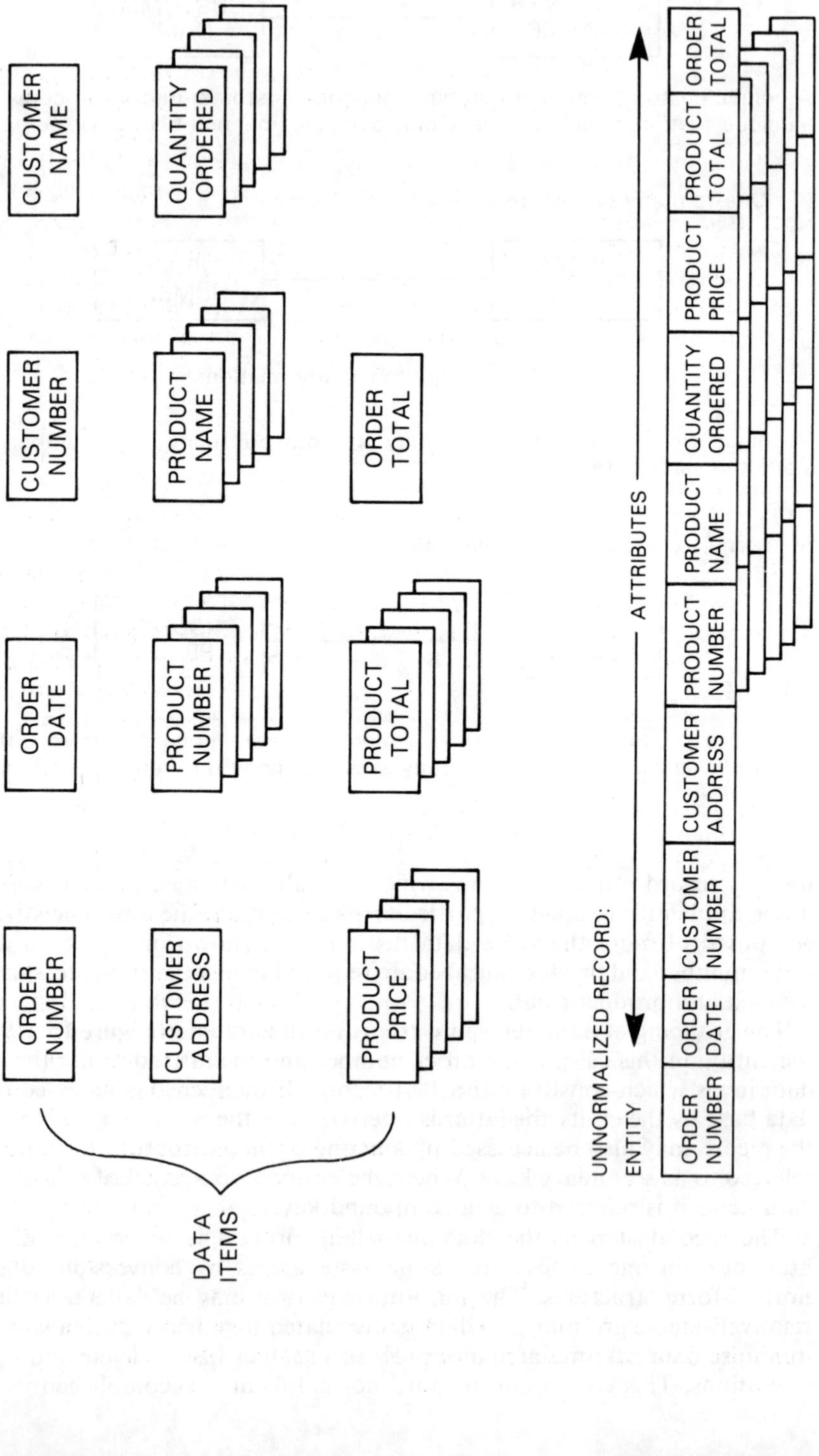

Figure 15 First step in data modelling: bring related data items together to form records

stages as illustrated in **Figure 16**. The objectives of normalisation are to:

(1) store each attribute once only;
(2) group data so that maintenance is simplified;
(3) provide a solid basis of stable features on which to build a conceptual data model.

The first stage of the normalisation process removes repeating groups, ie multiple values of the same items such as price and quantity in a stock record, into separate records. The second removes associations which do not exhibit full dependence, ie if the key is compound the data item should be dependent on the whole key.The third stage removes transitive dependencies, ie a data item which is not a key but which itself identifies other data items.

The normalised records can then be linked graphically to form a conceptual data model of which an example is shown in **Figure 31**, in chapter 7. The conceptual data model is a formal statement of how all relevant pieces of data relate to each other in a particular computing application. Its purpose is to provide a clear representation of the organisation's data and the relationships between the data.

The third step in the modelling process is to convert the conceptual data model into a global logical schema—or logical data model There is a number of automated modelling tools available, eg DATAMANAGER, DATADESIGNER, which will enable this process to be carried out rapidly and which also create third normal form structures.

The logical data model can be formed in several different ways according to the way the DBMS handles the records and examples of these are shown in **Figure 17**. A tree is composed of a hierarchy of elements referred to as nodes. This is shown in example (a) in **Figure 17**. The uppermost level of the hierarchy has only one node and is referred to as the root. Thus, a tree can be defined as a hierarchy of nodes with bi-nodal relationships such that:

(1) the highest level in the hierarchy has one node called a ROOT;
(2) all nodes except the root are related to one and only one node on a higher level than themselves called the PARENT;
(3) elements related to elements at a higher level are called CHILDREN;

Data files which are designed with a tree structure relationship between the records are referred to as hierarchical.

If a child in a data relationship has more than one parent, the relationship is described as a plex or network structure. This is shown in example (b) in **Figure 17**. A plex structure may be reduced to a simple tree structure by introducing redundancy, ie by duplicating some of the data items in the data records. This may be necessary if the data base management software (DBMS) cannot handle plex structures.

The third type of data model structure—the relational data model—is constructed by the process of normalisation which we have described above. Normalisation replaces tree and plex structures with relationships in two dimensional tabular form as shown in example (c) in **Figure 17**. The advantage of this is that it avoids the entanglements that can build up with tree and plex structures in large models. The relational data base is composed of two dimensional tables—which are referred to as relations—in which the rows are referred to as tuples and the columns as domains.

Figure 16   Second step in data modelling: convert un-normalised records to third-normal-form (TNF)

(a) first normal form: remove the repeating group

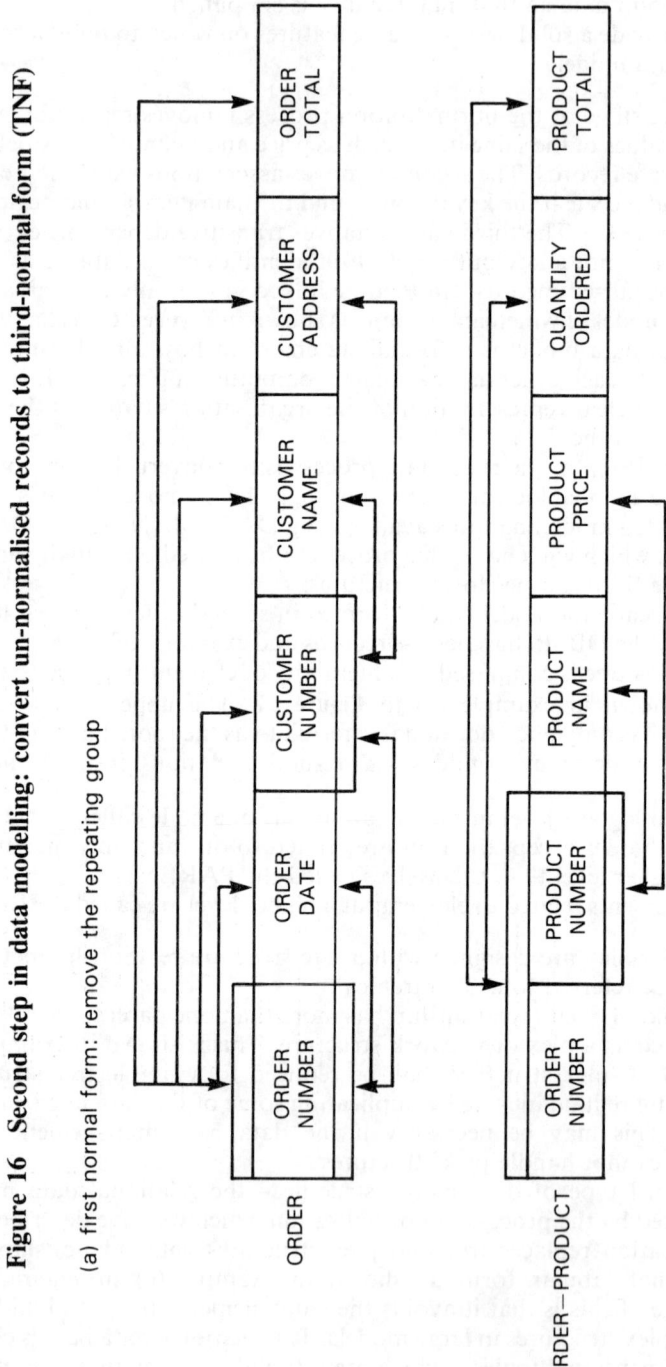

Figure 16 Second step in data modelling (cont)

(b) Second normal form: remove attributes not dependent on the whole of a compound key as in the ORDER—PRODUCT record above

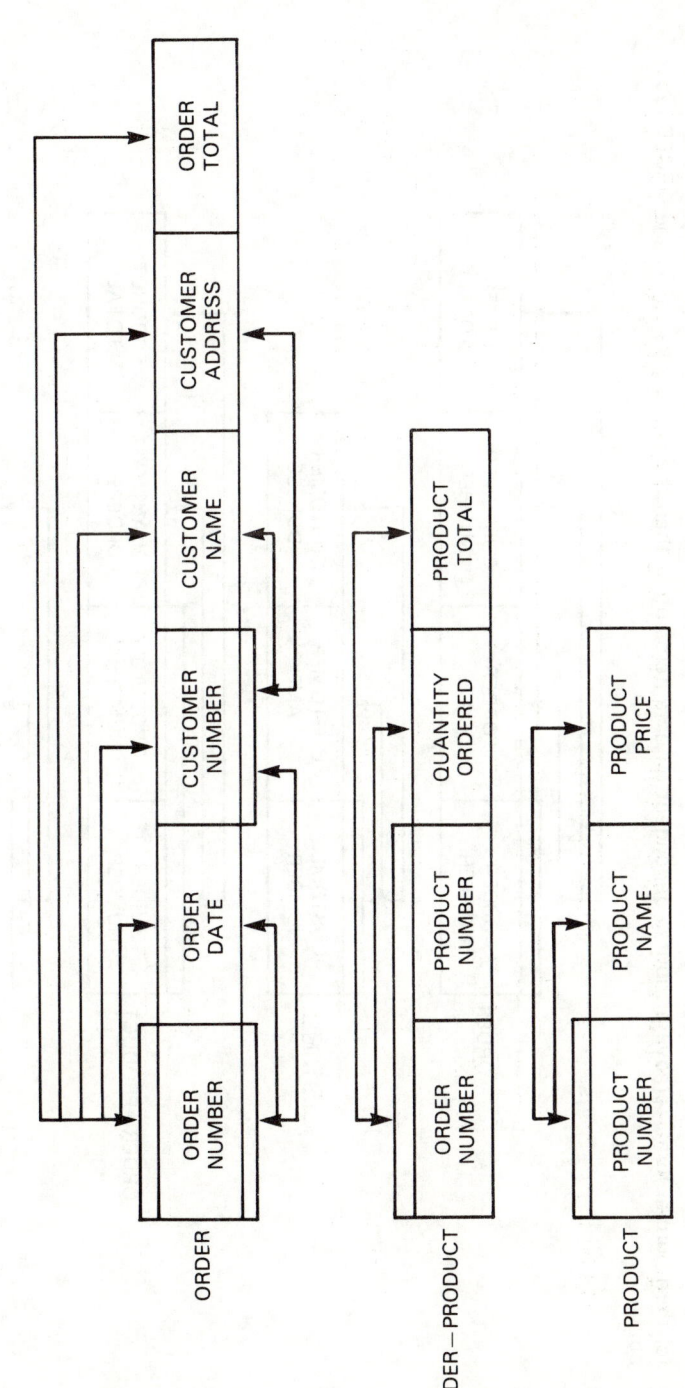

Figure 16   Second step in data modelling (cont)

(c) third normal form: remove attributes dependent on data items other than the primary key as in the ORDER record above

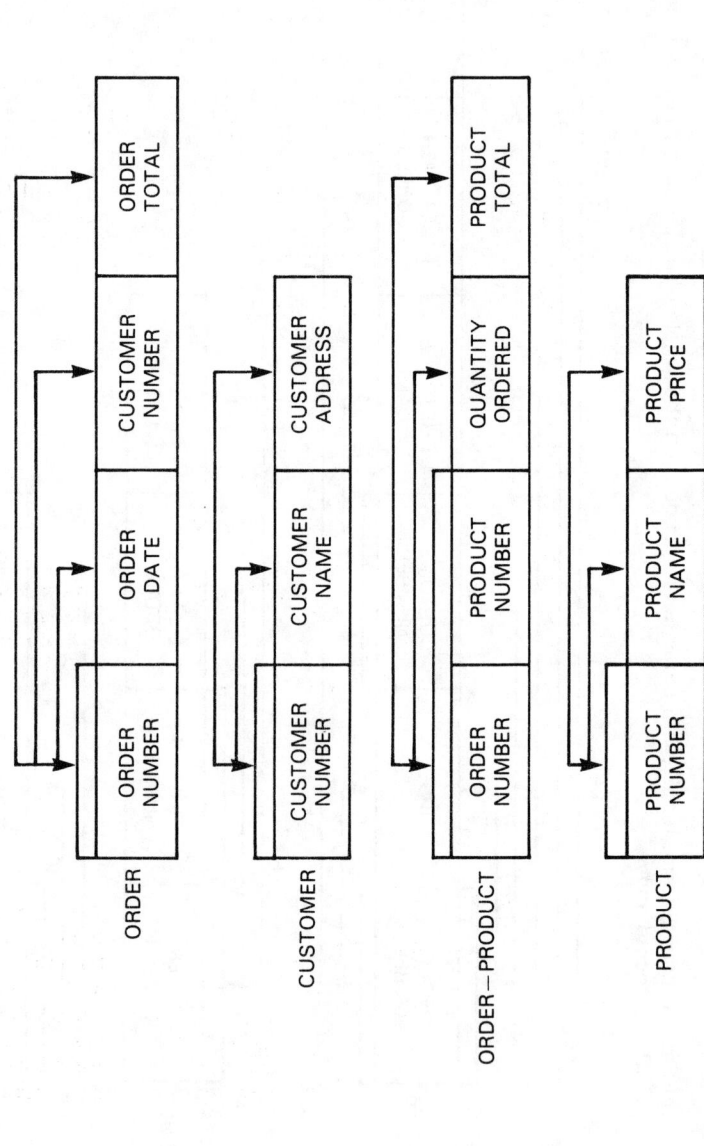

Figure 17   Third step in data modelling: convert the normalised records into a logical data model

(a) TREE or HIERARCHICAL model

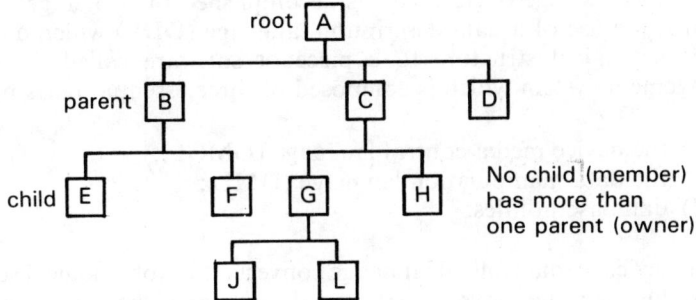

No child (member) has more than one parent (owner)

(b) PLEX or NETWORK model

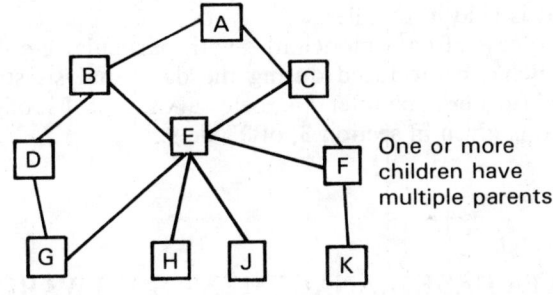

One or more children have multiple parents

(c) RELATIONAL model

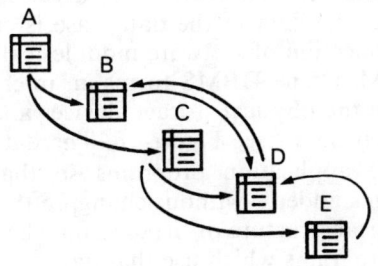

Two-dimensional tables (relations) having rows (tuples) and columns (domains). These flat files are associated to form a relational data base.

The final steps, in the data modelling process, are (i) to assess the model for future stability and (ii) to evaluate the effect of the model structure on machine performance by practical testing. The former is carried out by a careful appraisal of each data item to determine which of them could assume the importance of primary keys. However, before practical testing can be undertaken the logical data model must be converted into an actual physical model on a storage device. This is accomplished in two stages the first of which is the use of a data description language (DDL) which describes the global or logical structure to a piece of software called the data base management system which is composed of three essential parts namely:

(1) the device media control language (DMCL);
(2) the data manipulation language (DML);
(3) database utilities.

The device media control language converts the global logical schema into actual files on the physical storage devices and the data manipulation language,which is usually embedded in a host programming language, such as COBOL, is the interface between the application program and the DBMS. The end result of the processing, at this stage, is to produce a data base on the storage units which is independent of the application programs which use the data that is held in the files.

The process of data modelling—with particular emphasis on the deliverables which are produced during the data analysis stage of the SDC—is discussed further in chapter 7,**4.**, below. A sample list of essential controls, in this area, is given in section 3, of **Table 9**.

4. DATA BASE MANAGEMENT SOFTWARE (DBMS) SELECTION

A data base is an interrelated set of data items with controlled redundancy, ie duplication of data values, which may be used for a variety of applications and by a variety of users. The data in the data base is created, retrieved, updated or deleted by a collection of software modules called the data base management system (DBMS). The DBMS forms an interface between the collection of data items on the physical storage devices and the application programmes which use that data—see **Figure 18**. The data is, in this way, made independent of the application programs so that these may be rewritten—or new programs added—without changing the structure of the data. Conversely, the physical structure of the data may be changed without having to rewrite all the programs which use that data.

In auditing the data base environment, the computing auditor is likely to come across a variety of different terms. However, whatever terms may be used, there are essentially three viewpoints to take account of:

(1) the overall view of how the data is seen by the user, ie the global logical schema described in the previous section;

Figure 18 The function of a data base management system (DBMS)

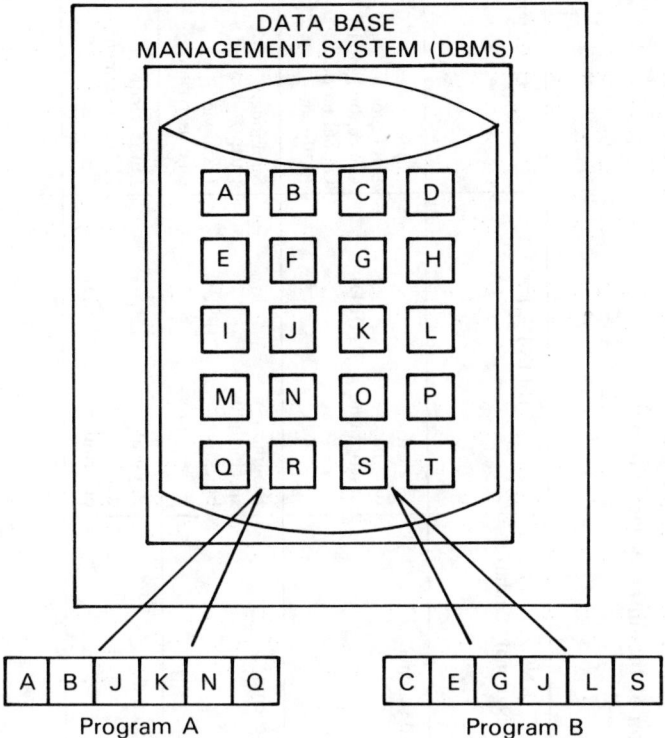

Program A   Program B

(2) a part of the global logical schema representing a specific application programmer's view;
(3) the actual physical representation of the data on the storage devices.

The different terms which have been adopted for these different views of the data structure are given in **Table 7**.

Although the terminology may differ, the processing components and the operation of a DBMS are standard across the range of different vendor products and are illustrated in **Figure 19** which shows the steps in the operation of a DBMS. The sequence of events is described by the following processes.

STEP	PROCESS
1	The user executes a transaction (enter data, retrieve information, etc) via a terminal connected directly or, indirectly through telecommunications channels, to the processor.
2	The relevant program is invoked by the transaction and issues a call to the DBMS to read a record.
3	The DBMS obtains the program data description or sub-schema used by the application program—in this case program **B**.

Table 7   Description of the different views of data

Description / Data View	CODASYL (Conference on data systems language)	ANSI (American National Standards Institute)	IBM's DL/l	Other terms
Overall logical view	Schema	Conceptual schema	Logical data base description (DBD)	Model Data model Conceptual model Global model Entity set
Programmer or application view	Subschema	External schema	Program specification block (PSB)	Submodel LVIEW Local view One user view
Physical view	Physical data	Internal schema	Physical data base description (DBD)	Entity records Physical segmented view

Figure 19 The operation of a data base management system

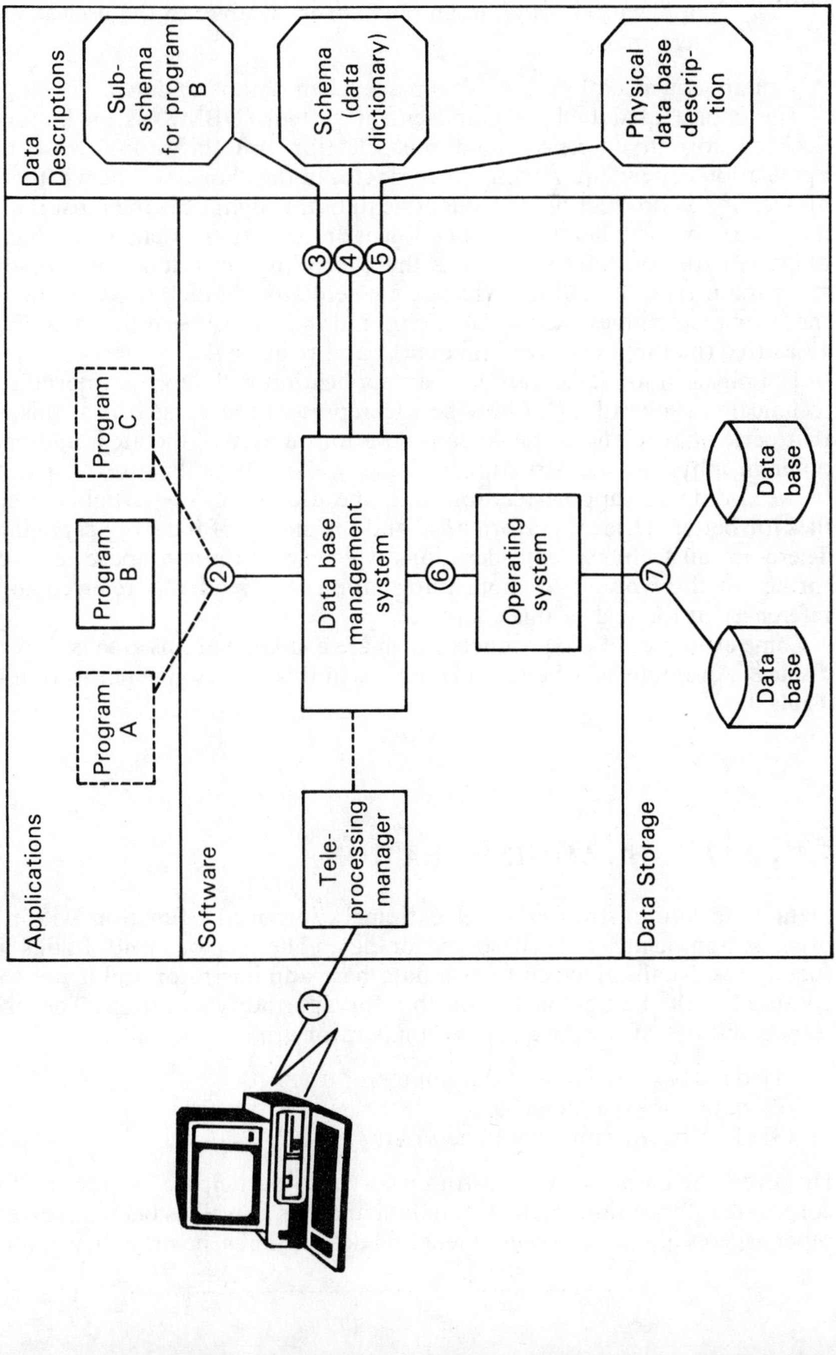

4	The DBMS then determines which logical data type(s) is required by reference to the global logical description or schema.
5	The DBMS examines the physical data base description and determines which physical record(s) to read.
6	The DBMS issues a command to the operating system instructing it to read the requisite record(s).
7	The relevant records are read and the data passed back to the application program and, where applicable, to the user at the terminal.

A similar sequence of events takes place when data is updated.

The choice of data base management system (DBMS) is an important decision for an enterprise and the selection criteria will be essentially application dependent. An important factor in the choice will be whether the application is production dependent, ie data throughput is the most important factor or whether the application is information-oriented so that the ability to sort on multiple keys is the overriding consideration. There are three main types of DBMS which are essentially characterised by the data modelling techniques used by each type and these have been shown in **Figure 17** as tree (hierarchical), plex (network) and relational.

The physical implementation of an application will depend, inter alia, on technical considerations of how best to represent the data. It is at this time that performance and retrieval considerations may well dictate a number of different physical file structures. These will include the use of pointers between data to support relationships, the use of full or partially inverted files for better retrieval performance and the choice of indexing capabilities. These are all technical considerations which we do not propose to discuss further in the work. For more information, the reader is referred to the references at the end of this chapter.

Some examples of the products which are available in this area is shown in **Table 8**. A sample list of essential controls in this area is given in section 4 of **Table 9**.

5.   DATA BASE ADMINISTRATION

Data base administration is an extremely important function within an organisation using data base technology. The person who fulfills this function is usually referred to as a data base administrator and is not to be confused with the person responsible for data administration. The prime responsibilities of the data base administrator are:

(1) data base design and development;
(2) data base maintenance;
(3) data base accuracy and security.

However, the database administrator may also participate in other areas of corporate information strategy and data analysis as well as being involved in other aspects of system development and design. Thus, he may participate in:

Table 8   Some DBMS products and their structure

DBMS	Structure	Hardware	Notes
ADABAS	Partially inverted files	IBM mainframes	Popular retrieval usage
ADR-DATACOM	Relational	IBM compatible	Relational market leader
dBASE II/III	Relational	Micros	CP/m, PC-DOS Operating Systems. Widely used
DB2	Relational	IBM mainframes	Yet to be announced for MVS environment
DMS-1100	Codasyl network & hierarchicial	Univac	
FOCUS	Flexible structures	Most mainframes, micros ICL, IBM, DEC	'User build' tool Requires skill in use
IDMS	Codasyl network		
IMAGE/3000	Network	HP 3000	
IMS-DL/1	Hierarchical	IBM mainframes	Complex, requires skill. DL/1 popular with CICS
NOMAD	Relational & hierarchical	IBM mainframes	'Natural language systems'
ORACLE	Relational	IBM mainframe DEC PDP-11, VAX	Mainly DEC installations
RAMIS II	Hierarchical	IBM mainframes	
RAPPORT	Relational	Mini systems	Used as a modelling tool
Relate/3000	Relational	HP 3000	
SQL/DS	Relational	IBM mainframes	VSE, VM environment
SYSTEM/38	Relational	IBM System/38	
TOTAL	Limited network and hierarchical	Most mainframes	Popular

(4) project selection,
(5) feasibility studies,
(6) selection and implementation of the DBMS,
(7) application programme design,
(8) application programming and testing,
(9) system implementation and testing.

The specialist nature of the data base administration role demands that there should be a recognised and trained functionary within the organisation and his responsibilities should be clearly defined. Further, there should be appropriate standards and guidelines governing all aspects of the responsibilities of the role which should be strictly complied with. In addition, appropriate reference manuals should be available, where appropriate, on the structure and use of the DBMS software that is available within the company.

In fulfilling his prime responsibilities of data-base design and development, maintenance, accuracy and security the data base administrator has a number of tasks to perform. He will be responsible, inter alia, for:

(1) determining the physical layout of the records on the storage devices;
(2) designing the means of restart and recovery;
(3) designing the means of reconstructing data in the event of loss of records or destruction of entire files;
(4) determining the security techniques that will be used and the detailed structures and techniques for maintaining privacy;
(5) monitoring machine performance, throughput and response times, selecting access methods and determining hardware requirements;
(6) monitoring the utilisation of the system bottlenecks such as the CPU, main memory, input/output (I/O) channels;
(7) measuring the capacity of the data base and balancing its facilities so that it can handle the highest throughput;
(8) measuring input volumes from end users, types of transactions, response times and rates of growth.

A sample list of essential controls, in this area, is given in section 5 of **Table 9**.

6. SYSTEM DESIGN AND CONSTRUCTION

This is the critical stage at which the analysis work and data modelling are converted into an application system. This is likely to prove the longest and costliest stage of the project. The stages in the design and construction of a data base system are shown in **Figure 20** and the processes are described in more detail in chapter 5 on the systems development cycle and in chapter 7 on systems development methods and deliverables.

There should be a clear idea, by now, of the final requirements from the system as well as of the eventual cost of the project. This has already been illustrated in **Figures 12** and **13**. Thus, the degree of error which is likely in any estimate of the cost of the remainder of the project should now be much lower than at the commencement of the project.

Figure 20 Data base design and construction

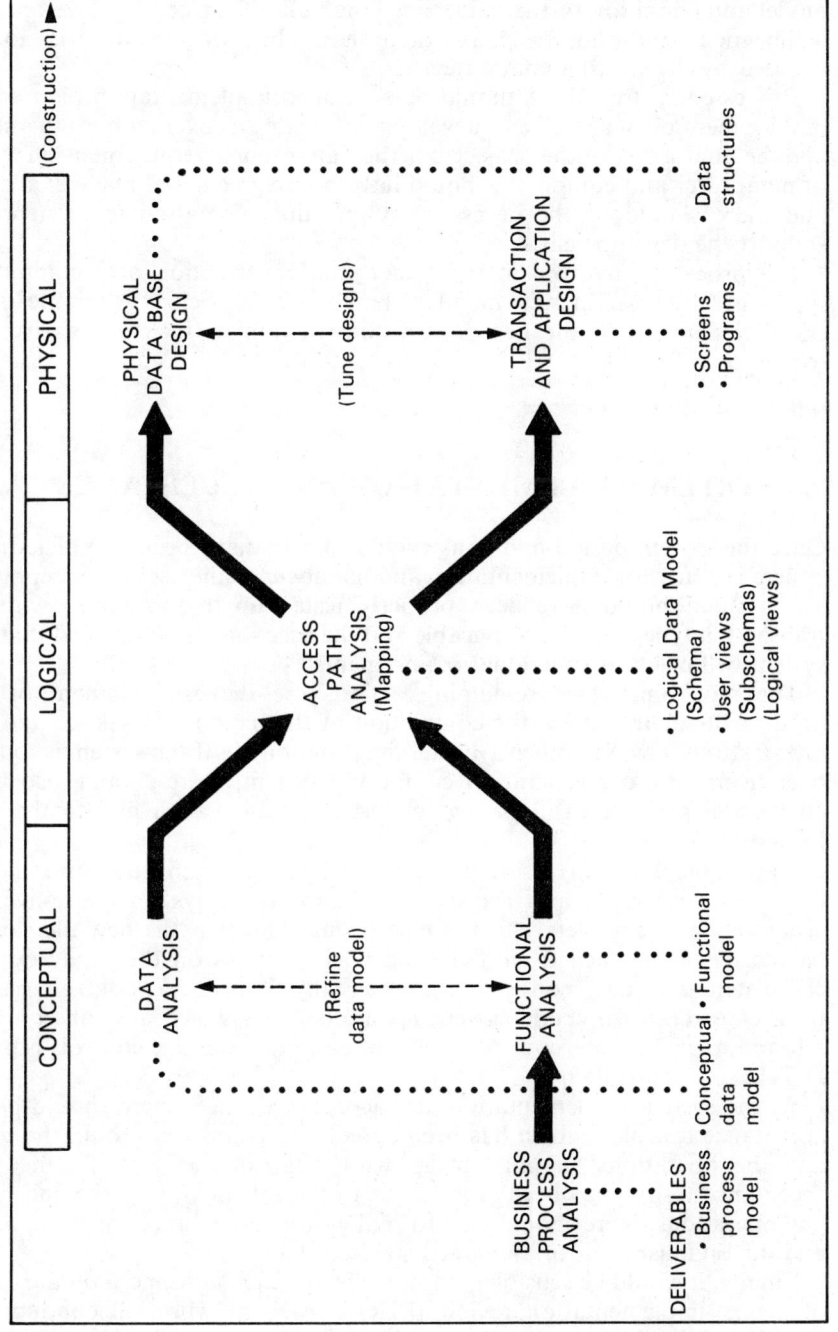

Before proceeding to the system design and construction stage, there should be a review, with the user, of the cost/benefit analysis, or other grounds on which the project has been justified, as well as the logical data model and definition of the data. Since the bulk of the cost of development will be incurred during this phase, there should be a written authorisation to proceed by the steering committee.

It is essential that there should be a detailed implementation plan and a development plan, as well as a development strategy, covering both this stage and the final stages of the project. Further, all resource requirements in terms of manpower and equipment should have been agreed, and made available, and there should be the necessary system documentation in existence,to support the development.

The processes involved in the design and construction of a computing system are discussed in more detail in chapter 5,7.-**10.**, below. A sample list of essential controls in the design and construction of systems, is given in section 6 of Table 9.

7.   SYSTEM IMPLEMENTATION AND ACCEPTANCE

Once the system design and construction phases have been completed, the system is ready for implementation and handover to the user for acceptance. The system should have been properly tested up to this point, with all transaction types that are applicable and the user should be satisfied that the system will meet his functional requirements.

The most important remaining actions are the establishment of the production environment, the completion of the handover package and the preparation of a comprehensive training programme. If the system is to take over from an older generation computing system, there should also be a conversion package available to convert all existing data files to the new format.

During the data conversion process, it will be important to ensure that all data—both reference and transaction—in the older system are converted accurately and completely to the new format and that the new file can be balanced and reconciled with the old. The controls on the accuracy and completeness of data conversion are basically the same as controls on the transfer of data from one system to another and which are subsequently referred to as interface controls. A list of essential interface controls is given in **Table 37**, scope item 6.

At the system implementation and acceptance stage, there should be an acceptance test plan which has been agreed by the project group, the users and the operations support group who will run the system. Once the acceptance testing has been carried out to the satisfaction of the end users and operations, there should be a formal written acceptance by both parties and the establishment of an agreed start-up date.

Finally, it would be sensible, at this stage, to reach agreement on the terms of a post-implementation review (PIR) as well as who will conduct the review, eg internal audit, quality assurance, project group, line management, etc.

The processes involved in the implementation and acceptance of computing systems are described in more detail in chapter 5,**10.–12.**, below. A sample list of essential controls in this area is given in section 7 of **Table 9**.

8. SYSTEM DOCUMENTATION

During the system development process, there will be a series of reports produced with detailed information on progress of the project at various stages. These reports, which are described in more detail in chapter 5 (the systems development cycle) are:

(1) project initiation report;
(2) feasibility report;
(3) system proposal;
(4) specification report;
(5) technical design report;
(6) construction report;
(7) implementation report;
(8) system review report.

Not all of these reports will be produced for every project. For a large project, which is digested in a number of stages, it may be desirable to produce them all but for small projects, which can proceed rapidly, only selected reports may be required.

In addition to the progress reports, there will be three other essential types of reports produced, namely:

(1) reports on management decisions;
(2) reports of a technical nature;
(3) the 'handover package'.

The first kind is generally to be found in the minutes of meetings of the project group and, if applicable, the steering committee for the project. The second type of reports is intended to form part of the system documentation and is represented by the functional specification, data structure guide, construction guide and controls specification. The third type, the 'handover package' represents the important documentation that the user and operations personnel require to operate the system and is represented by the operations manual, user procedure guide, user guide, etc A full list of the handover package is given in chapter 5, **10.**, below.

A sample list of essential controls, designed to ensure that the documentation is produced according to accepted standards and guidelines and is adequate to support both the development and operation of the system, is given in section 8 of **Table 9**.

Table 9   Systems development controls

Control reference	Key control area	Control details
1.	Systems development cycle	
1.1		There is a clear written request from the sponsor of the nature of the work to be performed.
1.2		There is a clear written statement of the costs/benefits for the project or other grounds on which the project is being justified.
1.3		There is a clearly established standard and guideline on the systems development methodology which is to be followed.
1.4		The role of all the following participants in the SDC has been clearly defined and understood:
		(1) project group,
		(2) end user,
		(3) sponsor,
		(4) steering committee,
		(5) project manager,
		(6) strategic planning,
		(7) operations,
		(8) technical services,
		(9) data administration,
		(10) data base administration,
		(11) internal audit,
		(12) quality assurance,
		(13) technical support,
		(14) system manager,
		(15) application support,
		(16) application manager (system custodian).
1.5		The terms of reference of the project steering committee and the project development group have been clearly defined in writing.
1.6		The project steering committee members are sufficiently familiar with the nature of their role and responsibilities.
1.7		The user representative(s) on the project steering committee have been trained in the application of the systems development methodology.
1.8		The user representative on the project group and the project leader have been trained in the application of the systems development methodology and in project development work.
1.9		The project manager has established a development strategy in terms of:
		(1) selection of checkpoints, formal and informal;
		(2) choice of development tactics;
		(3) choice of project control mechanisms,
		(4) project organisation, management and resourcing.
1.10		There is an outline implementation plan available covering;
		(1) phased implementation of the system;
		(2) the conversion or changeover requirements;

Control reference	Key control area	Control details
		(3) lead-times for new equipment, recruitment and training needs;
		(4) user re-organisation, recruitment and training needs;
		(5) contingency and fallback arrangements;
		(6) tasks, responsibilities and outline schedule.
1.11		There is a development plan available covering:
		(1) detailed estimates for the next phase,
		(2) machine resources required for the next phase;
		(3) outline estimates for remainder of project, phase by phase —and for each sub-project if appropriate.
1.12		For package solutions there is:
		(1) a short list of potential products and vendors;
		(2) an assessment of the degree of tailoring required;
		(3) a short list of available machines which can run the package;
		(4) an assessment of the impact on the current hardware strategy;
		(5) a package evaluation methodology;
		(6) a performance appraisal procedure;
		(7) a reporting procedure on package performance;
		(8) a user acceptance procedure.
2.	Project management	
2.1		User contacts have been appointed specifically for the consideration/development of the system, eg data analysis, information reporting, equipment requirements, organisational responsibilities, etc.
2.2		There is appropriate involvement by user representatives on the project steering committee and project development team and the user is fully conversant with his rights and responsibilities.
2.3		There is an appointed and experienced project manager recognised by both the user and DP functions.
2.4		There are appropriate standards and guidelines covering all aspects of the systems development process, eg
		(1) project planning and control;
		(2) program development and testing;
		(3) equipment acquisition;
		(4) controls in computing systems;
		(5) operational systems design;
		(6) data analysis and structure;
		(7) quality assurance;
		(8) operational systems construction;
		(9) documentation production;

Table 9—*continued*

Control reference	Key control area	Control details
		(10) access control and data protection.
2.5		The systems development standards are being followed and enforced.
2.6		There is a comprehensive and up-to-date development plan which is broken down into identifiable tasks for DP, the user and other departments involved, eg internal audit.
2.7		The project tasks are small enough to be effectively managed and there are established target start and completion dates set for every development phase and task.
2.8		There is an associated project control system in use, prefereably automated, which is used regularly to report the effort expended and effort still required to finish each incomplete task.
2.9		Control techniques such as critical path analysis (CPM) and network analysis are being used.
2.10		The steering committee and the user are being advised of progress, problems, and actual costs of the system development.
2.11		The steering committee and the user are monitoring any likely delays to implementation, especially if timing is critical.
2.12		The steering committee and the user are being advised of all changes, including formal authorisation procedures, revisions of budgets and timings.
2.13		The steering committee and the user are being advised of any increased cost estimates and required to give formal authorisation to proceed.
2.14		The steering committee and the user are monitoring the effect of any revised cost estimates on the original cost/benefit analysis and on the continuing viability of the project.
3.	Data administration	
3.1		There is a clear understanding by individual users of the responsibilities for, and ownership, of each data element.
3.2		There is a user with specific responsibility for assisting in the identification and definition of each data element.
3.3		There is a focal point within the DP function who has specific responsibilities for all aspects of data analysis and logical data model construction —the data administrator (DA).
3.4		There is a job description available describing the role and responsibilities of the DA.
3.5		There are standards and guidelines available covering the work of the DA, eg;
		(1) data analysis and data structure;
		(2) data dictionary;
		(3) access control and data protection.
3.6		The DA has been adequately trained in all aspects of strategic data planning methodologies as well as in the use of automated modelling tools.

Control reference	Key control area	Control details
3.7		There is an automated modelling tool being used which synthesises the optimal third-normal-form structures, documents them and assists in data base design.
3.8		Each data item in the final logical data model has been analysed by the DA, systems analyst and user to determine which might become future primary keys.
3.9		The likely future primary keys have been split out into separate records to ensure future model stability.
3.10		The logical data model and definition of data are being periodically reviewed with the user group during design and construction.
3.11		Adequate recognition of the effect of data model design on machine performance is being taken into account even if this requires deviation from third-normal-form structures.
3.12		The DA has formal responsibility for retaining and monitoring the definitive copy of the data dictionary.
4.	Data base management software selection	
4.1		There is an appropriate justification and approval procedure in operation to select the DBMS software.
4.2		There is effective use being made of in-house know-how and third parties (DBMS vendors) in selecting the DBMS.
4.3		The DBMS is selected to support either a transaction driven or a user driven data base, or perhaps both, providing that performance degradation in meeting two requirements is not unacceptable.
4.4		The operating system under which the DBMS executes is reliable and well controlled ensuring secure and continuous operation.
4.5		There are easy-to-learn high level development languages available to work with the DBMS which promise substantial productivity improvements over third generation languages like COBOL and PL/1.
4.6		There are easy-to-learn, flexible, end-user languages which can be employed with the DBMS, eg query languages, report generators, graphics generators, etc.
4.7		The DBMS is user friendly, which includes the following: (1) complete, clear, easy to understand documentation; (2) comprehensive training by the vendor; (3) ease of installation and maintainance; (4) operator friendliness; (5) support of multiple test files; (6) ease of use by programmers; (7) a comprehensive set of utilities;

Table 9—*continued*

Control reference	Key control area	Control details
		(8) ease of data administration to change structures.
4.8		The DBMS is flexible, to allow:
		(1) new data items to be added to a record without requiring program changes;
		(2) new data items to be added dynamically;
		(3) retrieval of records by more than one key;
		(4) dynamic addition of alternate keys;
		(5) use of secondary keys to be used on any data item;
		(6) growth without offload/reload to increase size of files;
		(7) addition of new associations without forcing rewriting of existing programs;
		(8) addition of new associations dynamically.
4.9		The DBMS maintains integrity by the use of:
		(1) automatic range checks and accuracy controls;
		(2) tight concurrency controls to prevent simultaneous updating;
		(3) protection from broken pointers, chains, indices, associations, etc;
		(4) tight security controls to correct data errors;
		(5) tight controls to prevent accidentally damaging data, loading wrong media,etc.;
		(6) controls on the use of query languages.
4.10		The DBMS ensures adequate security and privacy through:
		(1) data item, record or file protection;
		(2) powerful access controls;
		(3) possibilities to encipher sensitive data;
		(4) hierarchy of authority levels for different types of personnel;
		(5) good facilities for a security officer;
		(6) automatic creation of audit trails.
4.11		The vendor of the DBMS;
		(1) has a reputation for giving excellent support;
		(2) has local representatives familiar with the product;
		(3) offers a full range of good training courses;
		(4) is committed to future releases, enhancements and evolution of the product;
		(5) is financially sound;
		(6) has a sound base of installed systems.
4.12		There is a controlled DBMS implementation process in force including;
		(1) detailed implementation plan;
		(2) hardware and software requirements;

Control reference	Key control area	Control details
		(3) DP/user education and training; (4) vendor assistance and activities.
4.13		There are adequate data centre operations procedures in force to cope with the DBMS environment, namely: (1) change control procedures (new versions/ releases); (2) error message handling and procedures (under data dictionary control); (3) scheduling requirement (distributed processing); (4) statistical data collection requirements; (5) online/batch processing procedures; (6) testing and acceptance procedures; (7) restart, recovery and backup procedures; (8) fallback and contingency plans.
4.14		The organisational aspects are planned to ensure effective DBMS usage in production mode: DP organisation (1) DBMS responsibility and support; (2) data base administration/data dictionary; (3) network and terminal technical responsibilities; (4) hardware and communications resources and operations. User organisation (1) organisational changes; (2) input of on-line working; (3) user training and familiarisation.
5.	Data base administration	
5.1		There is a focal point within the DP organisation who has specific responsibilities for all aspects of data base administration—the data base administrator (DBA).
5.2		There are standards and guidelines available to guide the DBA in his work, eg: (1) data structure and analysis; (2) data dictionary; (3) data base design and operation; (4) access control and data protection.
5.3		The DBA has received adequate training in all aspects of data base administration as well as in the use of the specific data base management system selected for the application.
5.4		The DBA has copies of the DBMS vendors relevant reference manuals, understands these manuals, and is following them.
5.5		The DBA is responsible for monitoring and measuring the various aspects of performance to ensure an efficient level of service while maintaining data base integrity.
5.6		The DBA is responsible for the physical

Table 9—*continued*

Control reference	Key control area	Control details
		restructuring of the design and which methods of physical organisation best meet the performance criteria.
5.7		The DBA is responsible for designing the means of restart and recovery after system outages and the means of backup.
5.8		The DBA is responsible for designing the means of reconstructing data in the event of loss of records or destruction of entire files.
5.9		The DBA is assisting the systems analysts and programmers in the logical design of files.
5.10		The DBA is responsible for determining the security techniques that will be used and for designing the detailed structures and techniques for maintaining privacy.
5.11		The DBA is responsible for determining the policies for deleting or dumping old data, or data migration.
5.12		The DBA is responsible for determining whether the user's requirement is for a transaction-driven or a user-driven system, or perhaps both.
6.	System design and construction	
6.1		A review has been made of the cost/benefits for the project or other grounds on which the project has been justified.
6.2		There is a written authorisation to proceed, by the steering committee, to the system design and construction phases.
6.3		The logical data model and definition of data have been reviewed with the user group.
6.4		There is an implementation plan available, covering: (1) phased implementation of the system; (2) the conversion or changeover requirements; (3) lead-times for new equipment, schedule selection tasks and location of equipment; (4) user re-organisation, recruitment and training needs; (5) contingency and fallback arrangements; (6) tasks, responsibilities and outline schedule.
6.5		There is a detailed development plan available covering: (1) detailed estimates for the next phase; (2) machine resources required for the next phase; (3) outline estimates for the remainder of the project, phase by phase—and for each sub-project if appropriate.
6.6		There is a formal change control procedure for making amendments to the technical documentation, ie functional specification, construction guide and data structure guide, controls specification.

Control reference	Key control area	Control details
6.7		All requirements of both manpower and machine resources have been estimated and have been made available throughout these phases.
6.8		Programmers and, where appropriate, end users have been trained in the use of application development languages that have been selected for the DBMS software.
6.9		The operations group has been involved in all discussions relating to the hardware/software selection and implementation.
6.10		The application support group has been involved in all discussions relating to hardware/software selection and implementation.
6.11		The technical services group has been consulted on all aspects of hardware/software selection and implementation.
6.12		The involvement and role of quality assurance has been defined during the system design and construction phases.
6.13		All relevant system documentation that is required up to and including these phases has been, or will be, produced according to the accepted standard and guidelines.
6.14		There is a detailed development strategy covering: (1) division into sub-projects; (2) use and constraints of automated development aids; (3) tasks and checkpoints for remainder of the project; (4) resourcing of remaining phases; (5) terms of reference for remaining phases.
6.15		There is an outline acceptance test plan covering: (1) user acceptance criteria, test data and execution strategy; (2) operations acceptance criteria covering service levels, resource utilisation and performance, restart and recovery; operability and documentation; (3) DP, user and machine resources and the schedule.
6.16		There is a program test plan covering the testing method, sequence of testing and resources required and testing is continued until all conditions on the checklist have been successfully tested.
6.17		The interfaces, both between the programs and other systems, have been defined and a list of conditions necessary to test each interface, eg format, sequence, data values, has been drawn up.
6.18		There is a link test plan covering the testing method, sequence of testing and resources required and testing is continued until all

Table 9—*continued*

Control reference	Key control area	Control details
6.19		conditions on the checklist have been successfully tested. There is a system test plan covering the testing method, sequence of testing and resources required and testing is continued until all conditions on the checklist have been successfully tested.
6.20		The data analyst and application designer are using logical access maps (LAMS) in determining the access paths for each user application program.
6.21		The application programmers are using data base action diagrams (DADS) in order to create the program requirements of each user.
7	System implementation and acceptance	
7.1		There is a 'handover package' available which includes;
		(1) program source and load modules;
		(2) program specifications and listings;
		(3) system test files;
		(4) construction and data structure guides;
		(5) user guide and user procedure manuals;
		(6) operations manual and production job control statements;
		(7) data preparation and data control instructions.
7.2		There is a detailed implementation plan available covering:
		(1) phased implementation of the system;
		(2) the conversion or changeover requirements;
		(3) lead-times for new equipment, schedule selection tasks and location of equipment;
		(4) user reorganisation, recruitment and training needs;
		(5) contingency and fallback plans;
		(6) tasks, responsibilities and outline schedule.
7.3		There is a comprehensive training programme covering:
		(1) proposed education strategy and type of training required for different parties;
		(2) required education and training material;
		(3) resource requirements;
		(4) detailed training schedule.
7.4		The production environment has been established including:
		(1) delivery of all equipment, ie processor, terminals, printers, communications equipment, etc;
		(2) provision of adequate physical security in both the user and DP areas;

Control reference	Key control area	Control details
		(3) resource requirements, eg stationery; (4) delivery and despatch procedures for computer input and output.
7.5		There is a conversion package available—if applicable—to convert all existing data files to the new format and conversion procedures and practices for the balancing and reconciliation of the new files with the old.
7.6		There is a detailed acceptance test plan covering:
		(1) user acceptance criteria, test data and execution strategy; (2) operations acceptance criteria covering service levels, resource utilisation and performance, recovery and restart, operability and documentation; (3) DP, user and machine resources, and the schedule.
7.7		The acceptance testing is being carried out according to the satisfaction of the users and there is a written agreement by both end user and operations of successful completion.
7.8		There is a formal written agreement by the end user and operations of system acceptance.
7.9		There is a clearly established start-up date for live operations which has been agreed by both end user and operations.
7.10		There are terms of reference available for a post-implementation review (PIR).
8.	Documentation	
8.1		There is a separate reference file available containing all steering committee meeting minutes.
8.2		There is a separate reference file available containing all project group meeting minutes.
8.3		Where the end of a phase marks a formal checkpoint in the SDC one (or more) of the following management reports is available;
		(1) project initiation report; (2) feasibility report; (3) system proposal; (4) specification report; (5) technical design report; (6) construction report; (7) implementation report; (8) system review report.
8.4		There are the following documents available prepared in accordance with accepted standards and guidelines;
		(1) feasibility study; (2) functional specification; (3) construction guide; (4) data structure guide;

Table 9—*continued*

Control reference	Key control area	Control details
		(5) operations guide; (6) data control instructions; (7) data preparation instructions; (8) user procedure manual; (9) user guide; (10) controls specification.
8.5		There is a data dictionary, preferably on-line and active, which is maintained by the data administrator.

References

1   Martin J *An End-User's Guide to Data Base* (1981) Prentice-Hall Inc.
2   Martin J *Managing the Data Base Environment* (1983) Prentice-Hall Inc.
3   Martin J *Principles of Data Base Management* (1976) Prentice-Hall Inc.
4   Martin J *Computer Data Base Organisation* (1977) Prentice-Hall Inc.

PART 2

Systems development

5 The systems development cycle

This chapter describes a structured methodology for the development of computing systems which is generally known as the systems development cycle (SDC). The methodology is divided into eight phases each of which constitutes a potential checkpoint at which a go/no-go decision is required. The selection of checkpoints is part of the project management strategy and will depend, inter alia, upon the size and complexity of the project.

There is a listing in **2.** below, of the parties who are likely to participate in the SDC and a brief description of their responsibilities. The SDC is a formal process which requires the production of specified documents and these are described in **3.**

The application of the SDC is undertaken by the project manager who has responsibility for the selection of phases, tasks and checkpoints. This results in a development strategy which, if there is a project steering committee, will be endorsed by that body. The different types of strategies which may be pursued in the application of the methodology are discussed in **4.**

The remaining sections of this chapter—**5.–12.**—describe the tasks which are carried out in each of the separate phases of the SDC.

1. THE COMPONENTS AND PHASES

The systems development cycle (SDC) is a sequence of tasks which are grouped into phases. The end of each phase is a potential checkpoint where a go/no-go decision is required. In applying the SDC to the development of a system, the participants (or some of them) generate documentation which carries information between the phases.

A generalised SDC, as shown in **Figure 21**, is divided into eight phases, namely:

(1) project initiation;
(2) feasibility study;
(3) analysis;
(4) specification;
(5) technical design;
(6) construction;
(7) implementation;
(8) post-implementation review.

Figure 21 A generalised systems development cycle

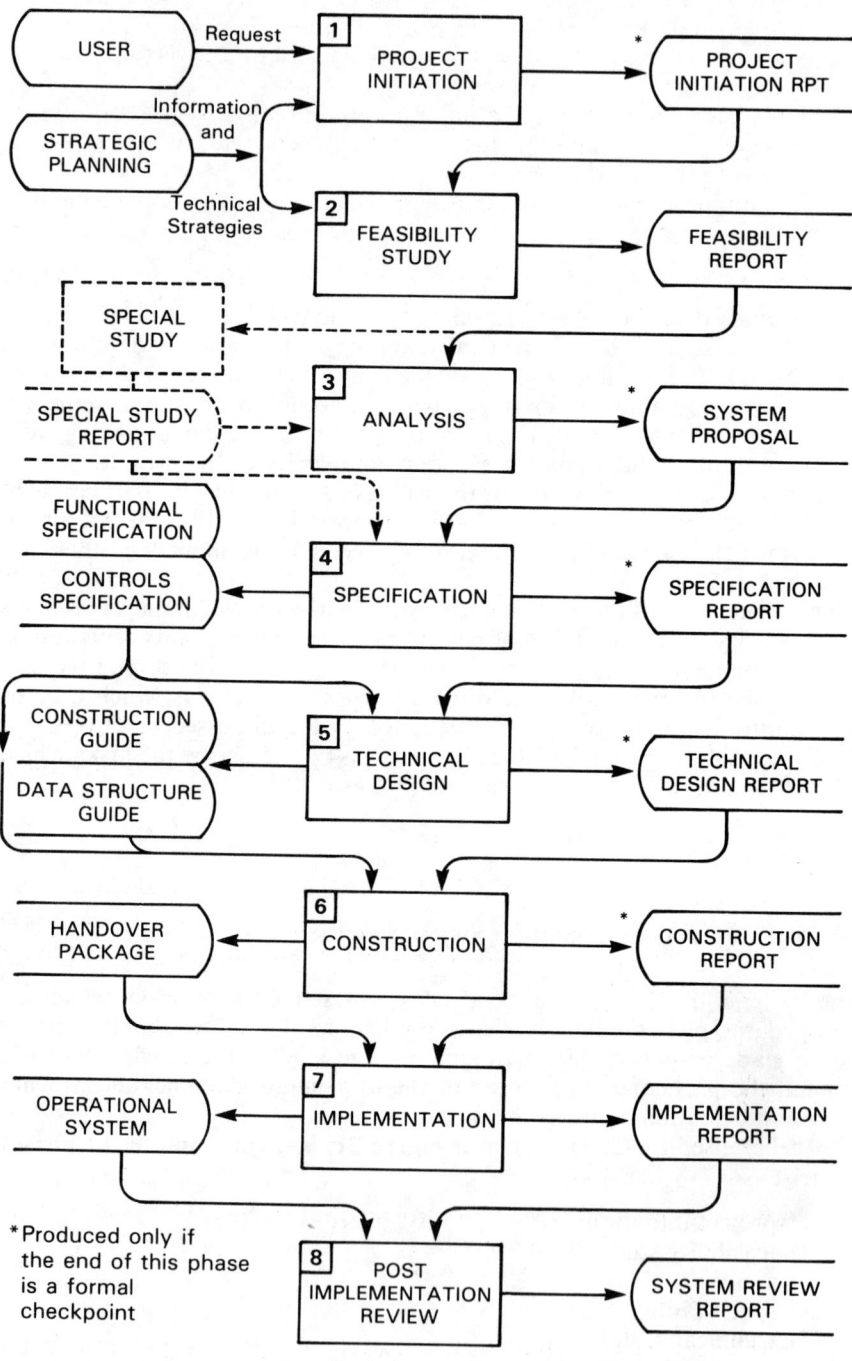

There is a potential checkpoint at the end of each phase whose purpose is:

(1) to confirm the continuing viability and relevance of the system;
(2) to reassess the required expenditure to complete the project;
(3) to reassess the required manpower effort and timing of the project to completion;
(4) to reconsider the justification for the estimated expenditure, manpower effort and timing as well as the direction of the development;
(5) making go/no-go decisions;
(6) to authorise progress to the next checkpoint against revised estimates.

The selection of checkpoints is part of the project management strategy and will depend, inter alia, upon the size and complexity of the project.

2. THE PARTICIPANTS

The SDC is a generalised schema of what needs to be carried out in systems development work and will be adapted by the project manager to suit the particular project being tackled. Thus, the persons or groups involved in the SDC will depend upon a project specific SDC. With this in mind, the following is a list of all the groups and individuals that can participate in the SDC process, with typical responsibilities.

(1) PROJECT GROUP

The group who largely carry out the tasks identified in the SDC. The project group is normally a partnership between users and computing staff.

(2) END USER

Users who will operate or benefit from the system and their line management who are responsible for agreeing specifications of the system at various stages as well as for testing that the system meets their requirements.

(3) SPONSOR

The senior user responsible for authorising progress beyond a formal checkpoint.

(4) STEERING COMMITTEE

A group responsible for monitoring the progress of a project. This group may include the sponsor.

(5) PROJECT MANAGER

The person responsible for the conduct of a project and reporting to the steering committee. He may be from either the user or the DP department.

(6) STRATEGIC PLANNING

A group responsible for defining the information and technical strategy within which systems are developed.

(7) OPERATIONS

The person or team who will be responsible for providing the computer service on which the operational system will run and who will accept the system for operation. For non-mainframe systems, operations may be run by the project group or by the end users.

(8) TECHNICAL SERVICES

A group which provides advice on hardware and software.

(9) DATA ADMINISTRATION

A person or group responsible for co-ordinating the data requirements of systems and for giving advice on data analysis and design.

(10) DATA BASE ADMINISTRATION

A person or group responsible for the design and operation of the data base(s).

(11) INTERNAL AUDIT

A group which has a dual role with regard to systems under development:

(a) to ensure that there are adequate controls on the effectiveness and efficiency of the systems development process;
(b) to give reasonable assurance to management that critical systems are implemented with adequate built-in controls for security and privacy of data, accuracy and completeness of processing and effectiveness and efficiency of operation.

(12) QUALITY ASSURANCE

A function which is involved in the monitoring of output throughout the project. The extent of QA involvement must be agreed and scheduled as part of project planning. It will depend upon the criticality of the system and upon the availability of QA resources.

(13) TECHNICAL SUPPORT

A person or group responsible for the maintenance of the system in the DP organisation.

(14) SYSTEM MANAGER

A person in the operations area who has overall responsibility for the proper functioning of the hardware and operating system software.

(15) APPLICATION SUPPORT

A person or group, in the user area, responsible for advising the users on the functionality of the system. Where a separate support group exists they must be brought into the project well before handover to familiarise themselves with the system they will have to maintain and to plan staffing.

(16) APPLICATION MANAGER (SYSTEM CUSTODIAN)

A person, in the user area, who has overall responsibility for the systems security, privacy, accuracy, completeness, effectiveness and efficiency.

3. DOCUMENTATION

There are three main types of documents generated during the system development process:

(1) management reports,
(2) specification documents,
(3) handover package.

Since the production of documentation is a time consuming process the aim is to produce the minimum documentation necessary to specify properly and control the development of the system. These three types of documentation are discussed further below.

(1) MANAGEMENT REPORTS

These assess the justification for the system at each formal checkpoint. There is a management report associated with each phase, but it will only be produced if that phase-end has been selected as a formal checkpoint. The full list of reports which may be produced is;

(1) project initiation report;
(2) feasibility report;
(3) system proposal;
(4) specification report;
(5) technical design report;
(6) construction report;
(7) implementation report;
(8) system review report.

The structure and contents list of each management report follows a standard format, as far as possible, so that each report can be derived from its predecessor by simply updating it with new information. This is particularly useful if the report is held on a word processor. The aim in updating should be to highlight differences from the previous report. An example of the format of a management report is given in **Table 10**.

Table 10   A management report—the feasibility report

PURPOSE

The purpose of this report is to provide information to enable a decision to be taken on whether to proceed with the proposed development. This report does not attempt to specify the full details of the recommended approach.

CONTENTS

(1) *INTRODUCTION*

—Background, terms of reference and scope of study;
—approach taken and acknowledgements;
—structure of the report.

(2) *MANAGEMENT SUMMARY*

—Existing system summary;
—system requirements summary
—outline of proposed solutions;
—development and implementation plans summary;
—costs and benefits summary and risk assessment;
—computer resources requirements and service level summary;
—limitations of the proposed solutions;
—conclusions and recommendations;
—terms of reference for the next phase.

(3) *EXISTING SYSTEM*

—Brief description;
—problems and limitations;
—summary of costs.

(4) *SYSTEM REQUIREMENTS*

—Business objectives;
—functional requirements;
—information requirements;
—security, contingency, audit and controls requirements;
—performance targets and service level requirements;
—business constraints.

(5) *PROPOSED SOLUTION*

—Justification for selection;
—requirements not met;
—system function;
—data model and data base strategy;
—coding systems;
—hardware/software requirements;
—distribution policy;
—implications for end-user and operations;
—implications for other systems;
—conversion and implementation;
—security, privacy, controls and contingency;
—risk and exposure evaluation.

(6) *OPTIONS CONSIDERED* (one section per option)

—Brief narrative description;
—summary of costs and benefits;
—reasons for rejection.

(7) *FUTURE REQUIREMENTS*

(8) *DEVELOPMENT STRATEGY*

—Projects, sub-projects and phases;
—prototyping;
—special studies and pilots;
—project management and steering committee structure;
—project group structure, membership and resourcing;
—specialist resource requirements, eg internal audit.

Appendix A   DEVELOPMENT PLAN

Appendix B   IMPLEMENTATION PLAN

Appendix C   COSTS AND BENEFITS

Appendix D   COMPUTER RESOURCE REQUIREMENTS

Appendix E   EXISTING SYSTEM

Appendix F   INITIAL HARDWARE/SOFTWARE EVALUATION (where appropriate)

Appendix G   INITIAL PACKAGE EVALUATION (where appropriate).

---

(2) SPECIFICATION DOCUMENTS

These define the system and any associated procedures. They are required for all systems developments although their size and scope will depend upon the size of the system and its proposed environment. The full list of reports which may be produced is:

(1) functional specification,
(2) controls specification,
(3) construction guide,
(4) data structure guide.

Wherever possible, specification documents are produced as a by-product of an automated development aid such as a prototyping facility or a data dictionary. They are held, maintained, and whenever possible used, within the automated environment.

(3) HANDOVER DOCUMENTATION

These are produced during the final stages of the SDC, as part of the 'handover package', and are of fundamental importance for the operation of the completed system. The full list of these is:

(1) computer operations manual;
(2) user guide(s);
(3) user procedures manual(s).

These should also be held, maintained and be produced in an automated environment.

4.   THE APPLICATION

The application of the SDC is undertaken by the project manager who has responsibility for the selection of phases, tasks and checkpoints for a particular project. The result of this selection process is a development strategy which, if there is a steering committee, will also be endorsed by that body.

The development strategy of the project manager sets out his intended approach to managing the project and must address the following issues:

(1) selection of phases, tasks and checkpoints;
(2) choice of development tactics;
(3) choice of project control mechanisms;
(4) project organisation, management and resourcing;
(5) use of 'intelligent' software for pre-specification (prototyping).

The ultimate objective will be to meet the user's requirements in the most cost-effective way.

The selection of phases, tasks and checkpoints is crucial to the success of the development process for a project. The end of every phase is a potential checkpoint but, unless the project is very high risk, it is unlikely that every one will be a formal checkpoint. The aim is to have as few as possible—achieved by merging phases—consistent with the proper management of the project since there is a significant overhead associated with each formal checkpoint. There are examples given of how phases may be merged in the system development process in chapter 10.

Development tactics are optional methods that the project manager can incorporate in his strategy if he thinks they will be of advantage in developing his particular system. Some examples of the tactical methods from which the project manager may choose are:

(1) overlapping phases;
(2) implementation by sub-project;
(3) special studies;
(4) application packages;
(5) pilot development.

The overlapping of phases is an attempt to avoid idle resources by starting on tasks in the following phase if the tasks of the current phase are largely completed. Approval to overlap phases must, normally, be given by the steering committee since there is a risk that the project could be wound up at the end of the current phase.

The development by sub-projects involves breaking up the main project into parts each of which is progressed separately through the SDC. This may also involve having separate project teams reporting independently to a co-ordinating steering committee. This approach will normally be suitable for very large projects such as the development of corporate finance systems which could be split up into projects covering sales ledger, purchasing ledger, debtors/creditors, budgeting and cost control, etc. This method was actually used in the development of the system for which the post-implementation review procedure is described in chapter 12.

Special studies address particular business or technical problems that cannot be adequately assessed within the agreed scope of the feasibility study. If the findings of the study are crucial to the further authorisation of the project then the study should be completed before the next phase of the SDC is started, particularly if the study is addressing a high risk area. In other cases, the study may be able to continue in parallel through, at least, the analysis phase and, in fact, until its findings are required.

The acquisition of a commercially available package, as opposed to custom building in-house software, has the advantage that it is a shorter route to achieving a working system even if not all of the system require- ments can be met in full or in the desired way. However, if the package can be customised by the vendor within a comparatively short time frame and at reasonable cost then there is much to recommend this option. The use of this particular method in a practical example is discussed in chapter 10.

The pilot development differs from prototying in that the pilot is used in live operations. A pilot is a development of part of the system only and is usually only installed in a few end user sites, often in parallel with existing systems. The aim is mainly to acquaint the project group and the end users with the facilities available so that possibilities and requirements can be clarified. It is also to some extent a check that the system will actually work in a live environment. This is the route that was followed for the system whose control framework is discussed in chapter 11.

The choice of project control mechanisms and project organisation, management and resourcing are covered in detail in chapter 6 on the management of computer projects.

5.   PROJECT INITIATION

The purpose of the project initiation phase is to identify the best way to handle a user's request, or a strategic requirement, and to establish the need, scope and organisational structure of the feasibility study. It is intended, at this stage, to form a very broad overview of the likely work and cost implications as well as the potential benefits which may arise.

The tasks involved are described below.

(1) ASSESS REQUEST

The broad benefits; major problems; potential contribution to infor- mation plan and technical strategy; interaction on other applications.

(2) DECIDE APPROACH

Steering committee and/or project team; structure and membership.

(3) PLAN NEXT PHASE

Terms of reference; staff and skill requirements; machine resources.

(4) DRAFT AND REVIEW DOCUMENTATION

Project initiation report; authorisation to proceed.

A checkpoint is almost always observed at the end of the project initiation phase because it involves authorisation to conduct a feasibility study which could be expensive. There will usually be a project initiation report produced providing sufficient information for a decision to be taken on whether to proceed to a feasibility study. However, the project initiation phase may be merged into the feasibility study so that no separate report will, in this case, be produced. This is demonstrated in Example 2 of a project specific development cycle shown in chapter 10, **2.**, below.

6.   FEASIBILITY STUDY

The purpose of the feasibility study phase is to assess whether the proposed development is practical in terms of technical and operational feasibility, the organisation's information system objectives and the balance of costs and benefits. During the feasibility study the broad scope, technical approach and development strategy for the project are settled.

The feasibility study adopts a 'broad brush' approach involving some analysis and some outline design. Its scope will be constrained by the terms of reference in the project initiation report. Its length will be determined by the nature of the project, its size and the risk involved.

For a small project in a well defined area the feasibility study should be particularly brief. For a very small project, where the relevant feasibility study tasks can be completed within the limits agreed for a project initiation phase, it may be combined with that phase. This is demonstrated in Example 4 of a project specific development cycle shown in chapter 10, **2.**, below.

The tasks involved are described below.

(1) DETERMINE SCOPE AND OBJECTIVES

Review terms of reference; establish business objectives; identify interfaces; agree involvement of other parties; produce project plan.

(2) EXAMINE EXISTING SYSTEM

Review existing documentation; analyse and document existing system; produce high level data model; evaluate current procedures, information provision, controls, security, audit and contingency arrangements; determine resources required and estimate costs; review and agree definition of existing system.

(3) DETERMINE REQUIREMENTS

Evaluate terms of reference and review with steering committee; analyse business objectives; identify constraints on change, eg security, legal, industrial relations; identify system requirements in terms of business functions, information requirements, performance; evaluate current system; review and agree overall system requirements with end users.

(4) EVALUATE SOLUTIONS

Outline the proposed system; revise high level data model if required; consider the various hardware, software and manual approaches which could be employed; consider packages; consider which approaches appear most favourable from cost/benefit aspect; evaluate each approach; assess risk and exposure.

(5) PREPARE IMPLEMENTATION AND DEVELOPMENT PLAN

(5.1) DEVELOPMENT STRATEGY

Consider special studies; standards development; pilot project; prototying; sub-projects; automated development aids; end-user computing; tasks and checkpoints; resourcing; terms of reference for next phase.

(5.2) IMPLEMENTATION PLAN

Consider phased implementation; conversion or changeover requirements; establish lead times for equipment; consider reorganisation, recruitment and training needs; contingency and fallback; decide tasks and responsibilities; prepare outline schedule.

(5.3) DEVELOPMENT PLAN

Prepare estimates for next phase and remainder of project; estimate machine resources for next phase; decide participants for this and remaining phases; prepare schedule for development.

(5.4) PROJECT JUSTIFICATION

Estimate development and running costs; expected system life; cost/benefits; make risk and exposure evaluations.

(6) DRAFT AND REVIEW JUSTIFICATION

Complete draft feasibility report and agree with project group and steering committee; issue final feasibility report and obtain authorisation from the sponsor to proceed.

The issue of the final feasibility study report ends the feasibility study phase and a checkpoint at this stage is mandatory for all projects.

7.   ANALYSIS

The analysis phase follows acceptance of the feasibility report by management and authorisation from the steering committee to proceed. The purpose of the analysis phase is to define the business requirements of the new system in detail and then to identify each business transaction and the way it will be handled. During this phase the application area is analysed in more detail and business requirements for the new system defined in full. An outline description of the new system in user orientated terms is produced. For small projects the analysis phase may be unnecessary or very brief if the feasibility study has defined the requirements and technical shape of the system sufficiently precisely for specification to take place.

The tasks involved are described below.

(1)   DETERMINE SCOPE AND OBJECTIVES

Review feasibility report and any other relevant reports; review terms of reference and agree scope and boundaries of phase; establish organisation and procedures for involvement and agreement by other parties; evaluate plans and schedule resources.

(2)   ANALYSE EXISTING SYSTEM IN DETAIL

Determine methods for data gathering; collect existing system data, eg volumes of transactions, expected growth, functions, files, timings, controls; produce overall definition of existing system; revise high level data model; establish performance and costs; summarise problems and deficiencies; review and agree definition.

(3)   DETERMINE DETAILED REQUIREMENTS

Analyse business requirements; establish system requirements; define security, legal, control and contingency requirements; identify system requirements that must be met; review and agree with end user.

(4)   DEVELOP OUTLINE NEW SYSTEM

Revise data model if necessary; define business functions, data stores and data flows, inputs and outputs; decide manual or automated functions, types of automation—batch, on-line mainframe, mini–data storage and data flow media; evaluate packages; define hardware/ software architecture; consider options;evaluate cost/benefits; re-assess risk and exposure.

(5)   UPDATE IMPLEMENTATION AND DEVELOPMENT PLAN

(5.1)   REVIEW DEVELOPMENT STRATEGY

Consider special studies; standards development; pilot project; prototying; sub-projects; automated development aids; end-user computing; tasks and checkpoints; resourcing; terms of reference for next phase.

(5.2) REVISE IMPLEMENTATION PLAN

Consider phased implementation; conversion or changeover requirements; establish lead times for equipment; consider reorganisation, recruitment and training needs; decide tasks, responsibilities and update plan.

(5.3) REVISE DEVELOPMENT PLAN

Prepare estimates for next phase and remainder of project; estimate machine resources for next phase; decide participants for this and remaining phases; update development schedule.

(5.4) REVISE PROJECT JUSTIFICATION

Estimate development and running costs; expected system life; review cost/benefits; re-assess risk and exposure.

(6) DRAFT AND REVIEW SYSTEM PROPOSAL

Complete draft system proposal report and agree with project group and steering committee; issue final system proposal report and obtain authorisation from the sponsor to proceed.

All of the tasks described above must be considered during the execution of the SDC but not all will be necessary for any particular project. Thus, if the end of the analysis phase is not a checkpoint, the need to update the development plan formally is reduced and there is no need to revise the project justification. Further, if there is no requirement for a checkpoint at the end of the analysis phase, the system proposal is not produced. A checkpoint may only be required for large scale developments, where requirements are uncertain or where more than one significantly different approach was brought through from the feasibility study.

8.   SPECIFICATION

The specification phase follows acceptance of the system proposal by management and authorisation to proceed (unless this phase has been combined with the proceeding analysis phase). The purpose of this phase is to define all the functions of the system in detail in user terms as well as the conversation structure of all on-line transactions, the data to be stored and the formats of inputs and outputs. For small projects the specification phase may be unnecessary, or very brief if previous phases have defined the required system sufficiently precisely for technical design to take place.

At the specification stage, internal audit should be actively involved with the project group in designing the system controls. The audit methodology to ensure that the controls framework is adequate to satisfy the objectives of security, privacy, accuracy, completeness, effectiveness and efficiency is described in chapter 11. During the specification phase, as with other phases, internal audit also tests that the project development controls are being applied and that the development process is proceeding effectively and efficiently to ensure the successful outcome of the project. The audit methodology to accomplish this is described in chapter 10.

The tasks involved are described below.

(1) DETERMINE SCOPE AND OBJECTIVES

Review system proposal and other relevant reports; consider automated development; agree involvement of other parties; review plans; schedule resources.

(2) COMPLETE DETAILED DATA ANALYSIS

Produce logical data model; assess implications for any corporate data models; refine preferred solution.

(3) DEVELOP DETAILED SYSTEM

Define procedures, eg validation, update and input control, terminal sign-on/sign-off, etc ; define menu hierarchy, conversation structure and use of function keys for on-line system; identify screens for each transaction; define business rules for all automated and manual activities; identify special features, eg controls; define and agree input/output layouts; tailoring of packages; hardware/software architecture; review and obtain agreement.

(4) PRODUCE OUTLINE ACCEPTANCE TEST PLAN

Appraise system requirements; agree acceptance criteria; define tests for systems requirements/acceptance criteria; define strategy, eg parallel running, etc; re-assess staff and machine resource requirements; agree acceptance test plan.

(5) UPDATE IMPLEMENTATION AND DEVELOPMENT PLANS

(5.1) REVIEW DEVELOPMENT STRATEGY

Consider special studies; standards development; pilot project; prototying; sub-projects; tasks and checkpoints; resourcing; change control procedures; terms of reference for next phase.

(5.2) REVISE IMPLEMENTATION PLAN

Consider phased implementation; conversion or changeover requirements; provision of premises; schedule equipment installation; decide reorganisation, recruitment and training; tasks and responsibilities; update plan.

(5.3) REVISE DEVELOPMENT PLAN

Prepare estimates for next phase and remainder of project; estimate machine resources for next phase; prepare estimates for subsequent phases; decide participants for this and remaining phases; update development schedule.

(5.4) REVISE JUSTIFICATION

Review costs/benefits; re-assess risk and exposure.

(6) DRAFT AND REVIEW DOCUMENTATION

Complete draft specification report and agree with project group and steering committee; issue final specification report and obtain authorisation to proceed from the sponsor; prepare draft functional specification and the controls specification.

All of the tasks described above must be considered during the execution of the SDC but not all will be necessary for any particular project. Thus, if the end of the specification phase is not a checkpoint, the need to update development and implementation plans formally is reduced and there is no need to revise the project justification. A checkpoint may only be required if the sponsor wants to sign off the functional specification before proceeding to the next phase; if an automated development aid is being used to specify the system enabling a firm estimate of development costs to be given; or if there was no checkpoint after analysis.

9. TECHNICAL DESIGN

The technical design phase follows acceptance of the specification report by management, the fuctional specification by the user and authorisation to proceed. The purpose of the technical design phase is to translate the functional specification for the automated part of the system into a set of programs, data bases and files. Where the functional specification has been defined using a high level language, this phase will need to concentrate on aspects such as performance rather than the specification of programs. The technical design phase will always be necessary even for a minor project. At the very least, the phase will be concerned with making any necessary amendments to program or file specifications.

The tasks involved are described below.

(1) REVIEW CURRENT POSITION

Review specification report and functional specification; review hardware/software approach; review plans; schedule resources.

(2) PRODUCE LOGICAL SYSTEM DESIGN

Check data documentation complete; define computer functions; ensure fields correctly derived; specify data accesses and data exchanges; specify outputs; review design.

(3) PRODUCE PROVISIONAL DATA BASE DESIGN (IF APPLICABLE)

Review data model; define scope of data base; apply DBMS to logical data model; estimate disc space requirements; define performance requirements; refine data base to meet performance requirements; test data base structure.

(4) DESIGN PHYSICAL SYSTEM AND COMPLETE DATA BASE DESIGN

Identify and agree physical constraints; set design objectives; create initial design; design security and recovery; size the design; refine to meet design objectives; review and agree

(5) COMPLETE DETAILED DESIGN

Determine file and program integrity controls; complete file and record specifications; specify changes to existing files and data bases; identify common routines and algorithms; specify utilities; finalise recovery and restart procedures; complete program and module specifications; review documentation.

(6) PRODUCE OUTLINE SYSTEM TEST PLAN

Define approach; define tests; specify test runs; specify test data; define device/file/machine requirements; review outline plan.

(7) UPDATE IMPLEMENTATION AND DEVELOPMENT PLANS

(7.1) REVIEW DEVELOPMENT STRATEGY

Consider pilot project; sub-projects; tasks and checkpoints; resourcing; terms of reference for next phase.

(7.2) REVISE IMPLEMENTATION PLAN

Consider phased implementation; conversion and/or changeover requirements; provision of premises; schedule equipment installation; decide user reorganisation, recruitment and training; review tasks and responsibilities; update plan.

(7.3) REVISE OUTLINE ACCEPTANCE TEST PLAN

Consider user acceptance criteria, test data and execution strategy; operations' acceptance criteria; resources required; timing.

(7.4) REVISE DEVELOPMENT PLAN

Prepare estimates for next phase and remainder of project; estimate machine resources for next phase; estimates for subsequent phases; decide participants for this and remaining phases; update development schedule.

(7.5) REVISE JUSTIFICATION

Review costs/benefits; re-assess risk and exposure.

(8) DRAFT AND REVIEW DOCUMENTATION

Changes have been agreed with user and incorporated in the functional specification and the controls specification; complete construction guide and data structure guide; complete draft technical design report and agree with project group and steering committee; issue final technical design report and obtain authorisation to proceed from the sponsor.

When carrying out the technical design, all of the tasks must be considered but not all will be necessary for any particular project. Thus, if the end of the technical design phase is not a checkpoint, the need to update development and implementation plans formally is reduced and there is no need to revise the project justification. A checkpoint may only be required for large scale developments; because performance requirements are critical; earlier resource estimates are uncertain; or if data is to be shared with other systems.

10.   CONSTRUCTION

The construction phase follows acceptance of the technical design report by management and authorisation to proceed. The purpose of the construction phase is to build and test the system specified in the technical design phase. This means designing, coding and testing each program; ensuring that the set of programs comprising an on-line transaction or batch job interact correctly; producing the procedure manuals needed to implement and run the system; and testing the system. The construction phase will always be necessary even for a minor project. At the very least, the phase will be concerned with making amendments to existing programs and testing them. At the end of the phase, the project group should be confident that the system meets its requirements and can be handed over to the end-users and Operations.

This phase can conveniently be subdivided into the following sub-phases:

(1) PROGRAM DEVELOPMENT

The individual programs are designed, coded and tested.

(2) LINK TESTING

This ensures that the set of programs comprising an on-line transaction or batch job interact correctly.

(3) PROCEDURE MANUAL PRODUCTION

The procedure manual(s) that are necessary to implement and run the system are produced. A full list of these and their purpose is as follows.

(i) OPERATING INSTRUCTIONS

To define the procedure to be observed for operating the system whether on mainframe or minicomputer. The actual structure and contents may be greatly affected by local hardware and software facilities.

(ii) DATA CONTROL INSTRUCTIONS

To define the procedures to be followed for the acceptance of input and the despatch of output. The actual structure and contents may be affected by local organisation and hardware and software.

(iii) DATA PREPARATION INSTRUCTIONS

To define the formats and keying instructions for all off-line inputs to be prepared by the data preparation unit.

(iv) USER PROCEDURE MANUAL

To define how the system is used to carry out one or more functions. The manual defines how to use the system not what the system is.

(v) USER GUIDE

To provide the non-technical definition of the overall system throughout its life and a reference manual for the users.

(4) SYSTEM TESTING

This covers any further link testing that may be required and general testing of the system by the project group.

The tasks involved are described below.

(1) PROGRAM DEVELOPMENT

(1.1) REVIEW DOCUMENTATION

Review program specification; agree timing; estimate testing requirements.

(1.2) PRODUCE LOGICAL DESIGN

Identify logical program modules; review use of common modules; design structure of each module; produce module hierarchy chart.

(1.3) REFINE DESIGN

Identify and extract common functions; optimise size of modules; review program design.

(1.4) CODE MODULES

Code and compile modules; review coding.

(1.5) DEVELOP PROGRAM TEST PLAN AND DATA

Prepare test checklist; prepare test plan; establish test environment.

(1.6) TEST PROGRAM

Test all items on checklist; review results.

(1.7) REVIEW PROGRAM DOCUMENTATION

Ensure documentation is complete.

(2) LINK TESTING

(2.1) PLAN LINK TESTING

Identify interfaces; group test runs; identify test data; review plan.

(2.2) CREATE LINK TEST ENVIRONMENT

Create test data; create job control statements; prepare test aids.

(2.3) CONDUCT LINK TESTS

Conduct/submit tests; correct program errors; retest; repeat as required; update documentation.

(2.4) PREPARE FOR SYSTEM TESTING

Review link testing; establish resource availability; test system; repeat as required; update documentation.

(3) PROCEDURE MANUAL PRODUCTION

(3.1) PREPARE OPERATIONS MANUALS

Produce operating instructions; produce data control instructions; produce data preparation instructions; produce manuals for operations, data control and data preparation.

(3.2) PRODUCE USER GUIDE AND PROCEDURE MANUALS

Define users by system function, on-line transactions and batch transactions; produce manuals.

(4) SYSTEM TESTING

(4.1) REVIEW OUTLINE SYSTEM TEST PLAN

Review proposed tests, test data, test run plan and schedule; reconsider resource requirements.

(4.2) CREATE SYSTEM TEST ENVIRONMENT

Create test data; prepare job control statements; schedule resources; prepare test aids.

(4.3) PERFORM SYSTEM TESTING

Conduct/submit tests; correct errors; retest; volume test; evaluate performance; test back-up, fallback and recovery procedures.

(4.4) REVIEW SYSTEM TESTING

Complete testing; review results; file test documentation; update system documentation.

(4.5) PREPARE HANDOVER PACKAGE

Ensure system documentation complete; arrange demonstration program; specify conversion and changeover requirements.

(4.6) UPDATE IMPLEMENTATION AND DEVELOPMENT PLANS
(4.6.1) REVISE IMPLEMENTATION PLAN

Review conversion and changeover requirements; provision of premises; equipment installation; user reorganisation, recruitment and training; tasks and responsibilities; update plan.

(4.6.2) REVISE ACCEPTANCE TEST PLAN

Consider user acceptance criteria, test data and execution strategy; operations' acceptance criteria; resources required; timing.

(4.6.3) REVISE DEVELOPMENT PLAN

Review estimates for next phase and remainder of project; machine resources for next phase; estimates for subsequent phases; participants for this and remaining phases; update development schedule.

(4.6.4) REVISE JUSTIFICATION

Review costs/benefits; re-assess risk and exposure.

(4.7) DRAFT AND REVIEW CONSTRUCTION REPORT

Complete draft construction report and agree with project group and steering committee; issue final construction report and obtain authorisation to proceed from sponsor.

When carrying out construction, all of the tasks described above must be considered during the execution of the SDC but not all will be necessary for any particular project. For example, if the system is relatively simple it may be practical to merge link testing with system testing. A checkpoint at the end of the construction phase is usually required to formally confirm that investment in implementation will be worthwhile and that the system is still justified. However, the construction report need only be produced if further budgeting and authorisation is necessary at the end of the construction phase.

11. IMPLEMENTATION

The implementation phase follows acceptance of the construction report by management and authorisation to proceed. The purpose of the implementation phase is to ensure that the system performs as required and to achieve a successful changeover. Planning for the phase begins at the end of the feasibility study phase and the implementation plan is refined at the end of each phase to reflect the more detailed definition of the system, as the project progresses.

The phase can be conveniently sub-divided into the following sub-phases;

(1) production environment set-up;
(2) acceptance testing;
(3) changeover.

The tasks involved are described below.

(1) PRODUCTION ENVIRONMENT SET-UP

(1.1) REVIEW IMPLEMENTATION PLAN

Review implementation plan with operations and end-users.

(1.2) DEVELOP TRAINING PROGRAM

Design appropriate education and training program; prepare training material; decide whether classroom training or on-the-job training; prepare detailed training schedule.

(1.3) SET-UP LIVE ENVIRONMENT

Install air-conditioning, physical security, hardware/software, backup media storage, communications network (if applicable); order special stationery.

(1.4) BUILD AND RUN CONVERSION PACKAGE

Build conversion or data take-on package; arrange back-up copies of files; run conversion; back-up converted files; check quality of conversion.

(2) ACCEPTANCE TESTING

(2.1) REVISE ACCEPTANCE TEST PLAN

Review tests; confirm acceptance criteria; update test data requirements and creation plan; update test run plan and execution strategy; prepare detailed testing plan; schedule resources.

(2.2) SET UP ACCEPTANCE TEST ENVIRONMENT

Review progress on production environment; create acceptance test data; start training.

(2.3) PERFORM ACCEPTANCE TESTING

Conduct/submit tests; evaluate performance; tune system; update documentation.

(2.4) REVIEW ACCEPTANCE TESTING

Review training, procedures, documentation, testing; request approval for changeover.

(3) CHANGEOVER

(3.1) REVIEW CHANGEOVER PROCEDURES

Review implementation plan.

(3.2) PERFORM CHANGEOVER

Ensure production environment is organised; conversion completed; software operational; operations prepared.

(3.3) OBTAIN FORMAL ACCEPTANCE

End-user and operations' acceptance; terms of reference for post-implementation review; support staff acceptance.

(3.4) DRAFT AND REVIEW IMPLEMENTATION REPORT

Complete draft implementation report and agree with project group and steering committee; issue final implementation report and obtain formal acceptance from the sponsor.

The implementation phase is by definition always necessary if the project has progressed this far. All the tasks described above must be considered during the execution of the SDC but not all will be necessary for any particular project. A checkpoint is not necessary since the project has been implemented.

12. POST-IMPLEMENTATION REVIEW

This is the last formal phase in the systems development cycle and will normally take place at least six to twelve months after the system goes live. It is preferable that the review should be carried out by an independent and objective party, such as internal audit, and the actual conduct of a PIR forms the content of chapter 12. The purpose of the post-implementation review (PIR) is essentially to review the implemented system in terms of its contribution to business objectives, its usability, operating costs and reliability.

The PIR may also review the development methods in terms of quality of estimating and the effectiveness and efficiency of the project organisation, procedures and techniques used. However, a review of the system development process is to be preferred immediately following the implementation of the system. This has the advantage of ensuring easy access to the project group members. Further, there should be a continual review during the system development process, by internal audit, to test the effectiveness of the project controls framework, as we describe in chapter 10, and by quality assurance to test the standard of the products, as we describe in chapter 6, **8**.

The tasks involved are described below.

(1) DETERMINE OBJECTIVES AND SCOPE

Agree with sponsor and DP department; agree timing; prepare audit programme.

(2) REVIEW OPERATIONAL SYSTEM

Business/system requirements satisfied; costs/benefits; operational performance; maintenance; security; back-up/recovery and fallback; interfaces; developments/enhancements; user satisfaction.

(3) FINALISE DOCUMENTATION

Complete draft post-implementation review report and agree with the system sponsor and DP department management; issue final post-implementation review report to the line management and a summary of the overall audit conclusions to the internal audit committee.

6 Management of computing projects

The management of every project can be viewed from two aspects, namely:

(1) activities and tasks;
(2) principles and practices.

This chapter concentrates on the principles and practices since the activities and tasks have been discussed in the previous chapter.

The principles and practices may be divided into five areas, namely;

(1) schedule planning and control;
(2) cost planning and control;
(3) quality assurance;
(4) change control;
(5) administration and team leading.

There is a discussion, in **2.**, below, of the management structure of a typical project—and the factors that will influence the project structure—as well as the project reporting mechanism. This is followed, in **3.**, below, by a listing of the eight essential requirements for proper project management. The project Manager's task is to ensure that all of the participants are aware of their responsibilities; remain committed through what may be a lengthy process and that the project control framework is working effectively and efficiently.

The principles and practices of project management are discussed in **5.-10.** of this chapter, below. The essential features of project control, in the five areas we have mentioned, are:

(1) a clear accountability at all stages with properly defined terms of reference;
(2) a proper level of authority delegated with the responsibility;
(3) active participation by the project manager—and steering committee, if applicable.

1. A PROJECT

We have already described a project in chapter 4, **2.**, above, as a set of interrelated tasks, organised to achieve a specific goal which has been recognised as desirable by the line Management in the company. The sequence of events which results in the conception and execution of a project and the delivery of a final product are:

(1) a potential project is identified by the information and strategic planning group or, by a request from a functional user who recognises the need for improved data processing and information requirements;

(2) a feasibility study is conducted by the requirements analysts for the business area to determine a favoured solution to the business needs;

(3) if the favoured solution is approved a project group is set up, and possibly a project steering committee, to carry out the work under an approved project manager;

(4) the project is executed in discrete stages—each of which may acquire approval by the project steering committee—under the supervision of a recognised project manager;

(5) the product is handed over to the functional users and the operations support group to run and maintain.

The management of every project can be viewed from two aspects, namely the:

(1) activities and tasks,
(2) principles and practices.

The activities and tasks which are performed during the execution of a project have been discussed in chapter 5 on the systems development cycle. The principles and practices are discussed in this chapter and chapter 7 on the methods and deliverables of the systems development process.

2. PROJECT STRUCTURE

The project management structure will depend upon the type of project that is being carried out. For a large project, which may take several years to complete, as well as being very costly, careful control is required at each stage of the systems development cycle to ensure the path of minimum time, cost and risk is selected. In this case, there may be a two tier hierarchical structure for the management of the project as shown in **Figure 22**.

The first tier is a project steering committee, composed of senior line management, whose principle task is to ensure that the objectives of each stage of the project have been clearly satisfied before granting approval to proceed to the next stage. The chairman of the project steering committee will usually be the head of the functional department for whom the system is being developed.

The responsibilities for ensuring that the activities and tasks associated with the project are correctly and timely carried out, within the approved cost constraints, are vested in a project manager who reports to the steering committee. The project manager usually attends meetings of the steering committee, as a non-executive member, to inform the members of progress, problems and delays, as well as to request permission for any modification to the original objectives and scope for the project phase.

The project manager's chief responsibilities will be to select the members of the project group; to ensure that they are briefed in their responsibilities; to ensure that there are approved objectives and scope for each stage of the

Figure 22   A typical project organisation structure

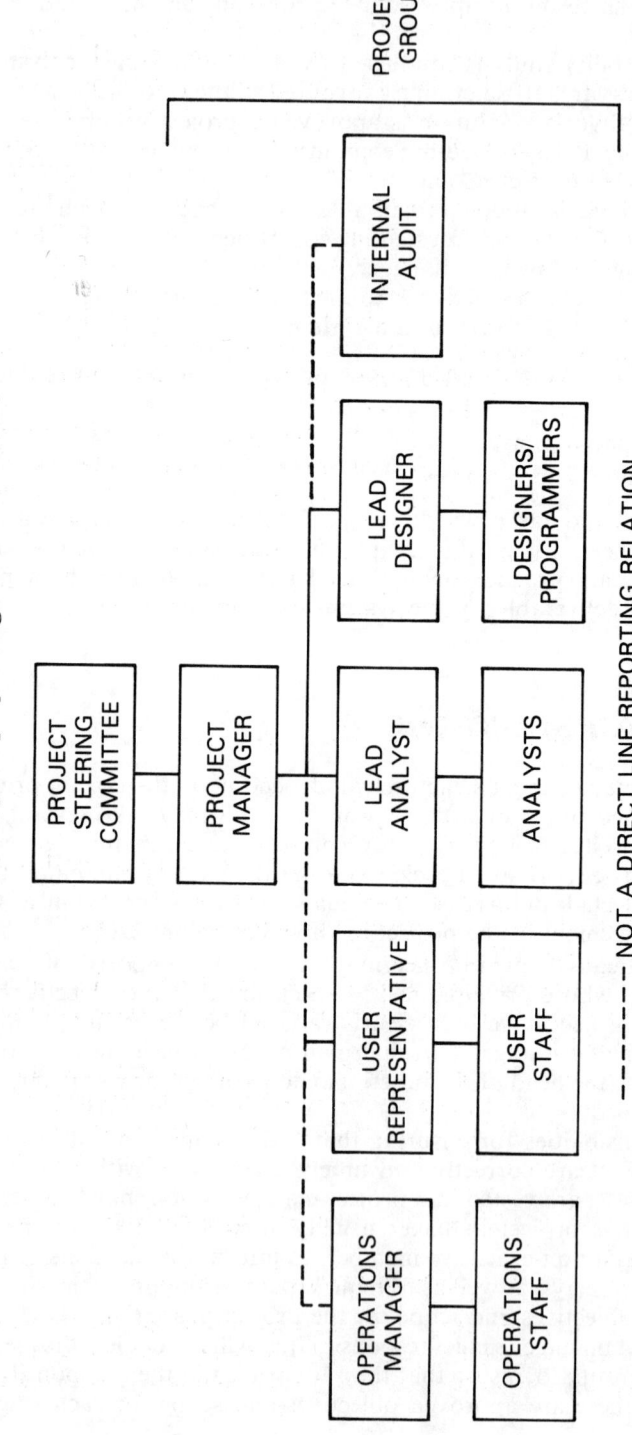

project; that there is an agreed plan in terms of activities and tasks; and that there is a control mechanism to monitor progress and make corrections.

The composition of the project group will depend upon which phase the project is passing through. Thus, the review of the project group structure will be a continual process as the project progresses. The requirements analysts will be active during the initial stages of the project and may well not be required at all in latter stages. However, the user representative(s) must remain with the project throughout to ensure themselves that the quality of the final product is satisfactory and meets their functional requirements.

The project reporting mechanism will operate on a three tier basis. The first tier will be the summary project reporting to the project steering committee which is made by the project manager when he attends the project steering committee meetings. There will be a second tier of reporting undertaking by the senior project group members to the project manager on a phase and activity basis and finally a detailed reporting of the individual tasks undertaken by the project group members. The way this reporting may be accomplished is shown in **Figure 23**.

For small projects, which are usually completed in several months, there is no justification for such a complicated project management structure. Thus, the involvement of senior management is largely unnecessary and the project is carried out without a project steering committee. Further, because the time frame is short, there is no necessity for dividing the project into phases. This is illustrated by Example 4, in chapter 10,**2.**, below, of a project specific development cycle for a small project.

3.   PROJECT MANAGEMENT

There are eight essential requirements for proper project management, namely:

(1) A defined objectives and scope for the work to be carried out.
(2) Clearly established terms of reference defining the authority and responsibilities of the project steering committee like those shown in the example in **Table 11**.
(3) Clearly established terms of reference defining the authority and responsibilities of the project group like those shown in the example in **Table 12**.
(4) A clear commitment by the functional users and a definition of the role they are to play in the development of the project.
(5) Clear, predetermined objectives covering time, cost and quality.
(6) A clearly established development strategy provided by the project manager.
(7) A clearly established development plan provided by the project manager.
(8) A clearly established framework of control reporting.

The project manager's task is to ensure that all of the participants are aware of their responsibilities; remain committed through what may be a lengthy process and that the project control framework is working effectively

Figure 23   A typical project organisation reporting structure

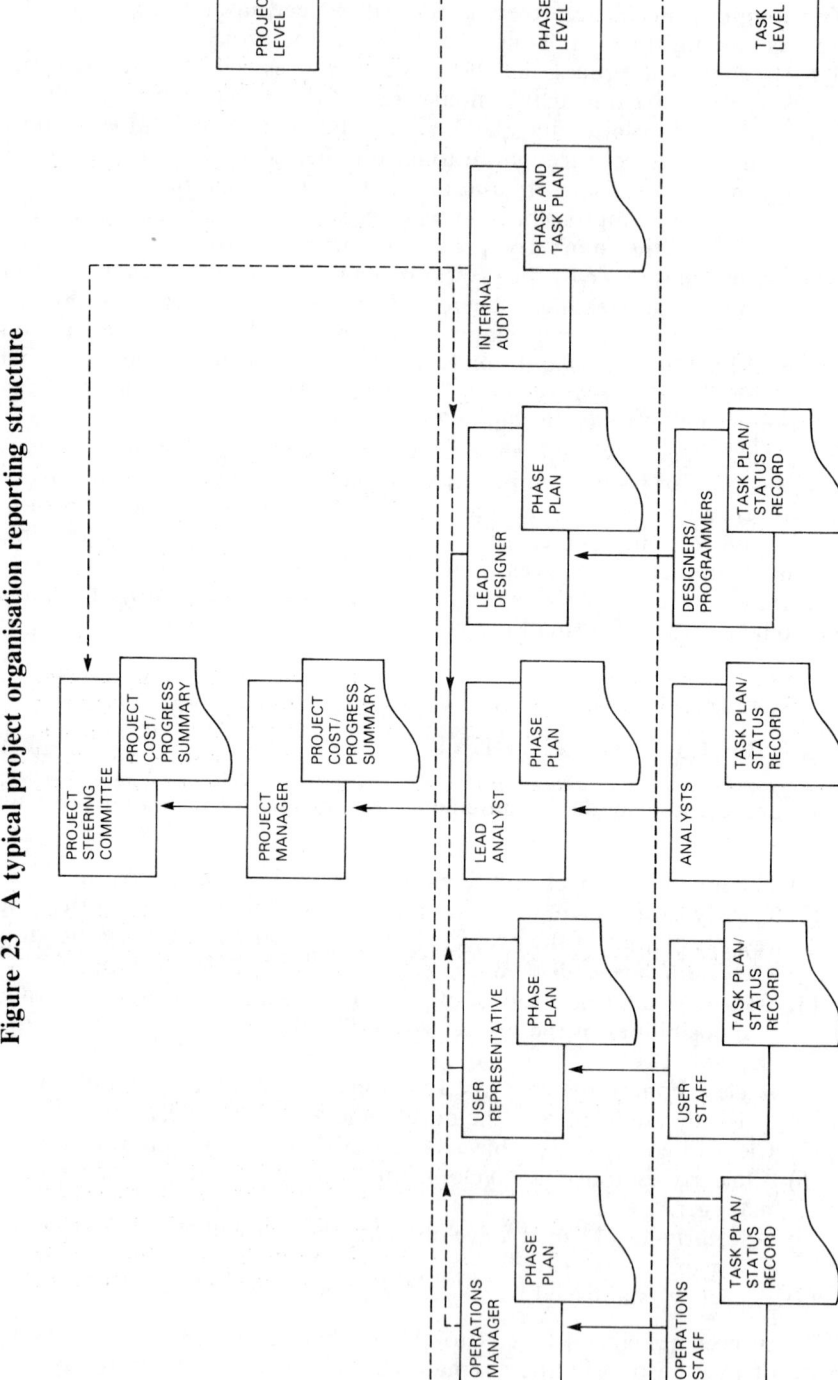

Table 11 Terms of reference of a project steering committee

(1) COMPOSITION OF COMMITTEE

Chairman	Director/senior manager of functional area.
Vice-chairman	Director/senior manager of data processing.
Project manager	DP representative/senior user representative responsible for the project development.
Sponsor(s)	Senior line management representative(s)—may be the chairman.
User(s)	Users who will be expected to apply the system.

(2) TERMS OF REFERENCE

The project steering committee will be responsible for:

—determining the overall system objectives;
—appointing the project group manager;
—reviewing progress of project against plan;
—formerly agreeing progress beyond each project checkpoint;
—assessing continuing project viability;
—approving any alterations in timing, costs or resources;
—approving the project development strategy;
—approving the project plans, ie development plan and implementation plan;
—approving the budget estimates.

(3) MEETINGS AND FREQUENCY

The project steering group will meet at least once a quarter and, in between meetings, there should be a regular liason between the chairman and the project manager in order that the former may be kept informed, on an informal basis, of progress, problems and costs. Minutes of meetings are prepared on the basis of an agreed agenda and circulated promptly after each meeting. The chairman may invite outside parties to specific meetings if he feels they have a contribution to make.

(4) REPORTING RELATIONSHIPS

The project steering committee is accountable to the company chief executive to ensure that the project is developed along a path of minimum time, cost and risk and that the objectives, and functional requirements, of the system are fully satisfied.

---

and efficiently. This is a daunting task which will be more assured of success, as we have suggested in chapter 4, **2.**, above, if the project manager has a successful track record behind him of similar projects and if the line management in the user area is firmly committed to making the project a success. Further, the availability of an experienced and committed internal audit function, to assist in establishing the project development controls, as discussed in chapter 10, is also an essential factor to ensure the successful outcome of the project.

Table 12   Terms of reference of a project group

(1) COMPOSITION OF THE GROUP

Project manager	DP representative/senior user representative responsible for the project development.
User(s)	person(s) who will apply the system.
Data analyst(s)	person(s) responsible for the construction of the logical data model.
Data base designer(s)	person(s) responsible for the physical data base design.
Programmer(s)	person(s) responsible for developing application programmes.
Operations	person who will be responsible for the day-to-day running of the operational system.
Internal audit	person responsible for monitoring the development controls framework and for advising on the application system controls.

(2) TERMS OF REFERENCE

The project group will be responsible for;

—carrying out the work of system analysis, design and construction;
—preparing a project development strategy;
—preparing project plans in terms of activities, tasks, time, cost and
  resources for approval by the project steering committee;
—preparing an implementation plan;
—reporting project progress formally to the project steering committee and
  informally to the chairman of the committee;
—ensuring that there are appropriate standards and guidelines available and these are
  being applied;
—preparing management reports at the end of each phase if appropriate;
—preparing the system technical documentation, ie functional specification,
  controls specification, construction guide and data structure guide;
—preparing the handover package.

(3) MEETINGS AND FREQUENCY

The project group will meet formally, at least once a month, in order to review progress since the last meeting and to consider any problems and possible changes in scope, timing and cost of the project. In addition, there will be daily/weekly contact between the project manager and his team members to review individual phase and task plans so that he is continually informed on project progress.

(4) REPORTING RELATIONSHIPS

The project group is accountable to the project steering group for the activities and tasks defined within the scope of the terms of reference set out above. The principal objective of the project manager is to ensure that the project is developed along a path of minimum time, cost and risk and that the objectives, and functional requirements, of the system are fully satisfied.

4. PROJECT ACTIVITIES AND TASKS

We have already discussed the project activities and tasks in chapter 5 on the systems development cycle. It will suffice to remind the reader that an important element in the success of project management is breaking down the project into sufficiently small and digestible tasks which can be realistically comprehended and executed. These tasks have been split into eight stages which have already been discussed, in the previous chapter, under:

(1) project initiation;
(2) feasibility study;
(3) analysis;
(4) specification;
(5) technical design;
(6) construction;
(7) implementation;
(8) post-implementation review.

5. PROJECT PRINCIPLES AND PRACTICES

This is the second of the two aspects of a project that we have mentioned in **1.**, above. These principles and practices apply across all stages of the project and may be covered under five headings, namely:

(1) schedule planning and control;
(2) cost planning and control;
(3) quality assurance;
(4) change control;
(5) administration and team leading.

The essential features of project control in all these areas are:

(1) clear accountability at all stages with properly defined terms of reference;
(2) a proper level of authority delegated with the responsibility;
(3) active participation by the project manager, and steering committee, if applicable.

6. SCHEDULE PLANNING AND CONTROL

6.1 Schedule planning

This is the important pre-project job of defining the principle project activities and of estimating a time scale for these activities and for the whole project. If this job is performed realistically, before the project commences, it will provide a valuable control mechanism during the course of the project life. The success at this stage of estimating a time scale will depend heavily on the project manager and especially his experience of developing similar systems. The outcome of schedule planning will be the production of a development plan for the project.

The steps involved in schedule planning and control are shown in **Figure 24**. The initial step is to define clearly the objectives for the work which is to be carried out as well as the scope of each stage of the project in as much detail as possible. In the beginning, there may be considerable uncertainty, except about the initial stage or stages of the project. As the work progresses, the scope should become clearer and there should be a revision of the development plan using the change procedures described in **8.**, below.

It is especially important, at this stage, to break down the work into realistic and manageable activities and the activities into tasks. Later activities in the project may be unclear at the commencement, but these may be defined later as the scope is clarified. A yardstick to use in defining tasks is that they should be capable of completion within ten days and each task should have a recognised start and completion date.

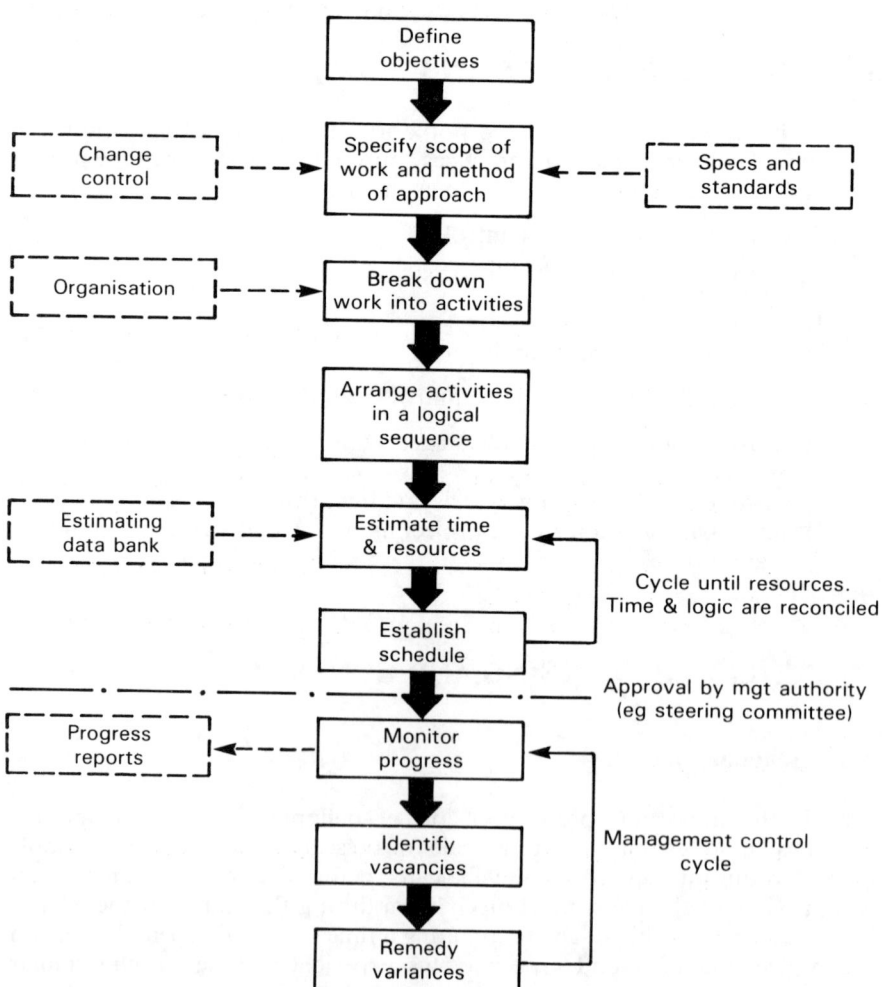

Figure 24 Schedule planning and control

All tasks should be clearly allocated to the responsibility of one single individual who should, preferably, be someone who has specific expertise to carry out that task. For example, the activity of data analysis and the tasks associated with it should be allocated to the person described as a data analyst who has the necessary training in data analysis techniques as well as the application of automated data modelling tools. An example of a task plan is shown in **Figure 25**.

However, if the objectives and scope of the stage or project are not defined at the appropriate level of detail, in the development plan, including the factors which influence the scope such as constraints, targets, priorities, two conflicts may arise:

(1) user management and the project team can have different views over what is being produced and change control becomes difficult because no one can agree what constitutes a change from the original scope— since cost and schedule targets are tightly linked to workscope, control becomes loose and poorly exercised;

(2) the project group are not clear how the objectives are to be achieved, which has a consequent effect on the accuracy of cost and schedule plans.

6.2   Schedule control

There are four essentials for effective control, namely:

(1) an agreed plan expressed in activities and tasks which can be measured;

(2) a simple recognised form of measurement which is accepted as providing evidence of performance;

(3) a regular monitoring of performance against plan;

(4) a means whereby variances can be corrected or agreement made on modifications to plan.

These steps are illustrated in the last part of the schedule planning and control review shown in **Figure 25**.

There are numerous ways of reporting actuals against plan but, whatever way is choosen, the reports should be:

(1) accurate,

(2) timely,

(3) easy to understand,

(4) clear as to the remedial action.

An example of how actuals may be reported against plan, at the phase level, is shown in **Figure 26**.

Figure 25   The task schedule plan

SCHEDULE PLANNING AND CONTROL — TASK PLAN

PROJECT REF. NO./DESCRIPTION:

PROJECT LEADER:

TASK REF NO/DESCRIPTION:

RESPONSIBILITY:

WEEK ENDING	EXPECTED COMPLETION DATE	EFFORT CURRENT WEEK (MAN DAYS)	EFFORT TO DATE (MAN DAYS)	EXPECTED EFFORT TO COMPLETION (MAN DAYS)	EXPECTED TOTAL EFFORT (MAN DAYS)	STATUS

Figure 26 The phase schedule plan

SCHEDULE PLANNING AND CONTROL – PHASE PLAN

PROJECT REF NO/DESCRIPTION:

PHASE REF NO/DESCRIPTION:

PROJECT LEADER:

REVIEW NO/DATE:

TASK REF NO	TASK DESCRIPTION	RESPONSIBILITY	START DATE		COMPLETION DATE			MANPOWER EFFORT (MAN DAYS)		
			PLANNED	ACTUAL	PLANNED	ESTIMATED FINAL	ACTUAL	PLANNED	ESTIMATED FINAL	ACTUAL
PROJECT TOTALS										

7. COST PLANNING AND CONTROL

7.1 Cost planning

Cost planning is the process of estimating the financial implication of executing the activities and tasks which have been sketched out in the process of schedule planning and is illustrated in the first part of **Figure 27**. This, to be truthful, is not an easy job and needs to be undertaken very realistically if a figure is to be arrived at which will be near the final actuals. The principal difficulties in the initial stages of the project are that the activities, at the later stages, are only vaguely defined since there is no clear system concept at this stage, and also that users may request a change of scope as the project proceeds. The latter needs to be carefully controlled for, if there are no change control procedures, the cost over-run could be horrendous.

The effectiveness of cost planning depends primarily on how effectively the schedule planning process has been carried out. If the results of the schedule planning process are a realistic and reliable development plan, there is a greater chance that the expression of this plan in cost terms will also be more realistic and reliable. The estimating process clearly becomes more difficult, the larger and longer the duration of the project, since there is more uncertainty in the estimates.

Thus, in building up the cost for each phase of the project, there are three essential factors to consider, namely the:

(1) technical target,
(2) contingency estimate,
(3) scope reserve.

The technical target will be the figure required to complete the activities described in the development plan for each stage of the project and will be the figure against which the project manager will be held accountable. The contingency estimate will be a reserve to cover unexpected occurrences and should, preferably, be greater the further ahead in the future for which the current cost estimate is being made. Finally, there will be a scope reserve which will cover changes of scope which do not prejudice the original concept and strategic purpose of the system.

In making an estimate of the technical target there are some basic rules which should be followed:

(1) clearly establish the scope and complexity of the project (or stage) and break it down into components;
(2) identify from previous projects the cost of completed components of similar type, scope and complexity;
(3) assemble the total project cost which represents the most probable final cost of the defined technical scope;
(4) make an allowance for components too small to individually assess;
(5) allow for float between tasks;
(6) allow for scheduling losses;
(7) allow for the learning curve;
(8) repeat the exercise with different component breakdowns;
(9) results should be within 10%, and if not obtain second opinion.

Figure 27   Cost planning and control

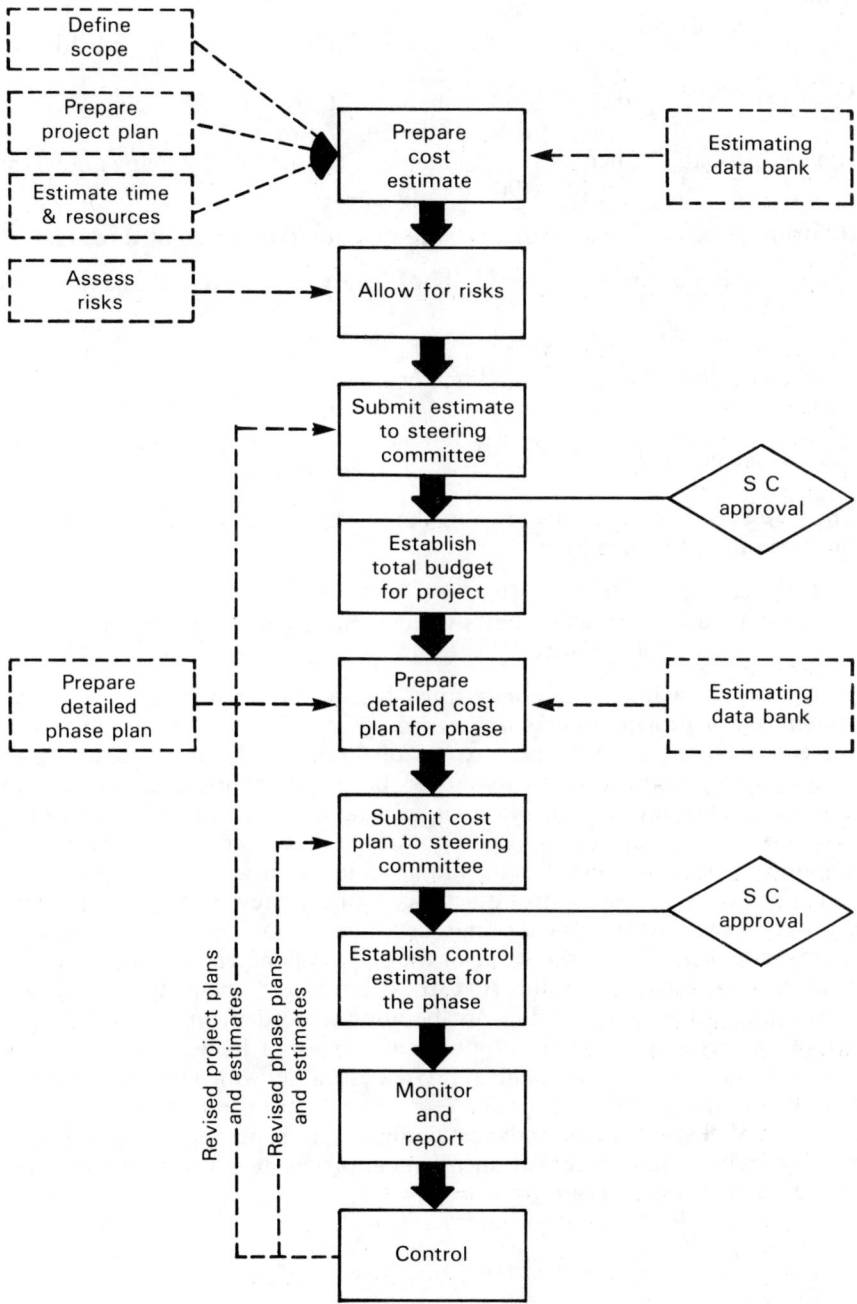

In deciding on the contingency and scope reserve three estimates should be made:

Lowest probable....there is a 10% chance of the actual cost being below this
                level (the 10/90 estimate)
Most probable.......there is a 50% chance of the actual cost being above or
                below this level (the 50/50 estimate)
Highest probable ...there is a 10% chance of the actual cost being above this
                level (the 90/10 estimate)

In formulating these risk estimates account should be taken of three factors:

(1) the highest realistic cost if almost every conceivable problem should occur;
(2) the lowest realistic cost if no problems occur;
(3) the most probable realistic cost.

7.2   Cost control

The process of control, as shown in the lower part of **Figure 28** consists of three essential features, the:

(1) recording of actual costs;
(2) comparison of actual costs with estimated costs and trends;
(3) reporting of variances.

In order to achieve this, there must be an appropriate cost accounting system and a proper process for recording costs within this system, to the correct activities and a proper process of reporting the actual costs. In the case of manpower costs, there should be an appropriate algorithym for allocating payroll costs, on the basis of a time key, to the different project activities. The important feature of control is that there should be a reliable system for the recording of costs and a reallocation where appropriate.

To be effective, cost control must incorporate a review of actuals against estimates as well as trends over time. Estimates should only be revised where there are real changes to the scope of the activity concerned or when they are outdated to such an extent that they have lost their motivating and controlling value. They should not be allowed to drift upwards, to follow actual increases in cost, due to poor cost control or ineffective working, so that comparisons are made against revised estimates which indicate that they may be on 'target'.

The final element in effective cost control is a proper reporting procedure which highlights important variances and appropriate remedial action. Good cost control reports should be:

(1) accurate,
(2) clear to read and understand,
(3) useful.

Accuracy depends upon an appropriate cost control system; clarity of presentation and usefulness depend upon identification of causes for variances. An example of a typical cost report is shown in **Figure 28**, at the project task level, and in **Figure 29**, at the phase summary and project level.

Figure 28 The task cost plan

COST PLANNING AND CONTROL — TASK PLAN

PROJECT REF NO/DESCRIPTION:

PHASE REF NO/DESCRIPTION:

PROJECT LEADER:

REVIEW NO/DATE:

TASK REF NO	TASK DESCRIPTION	MANPOWER COST (£K)			OTHER COST (£K)			TOTAL COST (£K)		
		PLANNED	ESTIMATED FINAL	ACTUAL TO DATE	PLANNED	ESTIMATED FINAL	ACTUAL TO DATE	PLANNED	ESTIMATED FINAL	ACTUAL TO DATE
	PHASE TOTALS									

AUTHORISATION, £K

PLANNED	EST FINAL	ACTUAL TO DATE	NEXT PHASE

SIGNATURE

Figure 29 The phase cost plan

COST PLANNING AND CONTROL — PHASE PLAN

PROJECT REF NO/DESCRIPTION:

SPONSOR:

PROJECT LEADER:

REVIEW NO:/DATE:

PHASE REF NO	PHASE DESCRIPTION	TOTAL COST (£K)			AUTHORISED (£K)			STATUS
		PLANNED	ESTIMATED FINAL	ACTUAL TO DATE	PLANNED	ESTIMATED FINAL	ACTUAL TO DATE	

PROJECT TOTALS

8. QUALITY ASSURANCE PLANNING AND CONTROL

The objectives of quality assurance are to ensure:

(1) the product(s) of the systems development process will comply in all respects with the user's requirements;
(2) the performance parameters established during the analysis phase are fully satisfied.

It is important to distinguish clearly between quality control and internal audit, with which it is sometimes confused. This is discussed further below, but suffice it to say at this stage that both quality assurance and internal audit are controls. However, the former is a technical control while the latter is a management control.

Quality assurance is a technical control aimed at user management to ensure they receive the product they require in terms of:

(1) cost being compatible with the benefits;
(2) ease of system implementation;
(3) functionality being complete and accurate;
(4) system being reliable and maintainable;
(5) system being efficient in operation.

It is applicable to all phases of the systems development process but, since its prime objective is to maximise benefits compared with cost and system suitability, the most constructive contribution to performance is made during the early stages of feasibility, analysis and design.

The first stage of planning, as shown in **Figure 30**, in the practical application of quality assurance to a project, will be to establish quality objectives, particularly in terms of performance, reliability, operability and maintainability. There must also be, at this stage, a clear recognition of the quality standards that will be applied during the project stages such as documentation, estimating methods, analysis techniques, design methods, change control systems, etc.

If the objectives and standards are clear, then it is possible to draw up a quality assurance plan for each stage of the project, identifying checks which must be made, timing of documentation, reviews, etc. This plan, and the procedures for applying the quality assurance checks, must be clearly communicated to the project group so they are aware of what is expected in terms of quality.

The final stage in application of quality assurance is to carry out the quality checks in accordance with the plan and procedures and report to project management on findings. If quality assurance is to be successful reports must be:

(1) clear in content,
(2) accurate in fact,
(3) useful with recommendations.

Further, line management in both the user area and the DP department should be prepared to act on the reports.

It has already been mentioned above that quality assurance is a technical control whereas internal audit is a management control. In some respects, the

Figure 30 Quality assurance

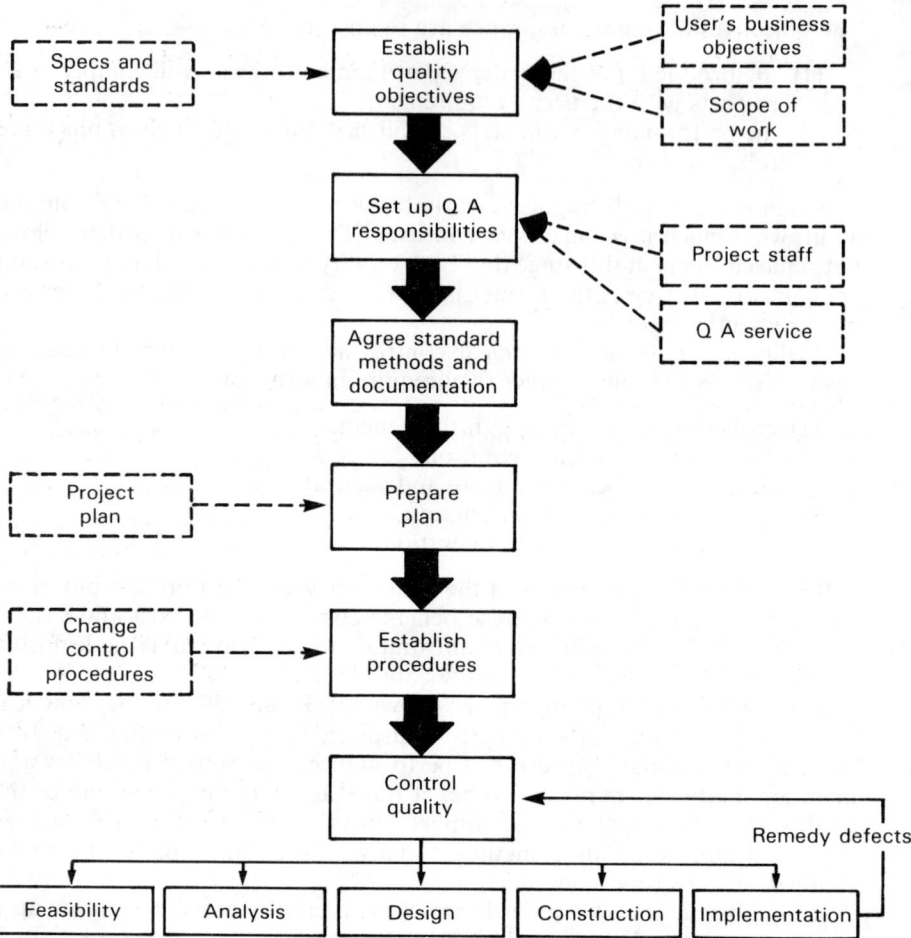

activities of the two will run partly in parallel for they are both concerned to ensure that the SDC is executed within minimum time, cost and risk to the company and the users are delivered the product(s) they require. However, the emphasis of quality assurance is on the quality and efficiency of the project team work in relation to agreed, or acceptable standards, while the emphasis of internal audit is on the system and system development controls.

The difference can sometimes be rather subtle and may not always be clear so an example may assist with clarification. The quality assurance role is to judge against agreed or acceptable standards so the most important first step in the involvement of quality assurance is the establishment of the objectives and standards. This then constitutes the control by which the quality of the actual work may be assessed. The internal auditor's involvement is not to judge the quality of the project group's work but to assess the adequacy of the controls by which quality assurance are working, ie the objectives and standards which they have set. However, in the absence of a quality assurance function, internal audit may be placed in the difficult position of actually carrying out the quality assurance role.

Finally, internal audit is a management control because it is concerned with evaluating the effectiveness and efficiency of the controls by which other groups are working, ie quality assurance and the project group and reporting on these controls, not only to the line management, but also to the internal audit committee. The reporting relationship of the quality assurance function will be to the project manager and to the sponsor of the system.

9. CHANGE CONTROL

There are no doubt many instances of project manager's who have struggled desperately to keep control on a project as deadlines have been passed and the deliverables still remain to be produced or prove to be unacceptable to the users. This often results in throwing out all formal planning, administration and control and falling back on despairing improvisation in an attempt to salvage something tangible from early expectant hopes. The result has usually been a disaster because changes are made without documentation and eventually no one knows, anymore, what the system is designed to achieve.

We must accept that change is a fact of life in the development of systems. This may result from a necessity to replan because the original estimates have proved too optimistic or because the users have requested a change in the scope of the work to be performed. However, in either case, change must be introduced in a controlled manner. The purpose of change control is to ensure that modifications are only accepted to any aspect of the project after adequate assessment of their impact on cost, timing and quality of the system and following a formal critical review.

The change control process involves six stages, namely:

(1) identification,
(2) assessment,
(3) change proposal,
(4) review,
(5) authorisation,
(6) recording.

The identification of change involves a potential revision of the agreed scope of work, or the agreed schedule plan, which will have an effect on the timing, cost and quality of the system. The result of the change should be assessed as to:

(1) requirement and potential benefits;
(2) estimated effect on system quality;
(3) estimated cost;
(4) estimated effect on the agreed schedule plan.

Following assessment of the change, a change proposal should be drawn up for review and authorisation at the appropriate level of project organisation.

The change proposal may then be reviewed at three levels:

1 individual team members......will generally decide on changes which have no impact on project objectives;

2 project manager...................will generally decide on changes which have a minor impact on project objectives;

3 steering committee................will generally decide on changes which have a major impact on project objectives.

Following the review the change proposal may be dropped; the change may be carried out as part of the project programme, or carried out as post-implementation maintenance. Whatever action is taken, the change proposal should be signed by a person(s) at the appropriate level of authority indicating whether approval has, or has not, been granted. Finally, it is important that the action that was subsequently taken should be recorded on the change proposal document.

10.   ADMINISTRATION AND TEAM LEADING

This is not intended to be a book on Management principles so, although this is an extremely important aspect of project success, administration and team leading will not be covered in any depth. There is, needless to say, a number of factors which are vital to success in this area:

(1) personnel selection;
(2) communications—within the project group and with other parties;
(3) motivation;
(4) administration control.

The first three are essentially concerned with the management of personnel while the last is concerned with how the project is actually run.

The running of the project is a vital element in project success and involves the manner and form of reporting, the frequency of reporting and the coverage of reporting. There have been examples already given, in this chapter, of the types of project reports which may be used to measure progress against the schedule plan. These project control reports should be clearly distinguished from the project reports which form part of the deliverables of the project development process. The frequency of reporting will depend upon the discretion of the project manager as well as the coverage, or distribution, of the project reports.

A particulary difficult aspect of the project manager's task is that a number of the members of the project group have no direct line management reporting relationship to the project manager—as shown in **Figure 22**. Thus, the project manager has responsibility without the authority to match this responsibility. The success of the project will, therefore, depend upon the skill of the project manager in handling his colleagues in other functional areas as well as their commitment, and motivation, to a successful conclusion.

7 Systems development methods and deliverables

This chapter contains a description of some of the methods which are applied in the development of systems, within the framework of the SDC, and the deliverables which are produced from the application of the methods. The selection does not claim to be exhaustive and other methods could be added, some of which we have described separately elsewhere, such as prototyping in chapter 8 and application package selection in chapter 11. The intention is to give the computing auditor a flavour of the work which is being carried out in the systems development process in order that he is better able to formulate his framework of controls.

The following system development methods are described in this chapter:

(1) analysis of objectives, goals and performance measures;
(2) constraint identification;
(3) problem analysis;
(4) data analysis;
(5) functional analysis;
(6) access path analysis;
(7) solution evaluation;
(8) specification analysis.

There are certain deliverables—and this is especially true of data and functional analysis—which have more applicability at one phase of the SDC rather than others. This is primarily due to the level of detail which is being sought at each phase. Thus, during a strategy study, the level of detail remains imprecise—broad groups of data and activities are examined rather than fine detail of attribute format and timeliness.

1. ANALYSIS OF OBJECTIVES, GOALS AND PERFORMANCE MEASURES

The purpose of this analysis is to identify business objectives, goals set to achieve those objectives and the performance measures used to monitor whether or not the goals have been achieved. The following deliverable is produced:

1 the table of objectives, goals and performance measures.

which is illustrated in **Table 13**. This serves to make clear which proposals are likely to be consistent with the business goals.

Table 13   Table of business objectives, goals and performance measures

BUSINESS OBJECTIVES, GOALS AND PERFORMANCE MEASURES Business area:				
Objective	Goals	Performance measures	Due date	Responsibility

The business objectives are a general statement of future results or conditions that the organisation wishes to achieve and which are usually defined by senior line management. Goals are specific targets to achieve a business objective whose results are measurable, and performance measures define the way in which the achievement (or otherwise) of goals will be assessed.

The business objectives have a direct effect on business activities and are usually analysed during the early phases of systems development, ie during the strategy or feasibility studies. A review is carried out throughout the system development process because the identification of constraints and problems may require some modifications to the initially formulated objectives.

2.   CONSTRAINT IDENTIFICATION

The purpose of this analysis is to identify the constraints, both business and technical, which might make a business solution infeasible or unacceptable within the business context. The following deliverable is produced:

1 the table of constraints.

which is illustrated in **Table 14.**

Table 14   A constraints table

Constraint list	
Constraint number	Constraint description

Constraints are usually analysed during the early stages of systems development, ie during the strategy study or the feasibility study but sometimes during the analysis phase. Those constraints which might affect the design are also analysed during the specification phase as, for example, limitations of hardware, software and resources.

3.   PROBLEM ANALYSIS

The purpose of problem analysis is to help the user to clarify and document his perception of the causes and effects of the business problems currently experienced or anticipated in the environment. The following deliverables are produced:

(1) problem table;
(2) interest group table;
(3) problem group table;
(4) needs for change table.

These are described in more detail below.

Since adequate identification of business problems is an essential prerequisite for the design of solutions to remove those problems, it is essential to check the problems with the user to ensure that the causes, and not the symptons, are identified. Problems are analysed during Strategy Studies and during the project initiation, feasibility and analysis phases of the SDC, clarification and additions being made as analysis proceeds through these phases.

During analysis of the current situation, the underlying problem causes will be clarified and categorised according to the business objectives and needs. A description of the deliverables is given below.

(1) PROBLEMS TABLE (Table 15)

A list of problems, clearly formulated, to show the effects of each problem and, when known, its causes. Effects should be quantified, if possible, so that one can assess how serious they are and prioritise them. When an effect or cause relates to more than one problem it will be necessary to develop separate tables of effects and causes.

Table 15   A problems table

PROBLEMS Business area:		
Problem number	Problem summary	Problem description

(2) INTEREST GROUP TABLE (Table 16)

Records the parties affected by each particular problem as, for example, end users, outsiders, DP specialists, etc to ensure that all groups of interested parties are represented, either by direct involvement or by inclusion, in the interviews conducted during analysis.

Table 16   An interest group table

INTEREST GROUPS Business area:	
Interest group	Problems
End users Public Funders Specialists	

(3) PROBLEM GROUP TABLE (**Table 17**)

Groups problems by prime business activities and shows where the most change is needed. Also shows which problems involve more than one area and whether solutions must involve several departments or activities.

Table 17   A problem group table

PROBLEM GROUPS Business area:	
Activities	Problems

(4) NEEDS FOR CHANGE TABLE (**Table 18**)

Summarises the key changes and their priorities to allow a request to be made for the removal of the causes of the problems identified. It is particularly useful when developing and evaluating proposed solutions.

Table 18   A needs for change table

NEEDS FOR CHANGE Business area:				
Needs for change	Goals	Objective	Problem number	Priority number

4.   DATA ANALYSIS

Data analysis is an essential technique for documenting data resources and is a wide subject which could occupy a book in its own right and, therefore, we do not propose to present more than a very concise summary of the subject. A brief mention has already been made of data analysis in chapter 4,3., above, under data administration, and a sample list of essential controls in this area has been given in section 3 of **Table 8**. The following deliverables are produced:

(1) the conceptual data model;
(2) model version;
(3) entity type;
(4) entity access authorisation matrix;
(5) model applicability by organisation unit;
(6) entity volumes by partition;
(7) attributes by entity list;
(8) relationship type;
(9) relationship end degree;
(10) relationship type exclusivity;
(11) attribute type;

(12) attribute type access authorisation matrix;
(13) attribute type permitted values;
(14) attribute type permitted ranges;
(15) attribute type to data item matrix;
(16) entity type to record types matrix;
(17) code values matrix;
(18) relationship types to sets/link path matrix;
(19) entity group to file type matrix;
(20) normalisation table.

The purpose of data analysis is to understand and document what the business uses in terms of entities, ie a data item against which we record other data items called attributes, during its operations, and the association between entities—or relationships. The deliverables of data analysis are primarily used to ensure effective data model design and also to assess the potential for data sharing, in application software evaluation, hardware planning and design, conversion and system management.

We have already shown, above, that there is a wide range of deliverables produced in the data analysis process and these are described in more detail, below.

(1) CONCEPTUAL DATA MODEL DIAGRAM

A pictorial representation of the entities, relationships and some of the deliverables of the relationships within the scope of the study. An example of a conceptual data model diagram is shown in **Figure 31** and the meaning of the symbols used in the process of data modelling is shown in **Figure 32**.

(2) MODEL VERSION

More than one data model may exist and the version is a number allocated to the data model which serves to uniquely identify it. Versions exist because any changes of business practices recommended may cause the data model to change.

(3) ENTITY TYPE

A data item, of interest to the enterprise, about which other data items, referred to as attributes, are recorded.

(4) ENTITY ACCESS AUTHORISATION MATRIX

This shows the organisational units which are allowed to access the different entity types.

(5) MODEL APPLICABILITY BY ORGANISATIONAL UNIT

This shows how the data item relationships can, and frequently do vary, between different organisational units of a functional organisation.

(7) ATTRIBUTES BY ENTITY LIST

This lists the attributes of each entity.

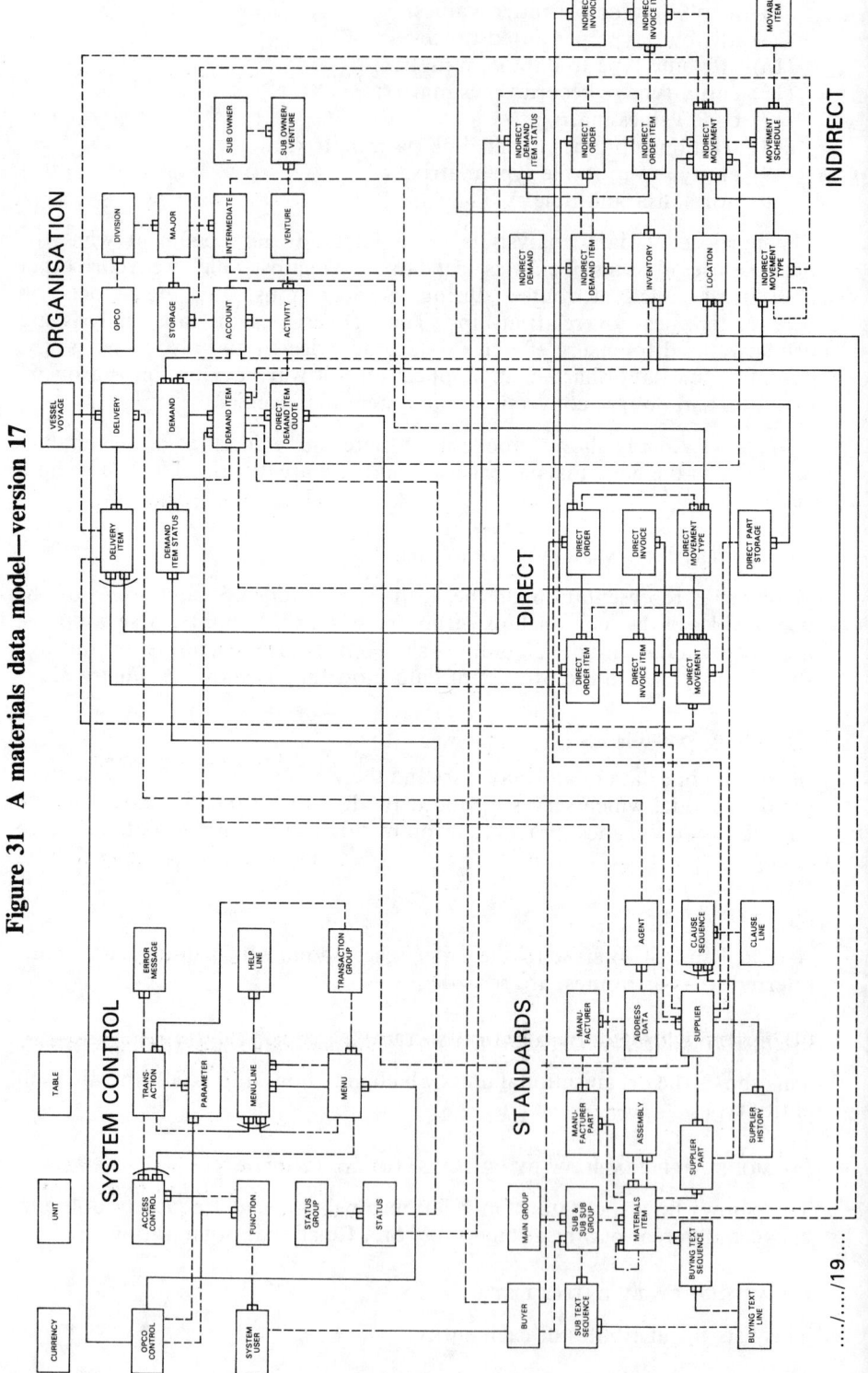

Figure 31   A materials data model—version 17

Figure 32 Conventions for data model diagrams

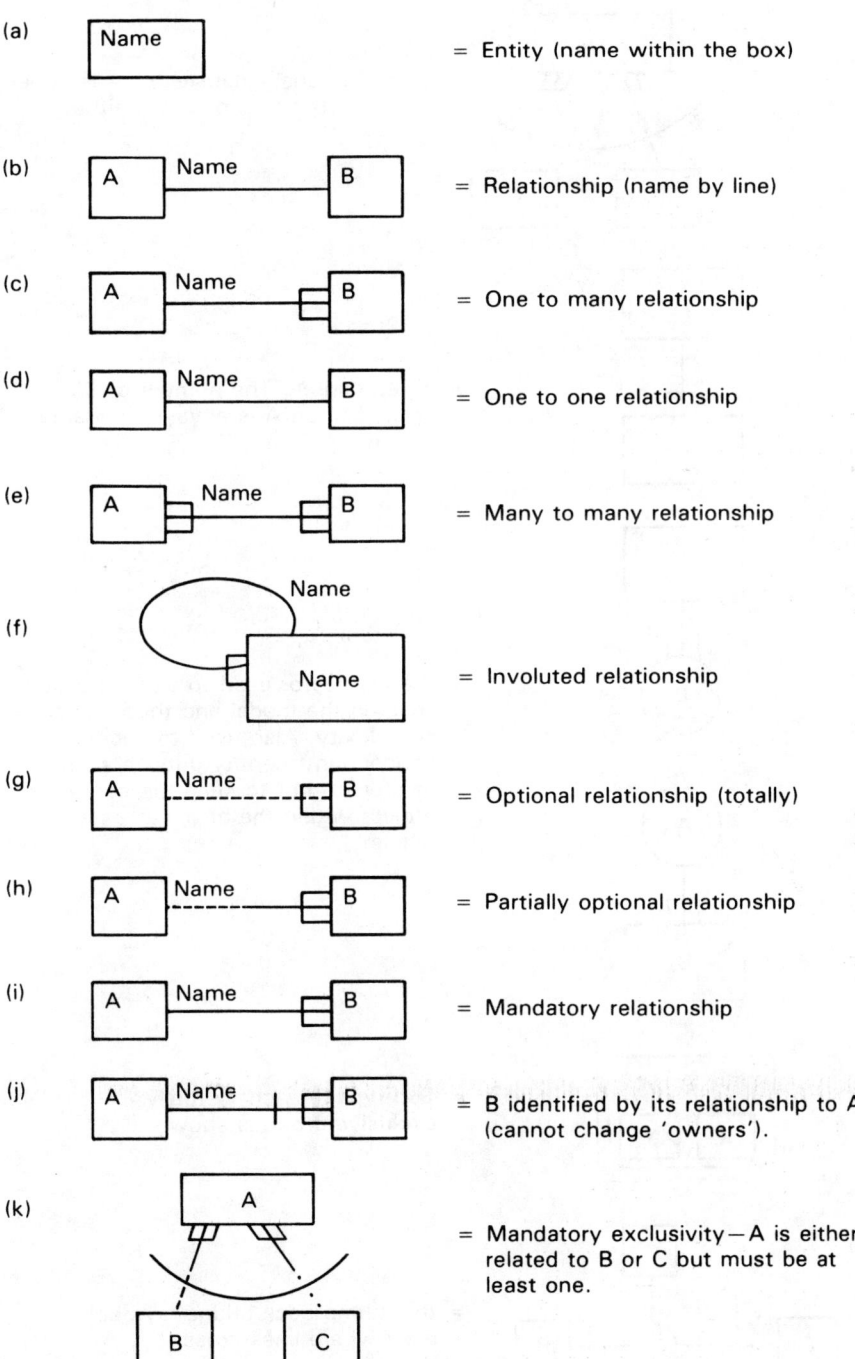

(a) Name = Entity (name within the box)

(b) A — Name — B = Relationship (name by line)

(c) A — Name — B = One to many relationship

(d) A — Name — B = One to one relationship

(e) A — Name — B = Many to many relationship

(f) Name / Name = Involuted relationship

(g) A - - Name - - B = Optional relationship (totally)

(h) A — Name - - B = Partially optional relationship

(i) A — Name — B = Mandatory relationship

(j) A — Name —|— B = B identified by its relationship to A (cannot change 'owners').

(k) A / B / C = Mandatory exclusivity—A is either related to B or C but must be at least one.

Figure 32   Conventions for data model diagrams (cont)

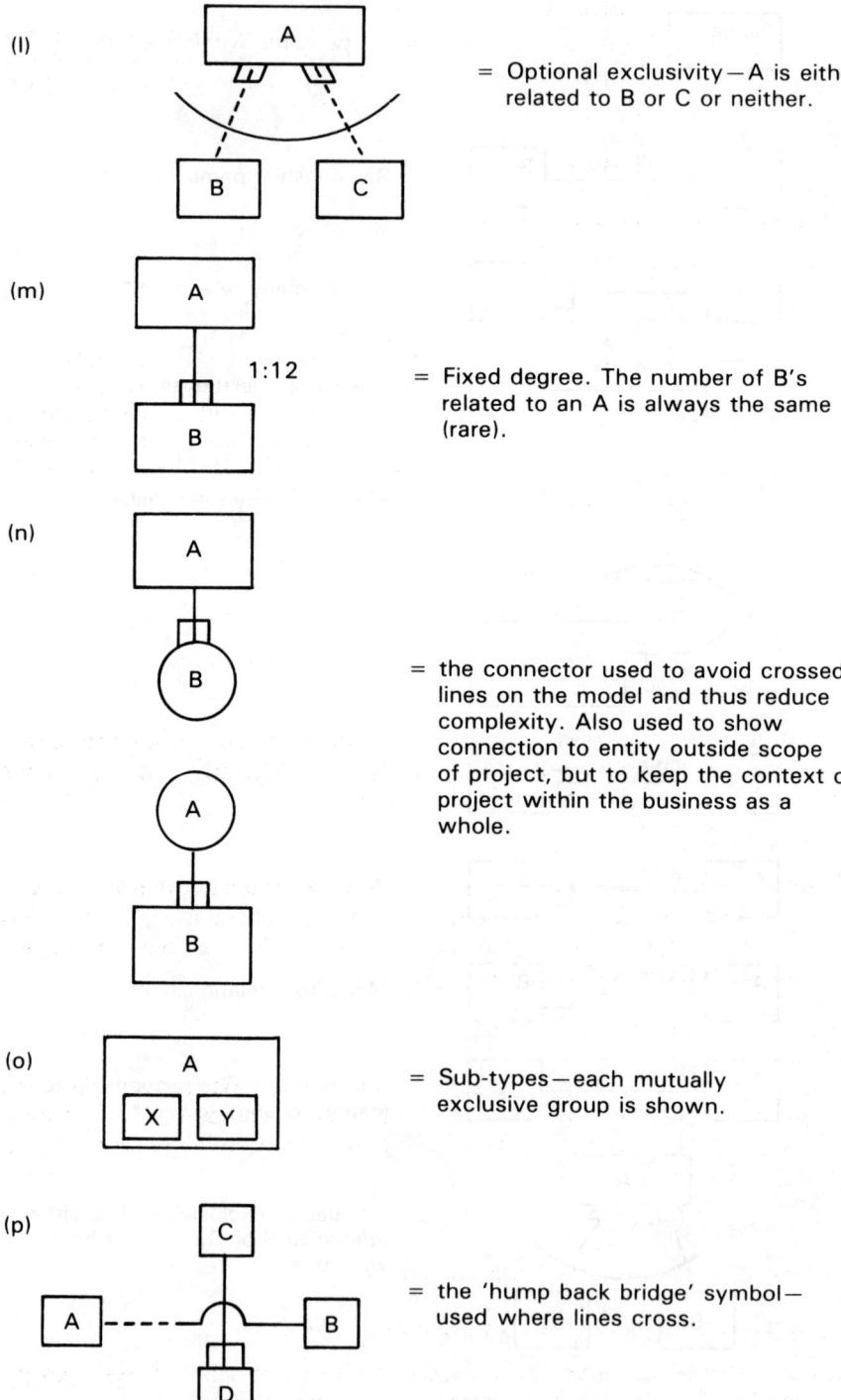

(l)

= Optional exclusivity — A is either
  related to B or C or neither.

(m)

1:12

= Fixed degree. The number of B's
  related to an A is always the same
  (rare).

(n)

= the connector used to avoid crossed
  lines on the model and thus reduce
  complexity. Also used to show
  connection to entity outside scope
  of project, but to keep the context of
  project within the business as a
  whole.

(o)

= Sub-types — each mutually
  exclusive group is shown.

(p)

= the 'hump back bridge' symbol —
  used where lines cross.

Figure 32   Conventions for data model diagrams (cont)

(q)

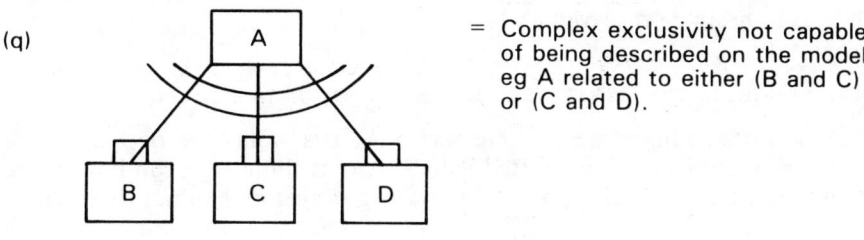

= Complex exclusivity not capable
of being described on the model.
eg A related to either (B and C)
or (C and D).

(r)

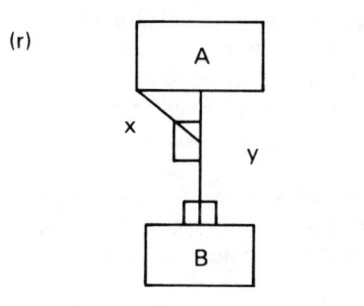

= Inclusivity
the relationship type x can only
occur if the relationship type y
occurs. x is effectively dependent
on y. This case is rare as it normally
occurs because of time which should
be removed from the model.

(8) RELATIONSHIP TYPE

A type of association between one entity type with itself or another entity
type and usually expressed as 1:1, 1:M or M:M form. This has been
previously illustrated in **Figure 14**, in chapter 4.

(9) RELATIONSHIP END DEGREE

These deliverables show precise quantitative information about how many of
an entity type A are related to an entity type B, eg if the relationship A to B is
1 : M then the degree relationship may be 1 : 10, 1 : 50, etc—only one degree
relationship will be applicable, at any one time.

(10) RELATIONSHIP TYPE EXCLUSIVITY

Relationship type exclusivity describes the rules of dependency between
relationship types where, for example, an item A is related to an item B, or C
or D. Examples of these relationship types are shown in illustrations (k), (l)
and (q) in **Figure 32**.

(11) ATTRIBUTE TYPE

A property or quality that defines an entity.

(12) ATTRIBUTE TYPE ACCESS AUTHORISATION MATRIX

This describes which users are allowed to access the attribute types of entity
types and is classified by the type of action/ access allowed.

(13) ATTRIBUTE TYPE PERMITTED VALUES

A permitted value is one of the allowed values an attribute type can take if there is a discrete set of values.

(14) ATTRIBUTE TYPE PERMITTED RANGES

The permitted ranges are discrete sets of values, which lie between finite limits, which define the permitted values. An attribute type can have more than permitted value range as well as having ranges and values together.

(15) ATTRIBUTE TYPE TO DATA ITEM MATRIX

The matrix of attribute types to data items shows where an attribute type is implemented as a data item in different record types as well as the name of the data item in each of the records.

(16) ENTITY TYPE TO RECORD TYPE MATRIX

The matrix of entity types to record types shows where an entity type is currently implemented as a 'record type'—it can also be a segment of a record type, depending upon the DBMS or file management system in use.

(17) CODE VALUES MATRIX

This shows where current code values for data items match, or not, against code values selected as appropriate for the system under development and, therefore, where changes will be required.

(18) RELATIONSHIP TYPES TO SETS/LINK PATHS MATRIX

This matrix shows how the relationship types, as shown in **Figure 32**, are implemented in the existing systems design. The different design methods that were chosen by the design group are listed horizontally and an indication is given as to the type—link path, record, etc

(19) ENTITY GROUP TO FILE TYPE MATRIX

This matrix shows how the broad entity groups, that have been identified, map onto existing file types.

(20) NORMALISATION TABLE

A table which enables the steps followed during the normalisation of data records to third-normal-form to be documented. The normalisation of records has already been discussed in chapter 4, 3., above.

Data analysis is the foundation stone on which the future system is based. If this activity is not carried out carefully and thoroughly, the resulting system may not be effective in meeting the user's requirements and neither will it be efficient if adding new entities and attributes necessitates a high level of maintenance work on the system.

5. FUNCTIONAL ANALYSIS

The purpose of functional analysis is to analyse what the business does now, or may want to do, and, within the SDC, is mainly applied during strategy studies and, feasibility studies and the analysis phase. Functional analysis is a top down method which aims to break down the activities of a business in a progressive way from very broad generalisations to the most detailed elementary activity. The following deliverables are produced;

(1) the functional decomposition diagram;
(2) the data flow diagram;
(3) the activity;
(4) the user/activity responsibility matrix;
(5) the user/activity detail;
(6) the event;
(7) the event/user frequency;
(8) source/sink;
(9) data flow;
(10) source element usage matrix;
(11) system/sub-system activity mapping matrix;
(12) transaction/elementary activity mapping matrix;
(13) sub-routine/module to common procedure matrix;
(14) activity/data usage matrices.

The activity analysis deliverables are used primarily in systems design and for determining strategies and feasibilities but they also have major importance in organisational planning and design, package evaluation, system software evaluation, hardware planning, conversion and systems enhancement. A description of the deliverables is given below.

(1) FUNCTION DECOMPOSITION DIAGRAM

A pictorial representation of how the functions of the business have been decomposed, by the analyst from broad generalised groupings into progressively more and more levels of detail. An example of this is shown in **Figure 33**. and the diagrammatic conventions used in functional analysis are shown in **Figure 34**.

(2) DATA FLOW DIAGRAM

A pictorial representation of how activities depend upon one another because they use the data created by other activities. These diagrams are complementary to the function decomposition diagram and show how the activities in each branch of the decomposition diagram are dependent.

(3) THE ACTIVITY

This describes what the business does—existing system—or wants to do—proposed system. At detailed analysis level an elementary activity is potentially one or more transaction types in design.

(4) USER/ACTIVITY RESPONSIBILITY MATRIX

A matrix showing which users are responsible for the activities.

Figure 33   A function decomposition diagram

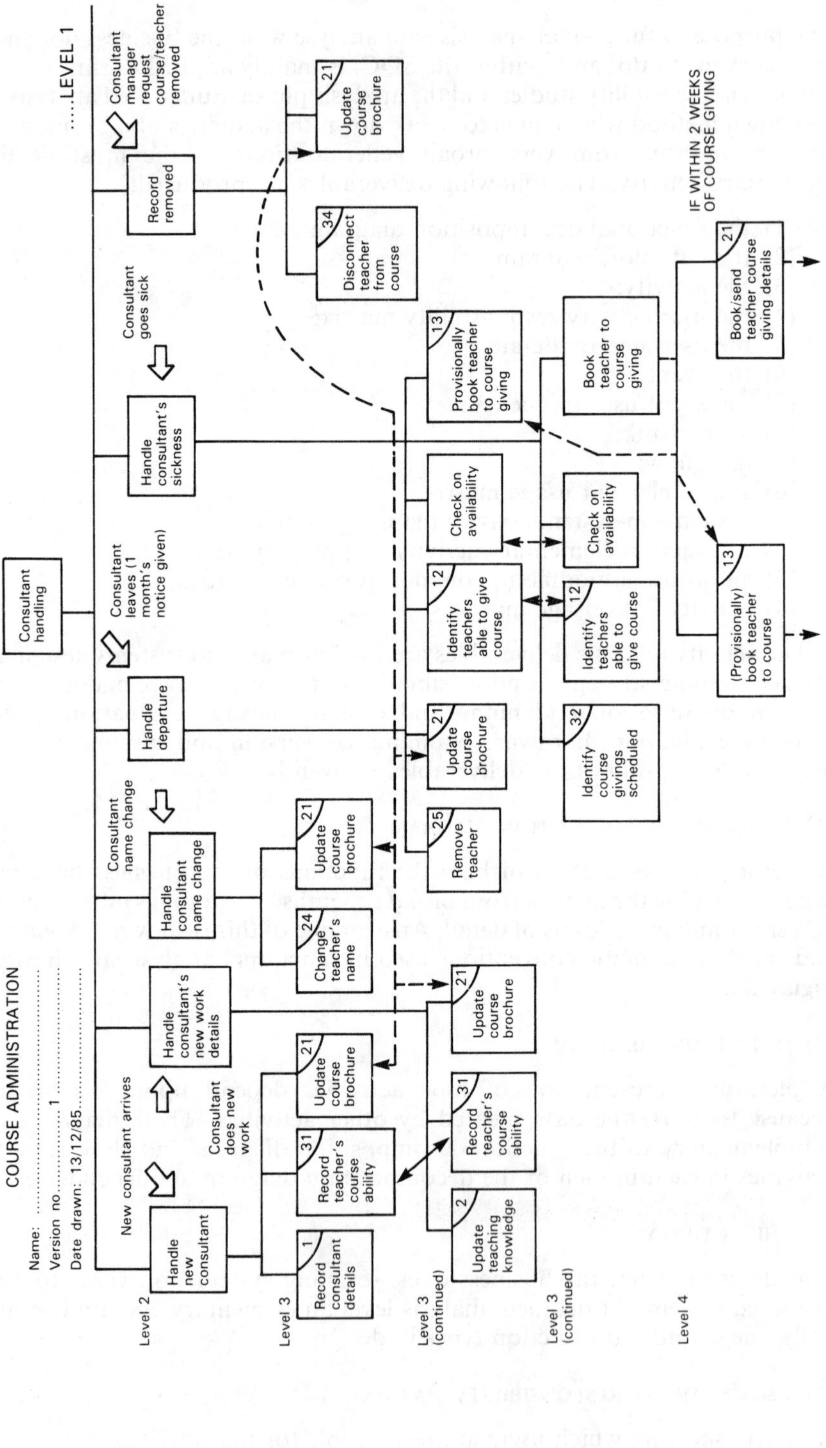

Figure 34   Conventions for function decomposition diagrams

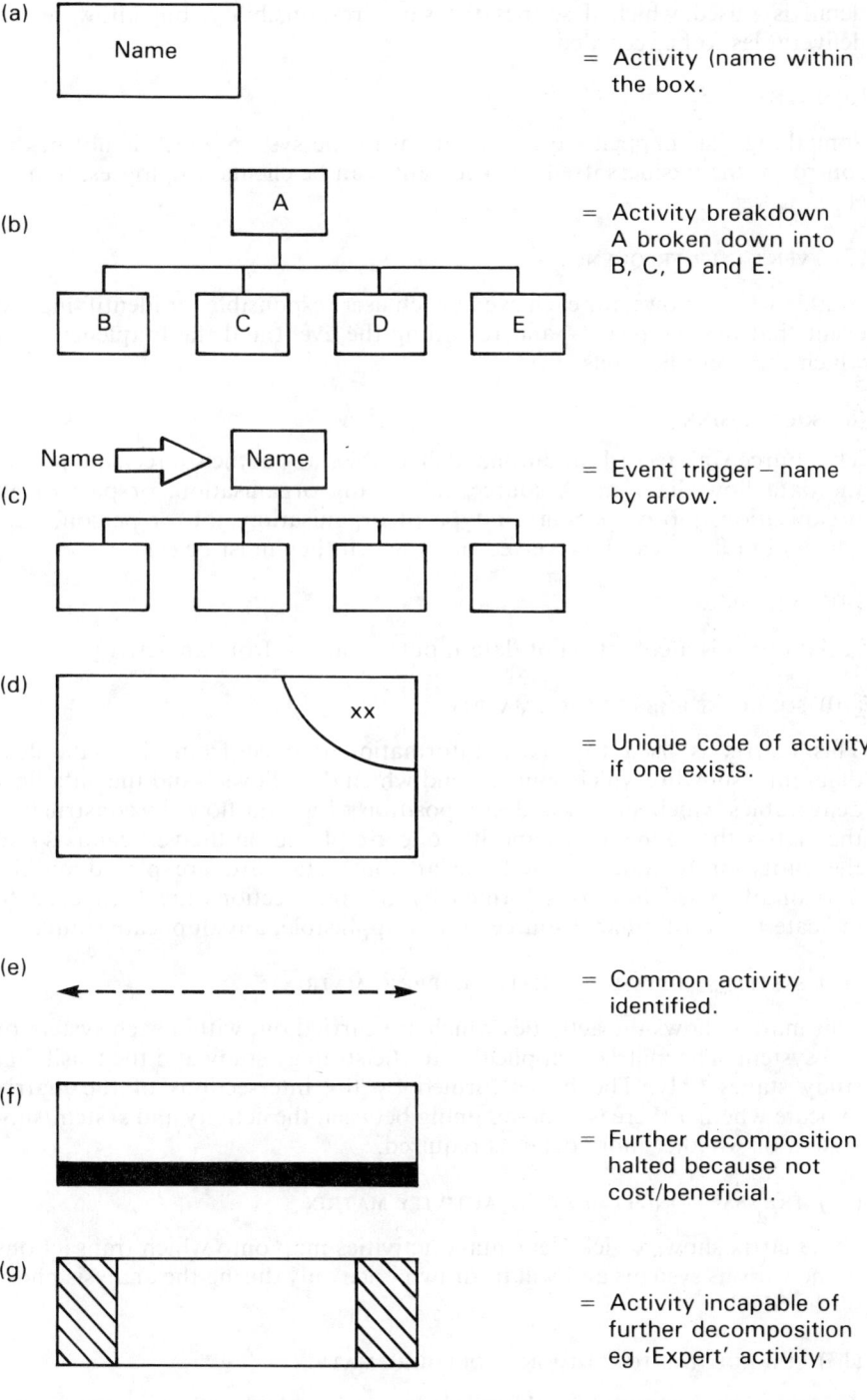

(a) = Activity (name within the box.

(b) = Activity breakdown A broken down into B, C, D and E.

(c) = Event trigger – name by arrow.

(d) = Unique code of activity if one exists.

(e) = Common activity identified.

(f) = Further decomposition halted because not cost/beneficial.

(g) = Activity incapable of further decomposition eg 'Expert' activity.

(5) USER/ACTIVITY DETAIL

For each entry in the user/activity responsibility matrix one user/activity detail is raised which describes the same responsibility, but allows extra deliverables to be recorded.

(6) EVENT

Something that happens to a participant in the system which is not in the control of the business itself. (Participants can be clients, employees, things, etc.)

(7) EVENT/USER FREQUENCY

A table which shows, for each event, each user responsible for identifying the event that has happened—and recording the event and the frequency with which the event happens.

(8) SOURCE/SINK

The source/sink records additional deliverables about the source/sink not on the data flow diagram. A source/sink is any organisation, or part of an organisation, job or person, or type of organisation, job or person from which data flows can be received or to which they must be sent.

(9) DATA FLOW

A data flow is a collection of data input or output from an activity.

(10) SOURCE/ELEMENT USAGE MATRIX

This matrix is used to record information derived from the data flow diagram—showing which sources send which data flows—and the data flow deliverables which show the decomposition of a data flow. In constructing the matrix the source name and its code are placed on the vertical axis and the entity or relationship and the attribute standard are placed on the horizontal axis. The boxes formed by the intersections are then used to indicate the most reliable source and, if applicable, any duplicate sources.

(11) SYSTEM/SUB-SYSTEM ACTIVITY MAPPING MATRIX

This matrix shows the activities which are carried out within each system or sub-system. The matrix is applicable to the strategy study and the feasibility study stages only. The boxes formed by the intersections of the matrix indicate whether there is good mapping between the activity and system/sub-system or whether more detail is required.

(12) TRANSACTION/ELEMENTARY ACTIVITY MATRIX

This matrix shows which elementary activities map onto which transactions in the various systems and will be drawn once only during the analysis phase of the SDC.

(13) SUB-ROUTINE TO COMMON PROCEDURE MATRIX

This matrix is produced for those existing design blocks of computer code—

sub-routines or modules—which are common callable routines and those blocks of logic—procedures—in the elementary activity which have been recognised as common blocks of logic. The matrix shows which routines map to which blocks of logic within a system and only one matrix is, therefore, produced for each system.

(14) ACTIVITY/DATA USAGE MATRICES

These matrices show the use by the activities of the deliverables of data analysis and are produced for each level of function decomposition once the decomposition is complete.

6. ACCESS PATH ANALYSIS

There are three fundamental objectives in access path analysis, to:

(1) provide a precise, complete and unambiguous specification of the logic of an elementary activity capable of being used in systems design;

(2) ensure that the logical data model which supports the elementary activities is also complete and that the accesses on it have been identified;

(3) quantify the accesses on the logical data model so that basic design decisions can be made, eg on-line or batch transaction and data base design can be made on quantified information.

The following deliverables are produced:

(1) elementary activity (part 1)—basic structure chart;
(2) elementary activity (part 2)—complete logic specification;
(3) elementary activity (part 3)—access path diagram;
(4) elementary activity (part 4)—user version;
(5) 'Procedure' form;
(6) list of messages;
(7) elementary activity access path usage.

Access path analysis is applicable only to the very detailed analysis phase of the SDC or may be delayed until the specification stage is reached. The elementary activity description is, therefore, still describing business logic, but in a precise, quantified way. The deliverables are described in more detail below.

(1) ELEMENTARY ACTIVITY (PART 1)—BASIC STRUCTURE CHART

These deliverables show how the elementary activity is broken down into a basic logical structure of what has to be done to achieve it. There are two methods which may be used to show the structure:

(a) showing the structure simply as a continuation of the functional decomposition diagram—as shown in **Figure 35**;

(b) showing the same information but uses different diagrammatic conventions; the decomposition diagram has effectively been turned

Figure 35a   Elementary activity form – part 1 (basic structure chart)

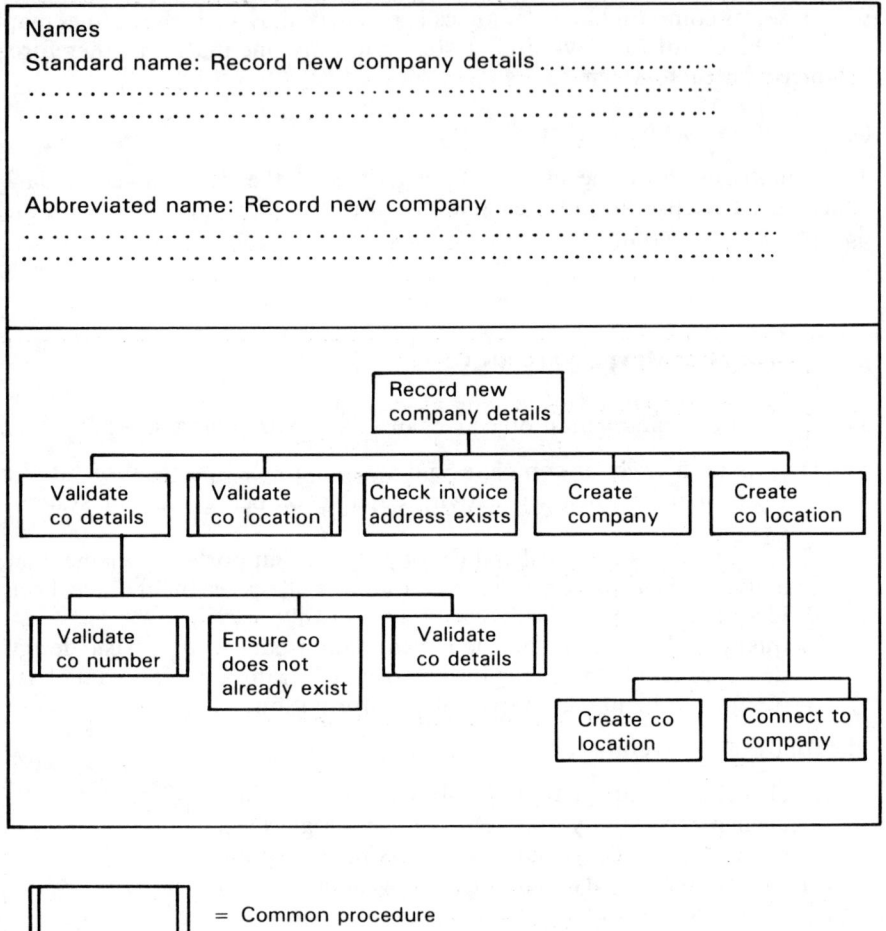

Names

Standard name: Record new company details...................
....
....

Abbreviated name: Record new company ....
....
....

= Common procedure

sideways—as shown in **Figure 35b**; The diagrammatic convention used in constructing the second of these basic structure charts is shown in **Figure 36**.

(2) ELEMENTARY ACTIVITY (PART 2)—COMPLETE LOGIC SPECIFICATION

This fills out the basic structures identified in Part 1 and provides a complete unambiguous description of what must be done. The logical business specification is written in structured English, building up the logic using a series of commands. A structured English command is simply a precise statement of what action must be completed at that stage of the activity.

(3) ELEMENTARY ACTIVITY (PART 3)—ACCESS PATH DIAGRAM

This shows on the logical data model the accesses which the elementary activity is making on the model.

Figure 35b   Elementary activity—part 1 (basic structure chart)

Names

Standard name: Record new company details ....
....
....

Abbreviated name: Record new company   ....
....
....

Record new company details

Validate company details
    Validate company number
    Ensure company does not already exist
    Validate company details

Validate company location
    Validate company location details

Check invoice address exists

Create company

Create company location details
Create company location
Connect to company

(4) ELEMENTARY ACTIVITY (PART 4)—USER VERSION

This records in ordinary user-oriented English what has been described in structured English in part 3.

(5) 'PROCEDURE' FORM

The common procedures, identified in the elementary activity, are specified separately using structured English commands and ways of expressing the logic.

(6) LIST OF MESSAGES

A message is a form of communication between activities and part of a data

Figure 36   Conventions for figure 35b

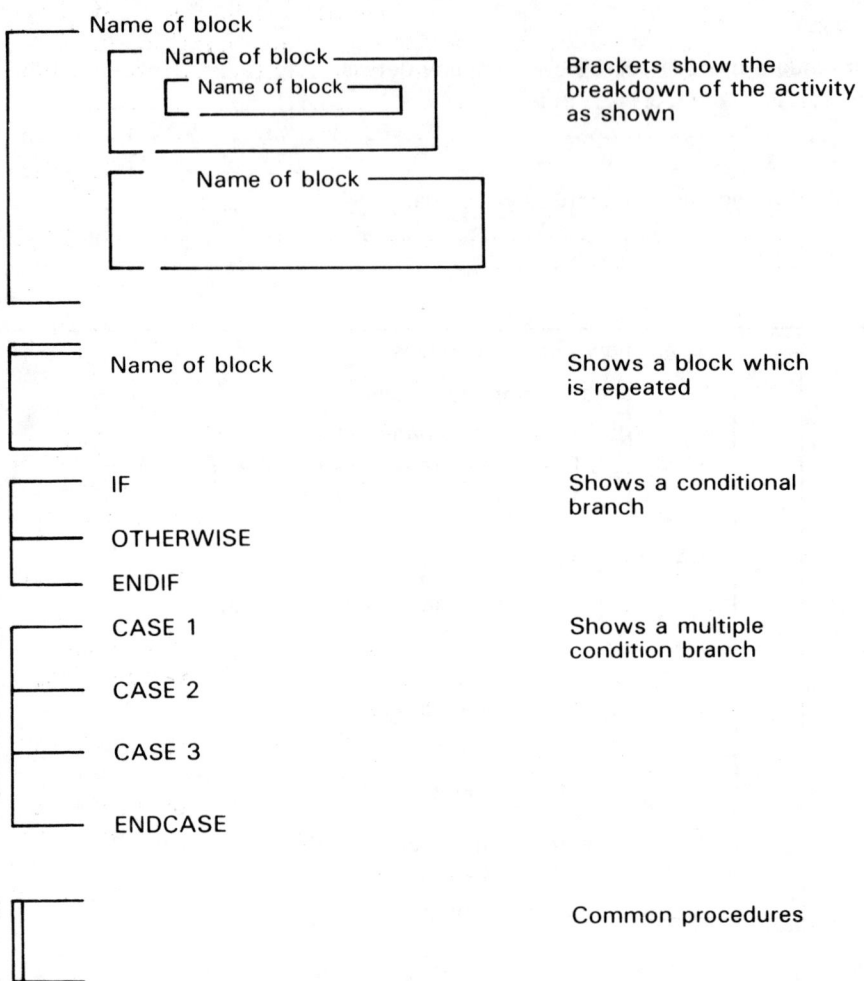

Name of block [nested: Name of block, Name of block, Name of block]	Brackets show the breakdown of the activity as shown
Name of block	Shows a block which is repeated
IF / OTHERWISE / ENDIF	Shows a conditional branch
CASE 1 / CASE 2 / CASE 3 / ENDCASE	Shows a multiple condition branch
	Common procedures

flow and the 'list' is simply a summary of all the messages used in the activities.

(7) ELEMENTARY ACTIVITY ACESS PATH USAGE

This deliverable records all the quantifiable information about an elementary activity and its use of data and should only be produced once the elementary activity and procedure descriptions are stable and have been agreed by the user.

7. SOLUTION EVALUATION

The purpose of solution evaluation is to ensure that the facts have been collected so that decisions can be made on the most desirable solution for the requirements. If the analysis has been completed, to the appopriate depth, the choice is normally relatively easy.

There are, however, other criteria to be input to the evaluation:

(1) the cost, benefit and risk of each particular solution should be assessed;
(2) impact that each particular solution will have on the organisation and its people must be analysed.

The following deliverables are produced:

(1) cost/benefit evaluation,
(2) social factor table.

The feasibility study is the prime development phase where different solutions are considered in detail. A strategy study will look at solutions globally. The analysis phase will re-assess the options after analysing the requirement in greater detail. A more detailed description of the deliverables is given below.

(1) COST/BENEFIT ANALYSIS

This is a detailed analysis showing the costs of developing, implementing and running the system against the expected savings in costs which are likely to be achieved by introducing the new system.

(2) SOCIAL FACTOR TABLE (TABLE 19)

The social factors table documents the impact of each alternative solution on people. Each different interest group is considered and the impact on members of the interest group is documented.

8. SPECIFICATION

The objective of specification is to produce an overall systems design covering the transactions, screens and listings and to show how they all fit together. It excludes the detailed design aspects of program specification and all aspects of file design. The concentration is on the initial mapping of analysis deliverables to a system design, as the user will see it, rather than the internal processing by which it will actually be achieved. Hence, there is considerable emphasis on screen and listings design.

Specification is a conglomerate of different methods and deliverables rather than being one unique method like the examples given in the previous sections. The final product of the methods are the functional specification and the controls specification. The methods and deliverables involved in the production of the functional specification are shown below and those for the production of the controls specification are described in chapter 11.

Table 19   Social factors table

SOCIAL FACTORS TABLE Business area: Alternative no:		
Interest groups and social factors studied	**IMPACT**	
	Positive	Negative

(1) ACTIVITIES TO TRANSACTION MAPPING

The activities identified during analysis are considered and grouped or split into meaningful units of work for the end user. These become transactions that will consist of some user activities and one or more on-line interactions or the submission of one batch transaction.

The deliverables produced are:

(1.1) ELEMENTARY ACTIVITY TO TRANSACTION MATRIX

—always used.

(1.2) TRANSACTION DEFINITION

—always used.

(1.3) SUMMARY OF USERS/TRANSACTION MATRIX

—used when important to define which users are responsible for each transaction.

(1.4) USER/TRANSACTION DETAIL

—used only when frequency of use by particular users is of critical importance.

(2) CONSTRUCT DATA MODEL TO BE IMPLEMENTED

The main aim of this method is to provide a data model to be implemented (computer) which the database designer can use and a data model to be implemented (paper) which the organisation and methods designer can use to produce paper forms and files. A subsidiary aim, which is a side-effect of the production of the data models, is to verify the transaction mapping results. This step is an essential one before batch flowchart construction and transaction network design as both these tasks use the verified transactions.

The deliverables produced are the:

(2.1) DATA MODEL TO BE IMPLEMENTED (COMPUTER)

—A sub-set of the complete (analysis) conceptual model showing a summary of accesses which will be performed during processing.

(2.2) DATA MODEL TO BE IMPLEMENTED (CLERICAL)

—As above, but showing the model which will be supported using 'clerical' means, eg forms, filing cabinets, etc.

(2.3) TRANSACTIONS USAGE MATRIX

—Shows how either each computer supported or each clerically supported transaction uses the entities, relationships or the attributes.

(3) DESIGN THE ON-LINE TRANSACTION NETWORK

The on-line transactions are structured into a top level dialogue structure. This will need to be integrated with existing transactions running in the same environment.

The deliverables produced are:

(3.1) ON-LINE TRANSACTION NETWORK DIAGRAM

—This is a pictorial representation of how the transactions which are on-line fit together as one integrated systems network.

(3.2) TRANSACTION NETWORK SUMMARY OF CALLING PARAMETERS

—Shows what transactions are called by what calling parameters and will only be produced if the calling and return parameters have not been shown on the transaction network; there are likely to be few calling parameters between transactions and ideally these should be minimised.

(4) DESIGN FIRST DRAFT INPUTS/OUTPUTS

In this step the input and output of the transactions is identified and a summary of input/output is produced.

The deliverable produced is:

(4.1) SUMMARY OF INPUT/OUTPUT

—This shows all the input/output of an elementary activity and the number of times each 'piece of data' is input/output by user.

(5) CONSTRUCT BATCH FLOW

In this step the details of the batch transactions are designed.
The deliverables produced are:

(5.1) BATCH SYSTEMS FLOWCHART DIAGRAM

—This show pictorially the interaction between user and computer for one transaction which will be implemented in batch.

(5.2) BATCH STEP DETAIL

—Shows the detailed logic of the batch processing.

(5.3) ROUGH PRINT LISTING LAYOUT

—Shows a rough layout of how a listing identified either in an on-line transaction network or part of a batch job should appear.

(5.4) ROUGH FORM LAYOUT

—Shows a rough layout of how a form identified in a 'clerical' system flowchart or 'batch' flowchart should appear; it may also be produced from the summary of input/output.

(5.5) DETAILED FORM'S LAYOUT

—Shows the detailed and precise design of a form's layout.

(6) DETAILED DIALOGUE DESIGN

In this step the details of on-line screen sequences are designed. Where possible, an application generator with good prototyping facilities should be used as the medium for recording and agreeing design details with the end-user.

The deliverables produced are:

(6.1) ON-LINE DIALOGUE DESIGN DIAGRAM

—This is used in the specification of the dialogue design for a single on-line transaction (rather than the complete structure menus) and shows the user tasks, the computer tasks and the screens through which interaction takes place.

(6.2) POTENTIAL EXCHANGE DETAIL

—This deliverable is optional and shows how the original elementary activity description has been cut up or altered to fit the logic of the dialogue flow for a particular transaction,

(6.3) ROUGH SCREEN LAYOUT

—This is a rough layout of how a screen identified in the transaction network should appear and is produced using the information on the summary of input/output form; it should preferably be produced using the screen painting software of the software tool that will be used to implement the production system.

(6.4) TRANSACTION/EXCHANGE USAGE MATRIX

—This matrix documents where exchanges have been rationalised (by combination) and where they are used in transactions; the purpose is to optimise on design and programming and to ensure that the user sees consistent results from the same actions thus making the system more user friendly and easier to learn and use.

(6.5) DETAILED SCREEN LAYOUT

—Shows the layout of the screen in absolute detail and should be produced using screen painting software.

(6.6) SCREEN SPECIFICATION

—Information about the details of the screen is entered directly into the screen painter, data dictionary or application generator and represent the permanent attributes of each field on the screen.

8 Prototyping—a development strategy

This chapter discusses the use of prototyping as a strategy within the broader framework of the SDC. It is sometimes suggested that prototyping is an alternative methodology which is to be preferred to the SDC because rigorous requirements definition has failed on so many occasions. We believe that this is very shortsighted since rigorous pre-specification is only one aspect of the SDC. We suggest that failure of structured development methodologies is due to a weak controls framework rather than the methodology itself. After all, the method of pre-specification has worked in other areas of engineering so why not in computing systems development?

The advantages which have been claimed for prototyping, as a development strategy, are listed in **1.**, below, and the assumptions upon which its use is based are discussed in **2.** The component parts of an idealised prototyping software package are:

    (1) integrated data dictionary;
    (2) flexible DBMS;
    (3) non-procedural report writer;
    (4) screen generator;
    (5) high level development language.

Prototyping is not suitable for all types of projects and in **3.**, below, factors are discussed which influence the decision to use this strategy within the SDC framework. There are five main steps involved in the application of the strategy, namely:

    (1) selection of suitable projects;
    (2) identification of data elements;
    (3) building the model;
    (4) tuning the model;
    (5) documentation.

The effectiveness of prototyping, as a development strategy, depends upon five essential principles:

    (1) most applications are derivable from a small set of structures;
    (2) most systems use a repetitive and well known set of model functions;
    (3) most input editing is derivable from a small set of edit models;
    (4) application reporting is based on four basic steps;
    (5) there are basic design structures that complement the prototype.

The introduction of prototyping into the company environment and its influence on project management are discussed in **5.-7.**, below. The final section of the chapter gives a sample list of controls that should be incorporated into the development controls framework when using proto-typing as a strategy within the SDC.

1. THE STRATEGY

There are four primary strategies for the development of computing systems:

(1) use software vendors;
(2) end-user development;
(3) conventional structured development with pre-specification;
(4) use of 'intelligent' software for pre-specification (prototyping).

We have already described prototyping in chapter 5, **4.**, as a technique for interactively building working models, with the users, of all, or part, of a system and the technique is particularly useful when requirements are unclear. Further, we have suggested that the main application of prototyping is during the analysis, specification and, to some extent, technical design phases although it may also be used during the feasibility study and to generate part of the functional specification.

The following advantages have been quoted for the use of prototyping as a strategy in the requirements definition process:

(1) adaptable to user styles;
(2) stimulates user participation;
(3) immediate validation of input/output;
(4) impact on the user environment can be immediately assessed;
(5) early assessment of user/system interface;
(6) consensus agreement can be obtained;
(7) reduces risk of unacceptable product;
(8) permits better communications;
(9) decreases time scale to completion of project;
(10) makes project management less complicated;
(11) synergy from experience of different systems;
(12) training mechanism;
(13) lower project cost;
(14) less risk of scope change.

There are advocates of prototyping who suggest that the strategy is an alternative development cycle to the methodology which we have described in chapter 5. This is an unfortunate interpretation which creates some confusion amongst those involved in the systems development process. It should be clearly understood that we do not consider prototyping as a separate methodology. We regard prototyping, instead, as a particular strategy which may be applied within the broader framework of the systems development process whose methodology is defined by the phases described in chapter 5. An example of the use of prototyping, as a strategy within the SDC, is shown in the project development plan, **Figure 37**, for an actual system under development.

Figure 37 A project development plan with prototyping

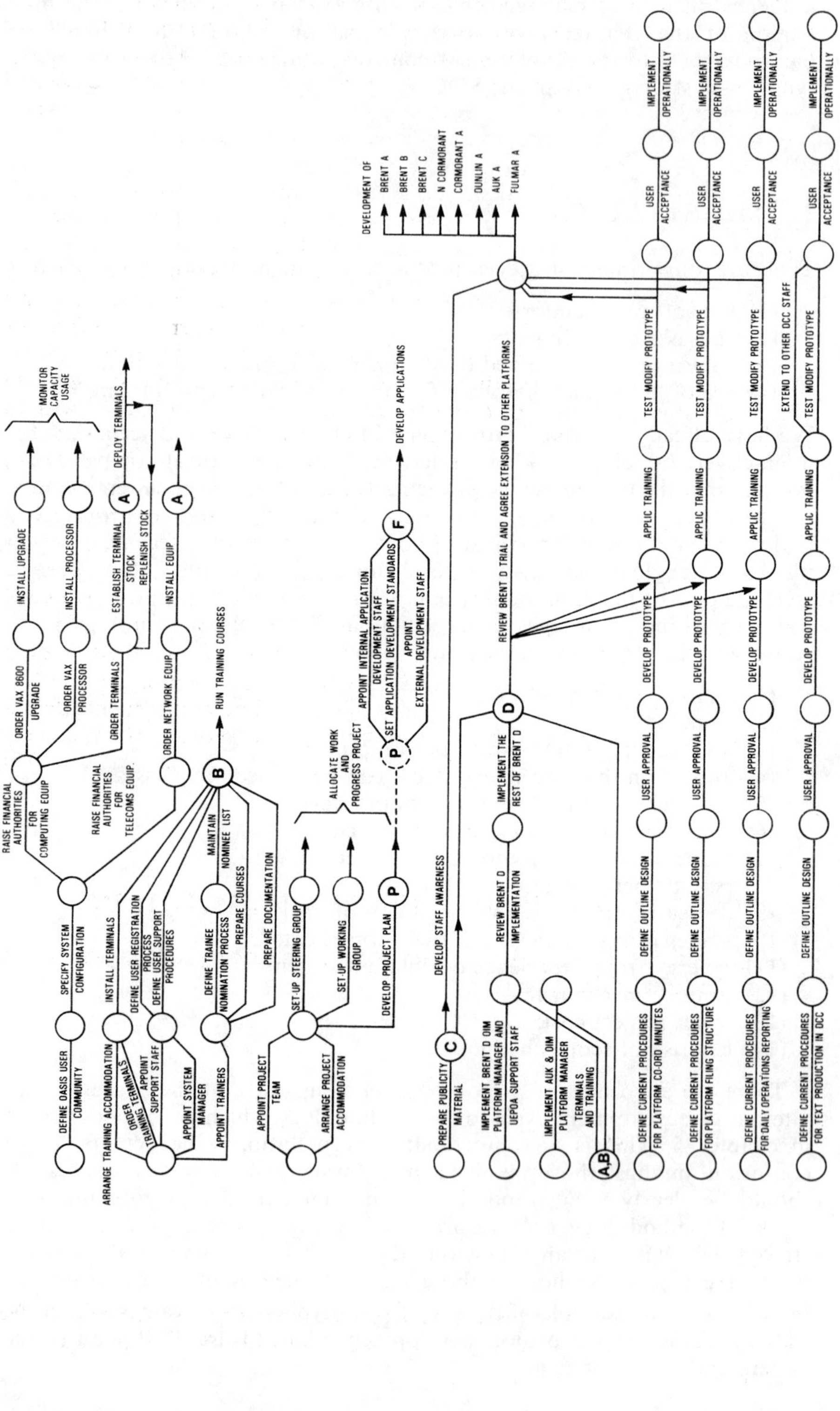

We have already suggested in chapter 5 that the objective in the initial phases of the SDC, ie the feasibility study and analysis phases, is to specify the user requirements as clearly and concisely as possible. This is ultimately manifested in the production of the functional specification which describes the technical requirements of the system in user-oriented terms. This same approach is used in other areas of engineering such as shipbuilding, aircraft construction, North Sea oil rig construction, etc.

If the outcome of the systems development process is to be successful, resulting in a product which meets the users requirements, the requirements definition has to be carried out, in the initial stages, with a high degree of precision. Lack of precision, at this stage of the development, will inevitably have repercussions at a later stage of the project in terms of time, cost and scope changes. Experience has shown that the majority of errors which occur in the development of systems arise at this stage of the development process. The implication is, therefore, that there is something wrong with the strategy of attempting rigorously to define requirements of the users in a written functional specification and some alternative approach should be considered.

However, this is rather akin to 'throwing out the baby with the bath water'. If the methodology does not work, ie does not produce the required product, this is no justification for discarding the methodology but it is a reason for questioning the framework of system development controls to see if the methodology is being applied correctly. The evidence frequently suggests that the methodology does not work because it is not being applied correctly and that the framework of system development controls is inadequate. This is not to say, as is frequently concluded, that we must be even more rigid in the application of the SDC methodology and attempt to define the users' requirements with even more precision. The requirements definition is only one control within the methodology and there are other, equally relevant controls, to which we need to pay attention, as we have suggested in chapter 4.

2.   PROTOTYPING IN REQUIREMENTS DEFINITION

The process of requirements definition involves specifying the factors that we noted in chapter 5, **7.-8.**, such as:

    (1) constraints;
    (2) system outputs;
    (3) system inputs;
    (4) data requirements;
    (5) data elements;
    (6) business functions;
    (7) controls framework;
    (8) performance/reliability;
    (9) conversation structure;
    (10) hardware/software.

In using prototyping as a development strategy, the process of defining the system requirements is carried out interactively with the user as shown in **Figure 38.**

Figure 38   Interactive requirements definition

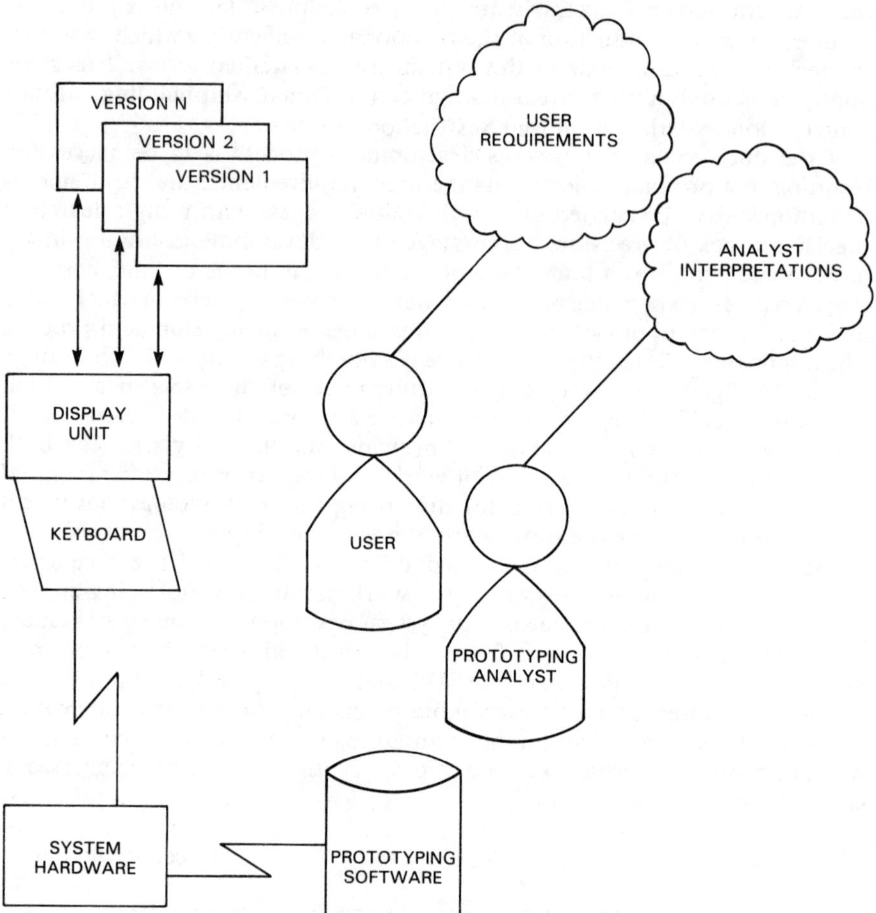

The basic assumptions underlining the use of prototyping as a strategy in the definition of requirements are:

(1) requirements cannot be precisely specified in writing;
(2) there are 'intelligent' software tools available for on-line development;
(3) there is a communications gap between project participants;
(4) requirements definition is more effectively performed interactively;
(5) the development process can be formalised when requirements are known.

The first of these assumptions is based on the premise that it is difficult for most people to define, with any degree of precision, business processes in an abstract way. If the reader has ever been involved in drawing a documentation or system flowchart they will be aware of how confused most participants in the business processes are of what actually happens, in practice, when there are many persons involved. Thus, the conclusion of the prototypers is that the requirements definition can be carried out more precisely if the users can be shown sample models of what will eventually be delivered to them, rather than an abstract written/graphical concept.

The second of the assumptions, on which the use of prototyping as a development strategy is based, is that there are appropriate software tools available for the conduct of the process. These tools—as for example EXCELERATOR which is available from Index Technology Corporation— and which can be run on an IBM PC consist of a basic set of software components such as the following:

(1) integrated data dictionary;
(2) flexible DBMS;
(3) non-procedural report writer;
(4) non-procedural query language;
(5) screen generator;
(6) high level development language (HLDL).

The core of the software module is the integrated Data Dictionary around which the other software modules revolve in the manner shown in **Figure 39**.

The third assumption, in the selection of prototyping as a development strategy, is that there is a communications gap between the systems development participants because the use of a communications language like English is less precise than the use of a software specification language. There are a variety of tools and techniques available, some of which have been discussed in chapters 4 and 7, to help in the systems development process. However, these, the prototypers claim, mean nothing to the normal end-user and are more likely to stimulate alarm than provide comfort when they are produced. The availability of working examples rather than flowcharts, logical access maps and data action diagrams, etc is more likely to gain the users' confidence. There is certainly, from the author's experience, a substantial amount of truth in this claim.

The fourth assumption is that the definition process is more effective if performed interactively with the users. The essential point is that requirements definition is an interactive process so that many steps may be necessary before the final needs of the users have been expressed with accuracy. This is more effectively achieved if the different possibilities that may satisfy the users requirements can be quickly and interactively developed as an on-line operation. The process of interactive development enables a better fit to be found for the users' requirements at an early stage in the development.

The final assumption is that, once the requirements are known, the development can be processed rapidly through the subsequent phases of the SDC because both users' and project group, including the computing audit function, now understand what the requirements from the systems development process should be. This we have illustrated in chapter 10, **2. (Figure 52c)**, which shows a customised SDC for a project where prototyping is the preferred development strategy.

Figure 39   Idealised prototype software

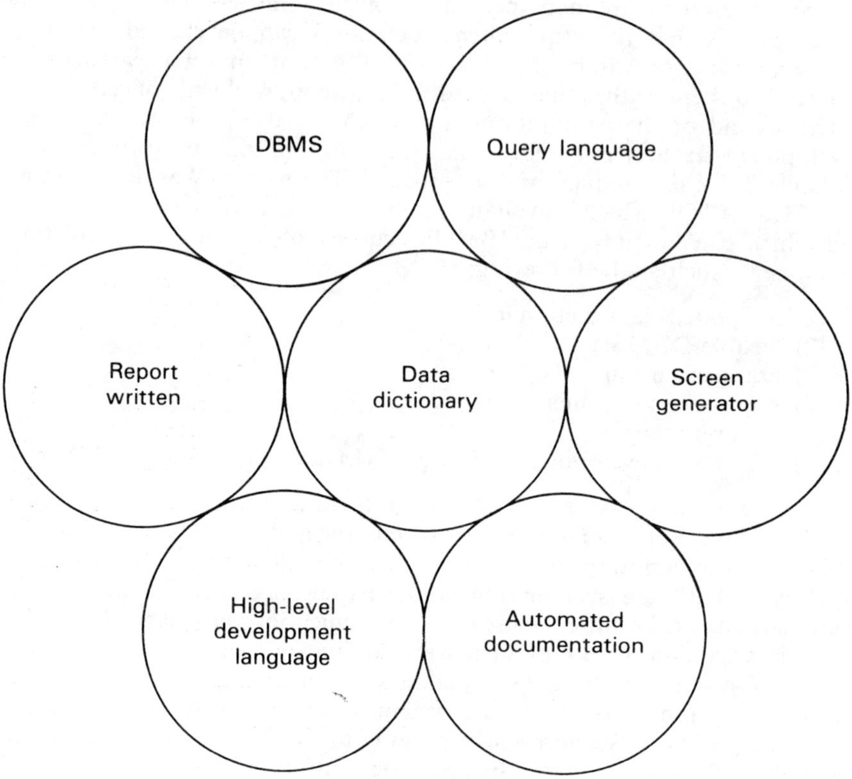

DBMS

Query language

Report
written

Data
dictionary

Screen
generator

High-level
development
language

Automated
documentation

3.   THE SDC WITH PROTOTYPING

The use of prototyping will normally follow the Feasibility Study phase of the SDC, as shown in **Figure 40**, since an important outcome of this phase will be the determination of the project development strategy. There are five main steps involved in the use of prototyping as a development strategy within the SDC:

(1) selection of suitable projects;
(2) identification of data elements;
(3) building the model;
(4) tuning the model;
(5) documentation.

These steps are illustrated in **Figure 41.**

The first step, in the use of prototyping, is the selection of suitable candidate projects for which the strategy is appropriate and this will depend, inter alia, upon the following factors;

Figure 40   The SDC with prototyping

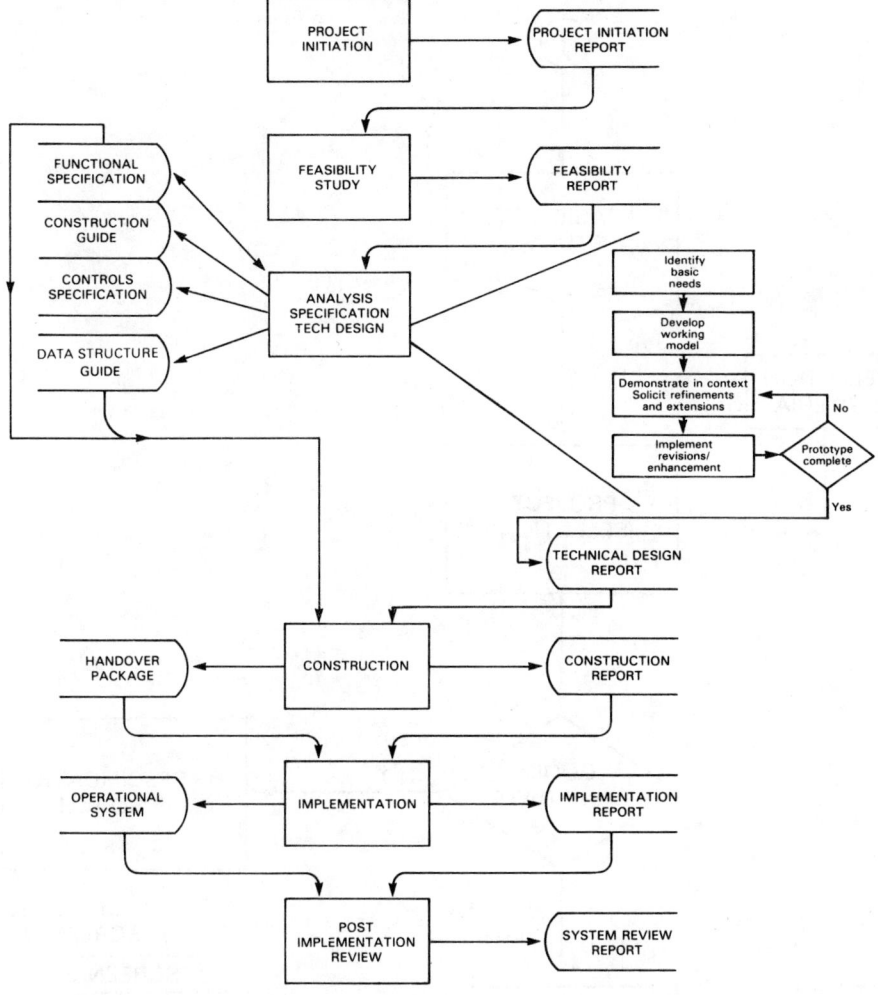

(1) system structure—suitable are on-line interactive, data base systems; batch processing systems are not;

(2) logic structure—suitable are applications with a well defined logic structure; applications that are heavily algorithmic, decision support systems or ad hoc retrieval systems are not suitable;

(3) user characteristics—applications for users who are computing literate and who can participate in, and understand, the prototyping process;

(4) time constraints—applications with crash target dates are unsuitable because they lead to incomplete definition;

(5) project management—the project manager is familiar with and experienced in the use of prototyping.

Figure 41   Stages in the requirements definition process with prototyping

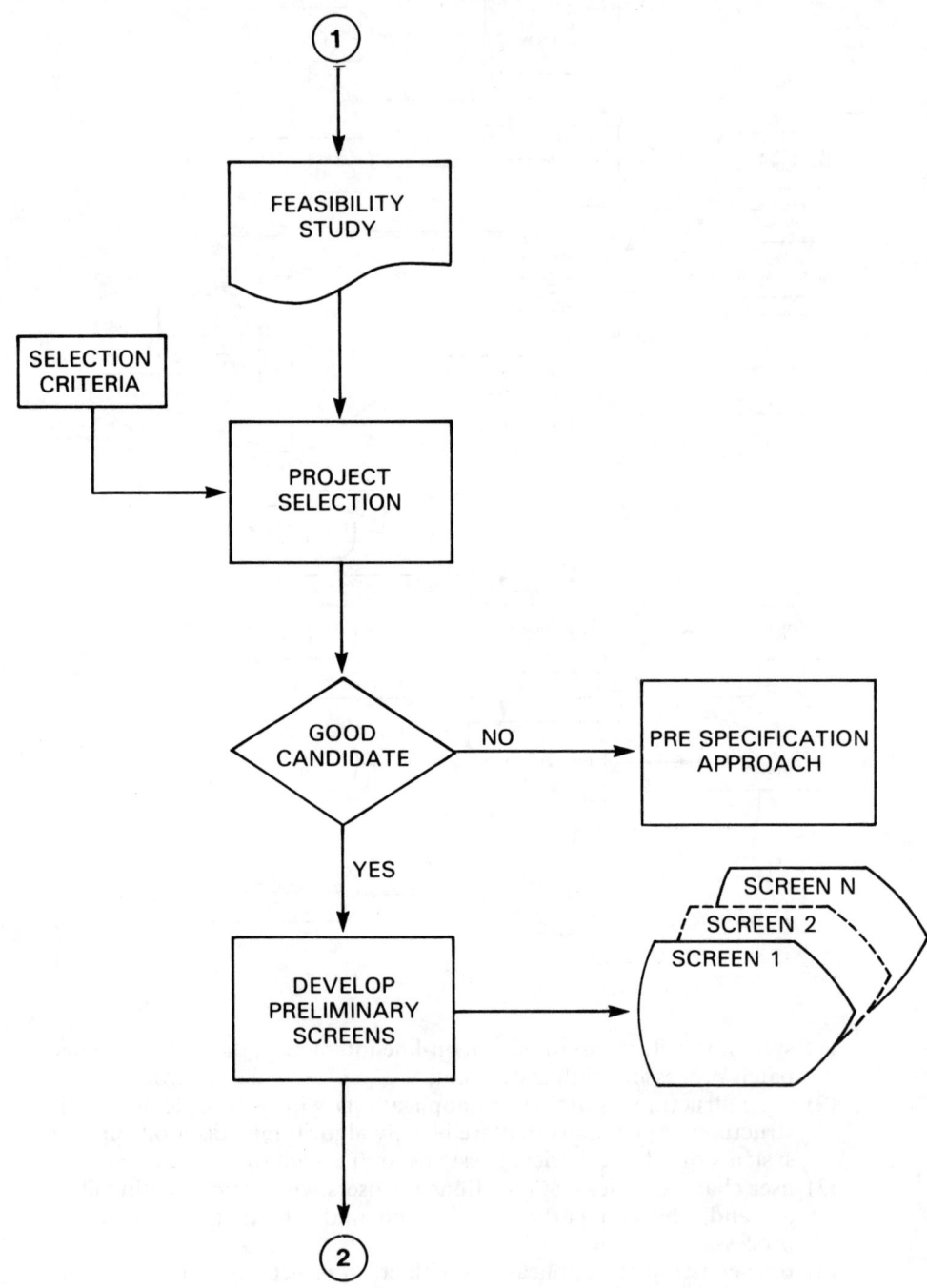

Figure 41 Stages in the requirements definition process with prototyping—*continued*

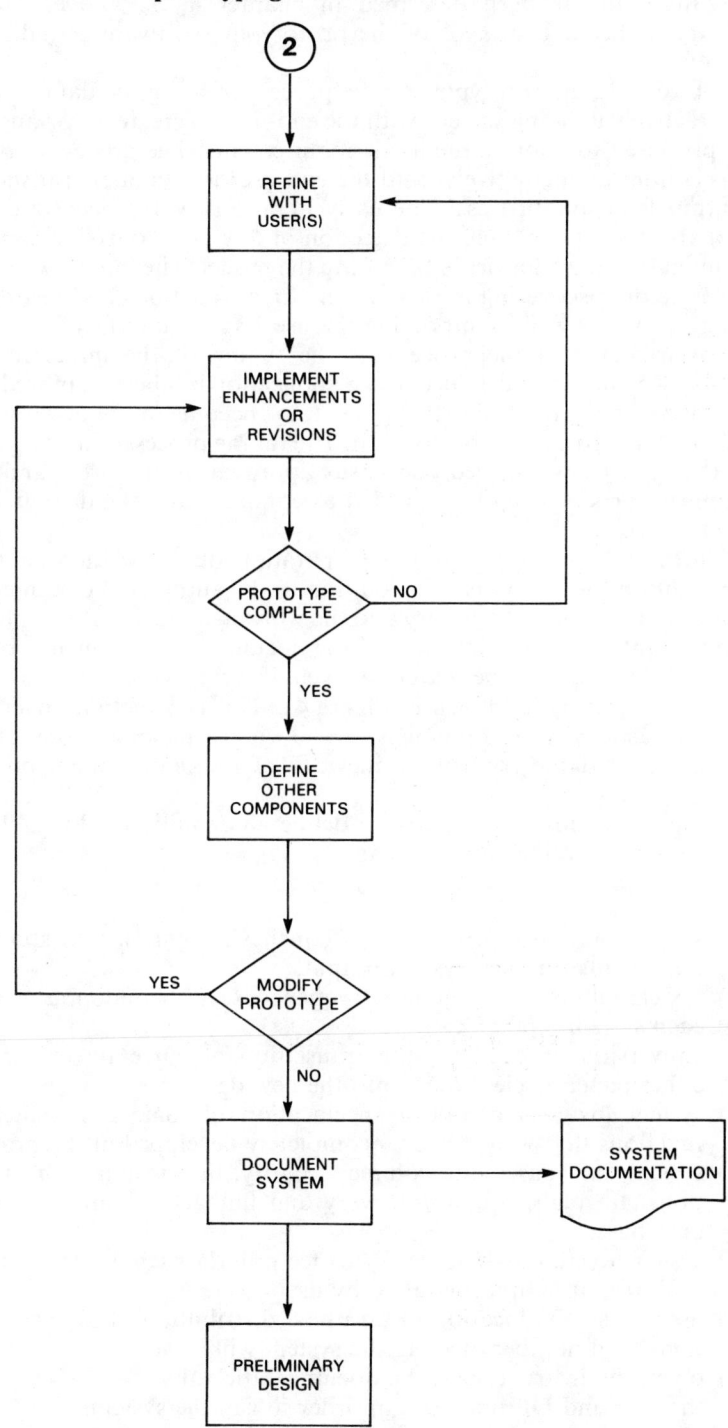

The second step, in the prototyping process, is the identification of all data elements and their cataloguing in an on-line, interactive data dictionary. This process has already been described in chapter 4, **3.**, above. The data dictionary is the central pivot of the prototyping software as indicated in **Figure 40.**

The third step, in prototyping, is the process of using the data dictionary for interactively building screens with the end-user to create a working model of the proposed solution to the users' requirements. The process of building screens continues interactively until the end user is ultimately satisfied with the output from the process. The early iterations will concentrate on the general appeal of the model, the detection of any gross oversights and with user familiarity and comfort in operating the model. The later iterations will concentrate on discovering missing or incorrect functions and testing ideas and suggestions as well as improving the user/system interface.

The fourth step in the process, is the tuning of the initial model to determine whether the substance of the application has been captured and to match users' revised expectations, as they become more aware of the practical possibilities available to them. The tuning process will be completed when the model has received consensus approval by the users and so the development process may be regarded as complete and the documentation can commence.

The fifth and final stage, is the preparation of the written supporting documentation for the system, in addition to the automated documentation represented by the data dictionary and the working model of the application. It is important to realise that most of the documentation, which is required for the SDC, will still be required even if prototyping is used as the development strategy as shown in **Figure 41**. This is sometimes overlooked and is one reason why prototyping is viewed with suspicion by some auditors who consider that the controls framework of the development process is somehow weakened.

The documentation is necessary to define all definition deliverables that require rigorous specification, such as:

(1) system outputs—the volume, frequency, retention and security requirements for each system output;
(2) system inputs—the volumes, frequency, security and input media for each system input;
(3) conversion procedures—the translation of currently existing files, either paper or electronic, into the new data base structure;
(4) system logic—a complete specification of logic requirements for functions that were not or incompletely developed in the prototype;
(5) system data base—the volume, security, integration with organisation data plan, backup/recovery and fallback specification for the data base;
(6) system reliability—the performance criteria such as downtime and peak response times required by users;
(7) user sites—the location of all users, distribution of allowable functions, and number of users the system will serve;
(8) operating instructions—the documentation that is required by both the user and DP functions in order to run the system;

(9) re-organisation, recruitment and training needs—the manpower resources, their disposition and skill requirements to run the system;
(10) hardware/communications links—the nature and capacity of the
equipment for handling the traffic flow.

4. PROTOTYPING PRINCIPLES

There are five essential principles that have been quoted for the effective
application of prototyping in systems development, namely:

(1) most applications are derivable from a small set of structures;
   (a) batch create/retrieve/update/delete;
   (b) batch reporting;
   (c) batch interface;
   (d) on-line create/retrieve/update/delete;
   (e) on-line reporting;
   (f) on-line interface.

(2) most systems use a repetitive and well known set of model functions,
such as, CREATE, RETRIEVE, UPDATE, DELETE;
(3) most input editing is derivable from a small set of edit models, such as:
   (a) field editing, eg data element numeric;
   (b) cross field editing, eg both date and transaction number present;
   (c) cross record editing, eg the same transaction number cannot exist
   twice;

(4) application reporting is based on four basic steps:
   (a) select and remove from data base;
   (b) sort by specification;
   (c) format and edit for printing;
   (d) print output;

(5) there are basic design structures that complement the prototype, such
as:
   (a) use of control totals;
   (b) help facility;
   (c) menu driven command structure.

5. PROTOTYPING AND PROJECT MANAGEMENT

The use of prototyping does not alter the validity and appropriateness of
applying sound project management principles and practices to the development of a system. Neither, as is sometimes suggested, does it alter the
principle that for successful development there must be a sound framework
of project development controls. The argument is that, because the process is
iterative and by its very nature, flexible, the framework of controls must be
loose and flexible too. This is a fallacy, which can be dangerous, because
processes which are flexible may require more rigid controls as we shall see in
8., below.

The principles of sound project management have been discussed previously in chapter 7. The use of prototyping as a development strategy will impact upon the project management process in four ways, namely:

(1) estimation procedures,
(2) cost recovery,
(3) change control,
(4) signing-off.

The use of prototyping is intended to shorten the SDC by amalgamating the analysis, specification and technical design phases. The expectation is that a two person team should be able to produce a deliverable product in between 2-6 weeks from the commencement of the requirements definition process. By compressing the time period for the development it should, in principle, prove possible to produce more realistic time and cost estimates following the procedures described in chapter 7, **6.** and **7.** Further, the more accurate identification of costs enables the charging out process to be carried out with a greater degree of precision.

The ease and flexibility of the prototyping process, in making changes, requires that there should be a careful control to ensure consensus of opinion is reached on the model and, finally, that once consensus has been agreed there must be a firm control on further changes. The signing off process, then, is the critical stage at which the model design should be 'frozen' and the users should be required to signify their acceptance of the prototype.

6.   THE PROTOTYPING CENTRE

The use of prototyping ideally requires the creation of a specialist unit in the DP organisation called the prototyping centre. The function of this centre is to combine, in the most effective and efficient way, the resources that are required for the prototyping process. These resources may be summarised under four headings:

(1) personnel,
(2) hardware,
(3) software,
(4) environment.

The personnel requirements are optimally limited to between 2-3 people. This is because of the communications gap that exists within large teams, the requirement for unity of vision and the demands for productivity. The ideal incumbent for the position of prototyper analyst is someone who has an all-round balance of understanding and skill in the DP development process rather than someone steeped in traditional expertise. The important factor is that once the initial model has been constructed the refinements can be carried out, later, by a specialist expert.

The hardware requirements of the prototyping centre are relatively simple and consist of a terminal and some form of hard copy output device which may be a terminal with a thermal printer or a separate list device. The ideal device is one which can be used as a stand-alone microcomputer, as well as a normal dumb terminal, by the use of the appropriate terminal emulation software. This enables the prototyper analyst to operate in both local mode with an appropriate microcomputer software package as well as to share more powerful facilities by operating in remote mode on a mini- or mainframe computer.

The software reqirements may be summarised under six headings, as follows:

(1) data dictionary driven;
(2) structurally encourages component engineering;
(3) enables 'cutting and pasting' of new components from existing components;
(4) provides an interactive prototyper workbench;
(5) permits declarative specification rather than procedural specification;
(6) automatically generates application documentation.

The most important requirement from the software is that there should be an integrated on-line data dictionary which drives the other components of the software as shown in **Figure 40**. The integrated and active data dictionary provides a records management system, for the prototyper, for data elements, records, screens, etc. The records are updated from two sources, namely:

(1) defining new entities directly to the dictionary;
(2) the integrated components update the dictionary during model building.

The prototyping process requires the creation of a work environment that is directly conducive to exceptional productivity. This work environment is composed of six main factors:

(1) work room;
(2) response time;
(3) library resources;
(4) demonstration/presentation facilities;
(5) centralised/distributed prototying centre;
(6) components classification.

7. INTRODUCING PROTOTYPING

Although we have referred to prototyping as a particular development strategy within the broader framework of the SDC it is, nevertheless, a strategy which is still unfamiliar or relatively new in many DP organisations. Thus, in order to convince both DP and user management that prototyping can be a valuable alternative to pre-specification, in the requirements definition process, there will have to be a period of learning and some history of successful application. This is more easily said than done because there will always be some scepticism about the introduction of new techniques until they have made their mark in the systems development process.

The essential question is 'How can we gain the necessary in-house expertise so that we have a cadre of experienced professional prototyper analysts?'. The answer, as always with personnel questions, is in a variety of ways, such as:

(1) recruitment of experienced prototypers from outside sources;
(2) training courses offered by vendors of prototyping software;
(3) training courses offered by consultants;
(4) in-house training carried out by experienced prototypers from vendors, consultants or agencies;
(5) direct hands-on experience.

There is no one unique solution to building up the in-house expertise and, in practice, a DP organisation is likely to use a blend of all these means in a combination that suits its own requirements.

Simultaneously with building up the required in-house expertise, the DP organisation must be prepared to allocate resources in the form of accommodation for the pioneer prototypers to work. This will require, as we discussed in **5.**, above, the provision of hardware/software, documentation library, demonstration facilities, etc. In the first instance, the hardware may be limited to the use of a microcomputer with a suitable software package such as EXCELERATOR. Later, as the DP organisation builds up the expertise, and provided the resources are available, more ambitious projects may be undertaken on mini- or mainframe computers that will greatly enhance the prototypers capabilities.

The selection of a suitable software package will then present itself and there are a number of candidates such as OADS (Cullinane), ADF (IBM), FOCUS (Info. Builders), MAPPER (UNIVAC), SL/1 (Thorne), etc. There are also packages such as the DEC 'All-in-1' software for office automation for which a very powerful application generator is also available from the supplier. The company will then do well to consider the types of controls which we have given in chapter 4, **4.**, as well as the specific prototyping controls given in **8. Table 20**, below.

8.   PROTOTYPING CONTROLS

We have already suggested in **1.**, above, that the successful application of the SDC depends upon the existence of an effective and efficient framework of development controls. Further, we shall explain in chapter 10 that the framework of controls depends upon the particular development strategy that we decide to select for our project. The use of prototyping creates a different development environment from that which exists when there is a rigorous pre-specification of requirements in written/graphical form and the controls framework needs to be appropriately adapted to this type of development environment.

A control has been defined in chapter 1, **10.**, above, as any means by which a business enterprise seeks to minimise or prevent an exposure by acting against the threats that cause that exposure. The success of prototyping as a development strategy in the project management process will, therefore, depend upon a framework of controls to combat effectively the potential threats that may work against the development. Thus, if the project manager has no experience of prototyping this will create a communications gap with the prototyper analysts and, perhaps, even with the end user.

A sample list of controls that the computing auditor should look for when prototyping is used as the development strategy is given in **Table 20**.

Table 20 Controls on the use of prototyping as a development strategy

Control reference	Key control area	Control details
1.	Project management	
1.1		The project manager has a thorough understanding of, and practical experience in the use of, prototyping as a development strategy.
1.2		The prototyping team is limited to 2–3 in persons in order to avoid communication gaps.
1.3		The prototypers are professionals who are fully experienced in the SDC.
1.4		The users are being actively involved in the prototyping process.
2.	Hardware	
2.1		The prototype hardware architecture uses the same type of terminals that are conventionally used by the users.
2.2		The prototyping hardware architecture includes the terminal types required to use the prototyping software most efficiently.
2.3		The prototyping hardware architecture includes high speed print terminals to enable quick access to batch output.
3.	Software	
3.1		The prototyping software architecture is dictionary driven.
3.2		The requirements are developed non-procedurally, ie a statement is made of the requirements and the software decides how to do it.
3.3		The prototyping software is complete and self-contained.
3.4		The software architecture is both menu and command driven.
3.5		The DBMS component of the software can model all common file structures.
3.6		The prototyping software is consistent across the components, ie dictionary, DBMS, report generator, etc.
3.7		There are adequate security features in the software.
3.8		The screen generator makes the creation and maintenance of screen maps a simple process.
3.9		There are user friendly end-user report generation tools.
3.10		The prototyping software has extensive de-bugging facilities.
3.11		There is a complete set of training and documentation facilities available to support the use of the software.
4.	Data modelling	
4.1		There is a clear understanding of who owns each data item and is responsible for its maintenance.

Table 20—*continued*

Control reference	Key control area	Control details
4.2		The data records have been developed using third-normal-form analysis.
5.	Component modelling	
5.1		The components of the system are being derived by using pieces from previous prototypes and new pieces are being created which are potentially re-usable.
5.2		The components of the system are being assembled by 'cut and paste' techniques.
5.3		The components of the system are being built up by drawing on previous examples, ie demonstration models from previous work.
6.	Automated documentation	
6.1		There is an alphabetical listing by entity type of every application entity and its description.
6.2		There is an alphabetical listing of every data element used by the prototype.
7.	Work environment	
7.1		There are appropriate visual aids available to aid memory recall.
7.2		The hardware/software provides rapid response time, eg within three seconds when used interactively.
7.3		The prototyping centre has access to both technical and business libraries.
7.4		There are adequate demonstration/presentation facilities available to present working models to the users.

References

1   Boare BH *Application Prototyping* (1983) John Wiley & Sons.
2   Martin J *Application Development Without Programmers* (1986) Prentice-Hall Inc.

PART 3

Systems development auditing

9 Audit methodology, tools and techniques

This chapter discusses the planning of audits and a methodology for the conduct of individual audits within the framework of the overall plan. There is also a discussion of some valuable audit tools and techniques that can be applied to the audit of computing systems. The objective of this chapter, is to draw out the similarities and differences between systems development auditing and other areas of audit.

A standard 'Objectives and Scope' for the audit of a system under development is given and this is followed by a description of how the audit programme is evolved from this foundation. The audit programme is the central pivot around which the discharge of the scope of work will revolve.

There is a listing of the type of working papers that the auditor will accumulate during the course of his audit involvement, and emphasis is made on how the working papers provide valuable background for making an assessment of the controls framework.

Finally, the reporting of audit findings and conclusions is discussed. The audit report is, usually the final stage of the auditors involvement in a project and is, eventually, the only visible product which remains when the audit is complete. A format for the presentation of the audit investigations is shown, which may be used for a post-implementation review (PIR), and mention is made of how this differs from the reporting on systems under development.

The audit reports produced during the audit of systems under development are of two kinds, namely:

(1) progress reports on the application system controls and the system development controls to line management;
(2) summary reports to the internal audit committee expressing an audit opinion on the adequacy of the controls.

1. AUDIT PLANNING

The audit of company activities is demanding on manpower resources of both internal audit and the auditee organisation. Thus, there must be a careful planning process which takes account of when and how frequently audits should be carried out. There are two levels to the planning process, an annual cycle of planning, and the planning of individual audits which are part of the annual plan. In both cases, the essential purpose of planning is an attempt to match resources against an agreed scope of work.

The first level of planning manifests itself in the preparation of an annual plan whose purpose is to:

(1) enable the internal audit committee to ensure that a continuous and effective level of internal audit activity is maintained;
(2) enable internal audit management to:

    (i) establish the scale and scope of the internal audit activity;
    (ii) match the proposed internal audit activities with the manpower available;
    (iii) monitor the progress of work against plan and report thereon to the internal audit committee.

A format which may be used to draw up an annual plan for an internal audit department is shown in **Figure 42**.
The computing audit plan may be broken down into main audit areas as follows:

(1) DP organisation;
(2) DP information and strategic planning;
(3) computer operations centre;
(4) computer application systems;
(5) systems under development.

There is the date shown when the last audit was carried out, an assessment of the current risk, the recommended frequency of the audit, the timing of the next audit and the manpower effort required.

In carrying out the audit of a computer operations centre, an audit of the DP organisation, an audit of information and strategic planning processes or of application computing systems, it is possible to agree with the auditee management how frequently, and when, the audit will be undertaken. This will depend on the assessment by both line and corporate management of the degree of risk involved. An acceptable time frame for the annual planning process is five years; with high risk activities being audited once a year and medium to low risk activities between three and five years.

For example, the audit of the computer operations centre may be carried out once every three years, which would be a reasonable time scale for this activity. However, if the audit indicated that there was some cause for concern in various areas of control, eg production scheduling, environmental control, media library control, etc then there could be a justification for repeating the audit again, after a year, to test whether the controls have been improved. Further, if the computer operations centre had been expanding rapidly because of increasing use by the company of electronic data processing, either on account of the company expanding rapidly, or replacing manual systems by automated systems, then there may also be justification for an annual audit. The essential point is that there are only general guidelines and the auditor must use his discretion as to how frequently he carries out an audit, bearing in mind that his activities should be cost effective.

Once the frequency of the audit has been agreed upon by both line and corporate management it is then necessary to agree with the line management the timing of the actual audit itself. This will depend, inter alia, upon:

Figure 42 The annual audit plan

Class-ification	Subject	Risk	Last carried out		Fre-quency in years	Remarks/ UNITS - MAN DAYS /Complementary audits
			Audit Ref	Completed		

(1) availability of audit manpower resources;
(2) estimated time for audit;
(3) convenience to line management;
(4) other audits;
(5) changes in priorities/frequencies;
(6) new activities in the company;
(7) changes in systems or organisation;
(8) special assignments.

The objective is to agree with the auditee management a starting date for the commencement of the fieldwork and an estimate of the likely duration. The auditor should also plan to give the auditee management an estimate of when the first draft of the audit report is likely to be available as well as the target date for the final report.

The audit of systems under development differs from the other four areas of audit in that the audit involvement is not a discrete process with defined start and completion dates. The audit involvement will be a continuous activity during the development of the system which may be spread over several years. The author has personally been involved in computing systems which have taken more than four years to develop. Thus, the nature of the audit involvement in systems under development, is evidently different from that of audit involvement, in other areas, and this distinction clearly marks out systems development auditing as a separate area of control.

In a small corporate environment, it may be possible to include all systems under development in the annual plan, although this would not necessarily be an effective use of audit resources. In this type of environment, the auditor would be more of a general purpose figure rather than a specialist computing auditor and the more time he devotes to systems development work the less effort he can spend on other activities.

In a large corporate environment, there is very likely to be a number of projects being carried out simultaneously, all of which could be of a substantial nature. To include all these projects in the auditor's programme could be highly demanding on the auditor bearing in mind that, if he is to play the prominant role in designing the system controls, he needs as much knowledge about the functionality of the system as the project manager. Thus, it would be a far better utilisation of the computing audit resource if the auditor used some method of risk assessment in deciding upon which systems to incorporate in his plan such as the risk and exposure methodology described in chapter 1.

When there is an agreed annual plan with regard to systems development auditing, the computing auditor must then plan his involvement in each individual project that has been incorporated in his plan. This he will do taking into account:

(1) stage of the project;
(2) other audit work;
(3) convenience to project management;
(4) convenience to line management;
(5) new activities.

This is no easy task because there may be conflicting demands as projects reach equivalent stages together and the auditor is expected to make an assessment of system documentation, which could be very substantial. Further, projects at different stages will require an independent audit assessment to be made, so that the auditor must be up to date on each project's progress. Another complication is that the manpower effort that the auditor has allocated in his agreed audit plan may have been exceeded so that a complete rescheduling of the plan is required.

2. AUDIT METHODOLOGY

Once a firm plan has been established, the auditor has the responsibility for the discharge of the audits which have been approved by the internal audit committee in the annual plan. The audit methodology is the series of steps by which each individual audit is carried out. A typical example of a generalised audit methodology consists of 17 steps, as follows:

STEP	TASK	STAGE
(1) define objectives and scope;		establish objectives and scope
(2) agree with auditees;		
(3) revise objectives and scope (if necessary); or		
(4) initial familiarisation;		prepare audit programme
(5) construct audit programme;		
(6) agree with auditee;		
(7) revise audit programme (if necessary) or;		
(8) redefine objectives and scope (if necessary); or		
(9) select audit tools/techniques;		
(10) detailed familiarisation;		test and evaluate controls
(11) identify and test the controls and potential exposures;		
(12) evaluate the results and form opinion;		
(13) re-assess controls (if necessary); or		
(14) prepare draft audit report;		prepare audit report
(15) review with auditee(s);		
(16) revise audit report (if necessary); or		
(17) report on controls.		

These steps in the generalised audit methodology are shown in flowchart form in **Figure 43** and the application of the methodology is discussed further in the remaining sections of this chapter. The important point to note about the methodology is that the four essential stages namely, the definition of the objectives and scope, preparation of the audit programme, testing and evaluation of the controls and preparation of the audit report are all iterative processes and the steps may be repeated a number of times during the course of the audit.

The auditing of systems under development follows, in broad terms, the same methodology, although there are some nuances because of differences in the time frame due to uncertainty, at the beginning, of how long the audit involvement will last. Further, the objectives and scope for the audit involvement are essentially the same for all systems development audits and have been set out in **3.**, below. Thus, the auditor may start from the basis that this part of the audit is a fixed parameter.

Figure 43 A generalised audit methodology

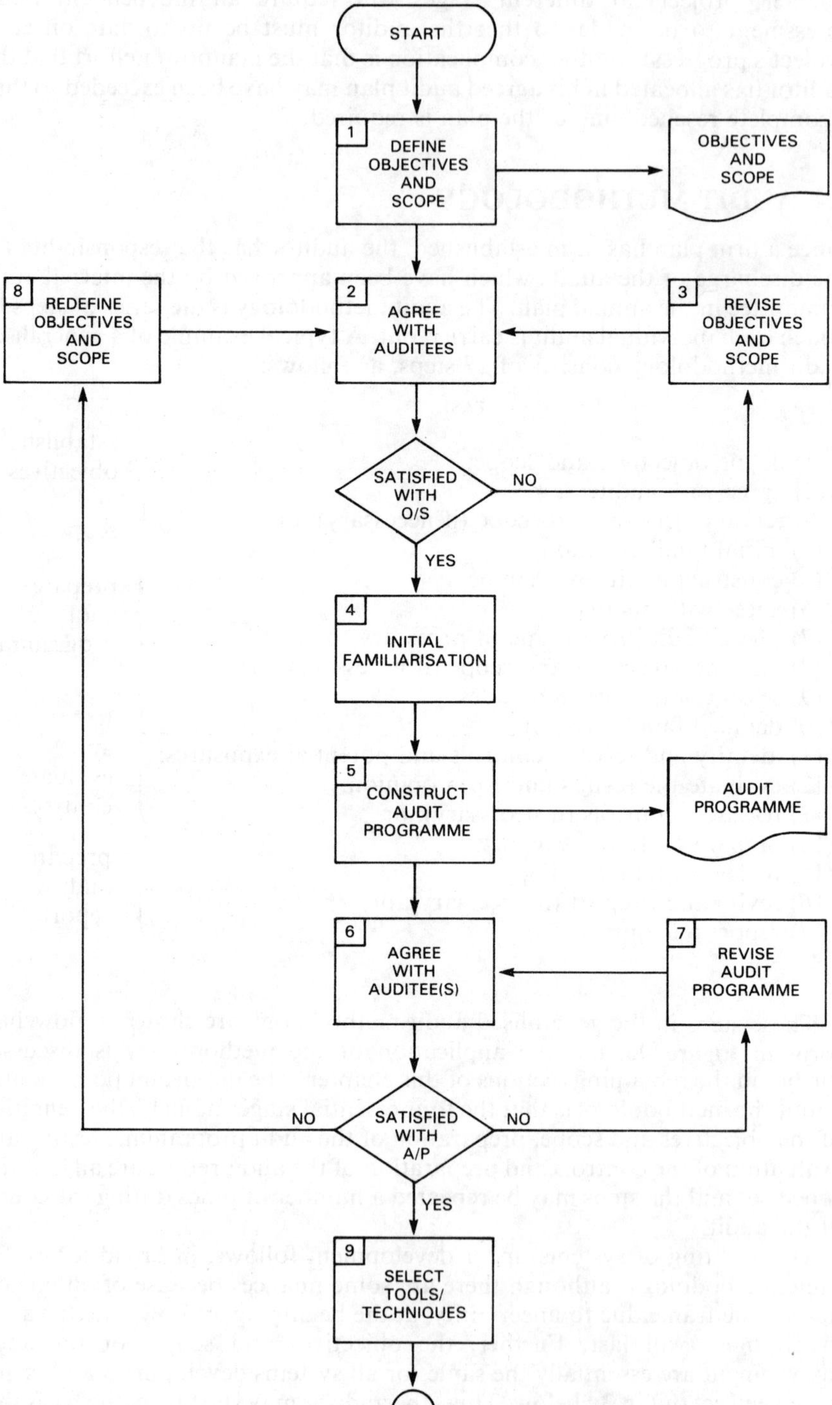

Figure 43 A generalised audit methodology—*continued*

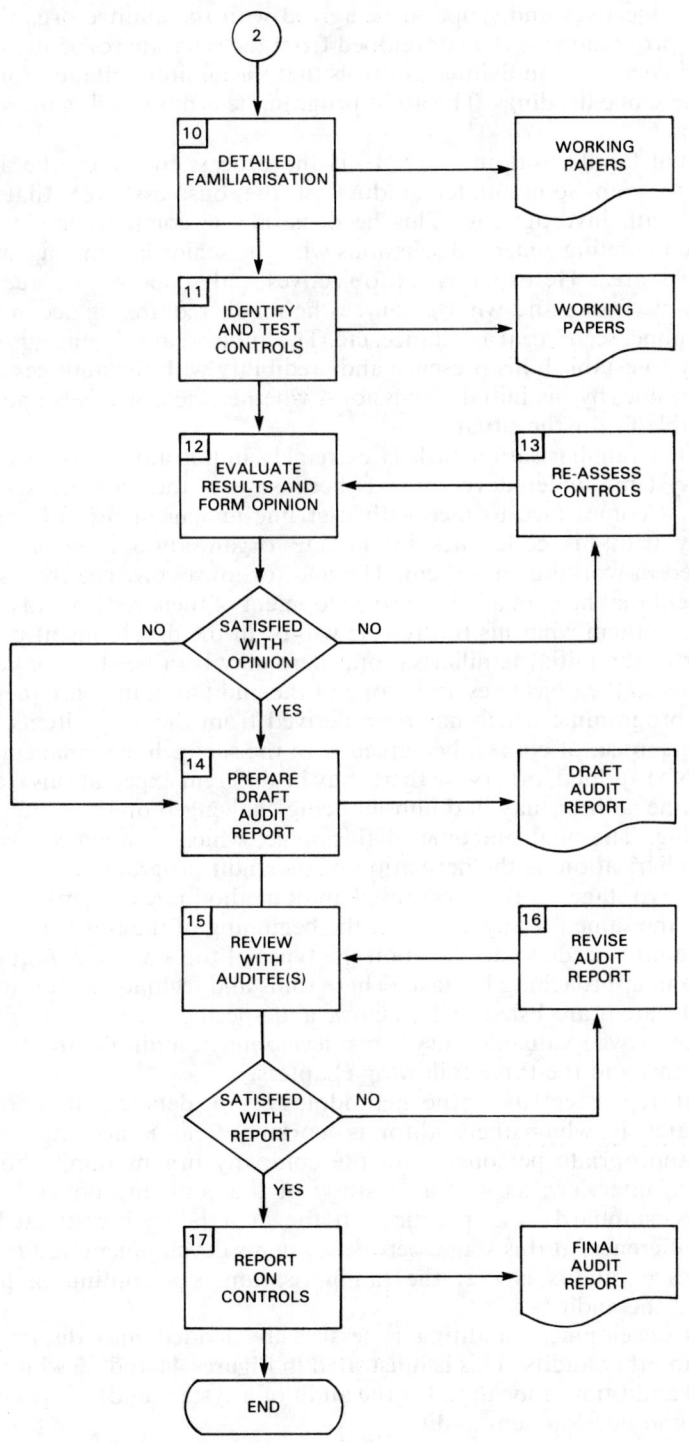

The first stage in the generalised audit methodology—steps 1-3—is to define the objectives and scope to be agreed with the auditee organisation. The audit programme is then developed from the separate scope items for it describes in detail the individual controls that the auditor will look for under each of the scope headings. The audit programme is discussed in more detail in **4.**, below.

The initial familiarisation—step 4—is the process by which the auditor attempts to gain some understanding of the business area that he is concerned with investigating. This he does, at the commencement of the audit, by conducting general discussions with the senior line management in the business area. He explains the objectives and scope of the audit, the expected time frame and what resources he might require, eg accommodation, telephone, secretarial assistance, etc. The auditor, at this stage, is simply attempting to establish his presence and credibility with the auditees as well as to determine, by his initial discussions, whether the objectives and scope are a suitable fit for the situation.

The initial familiarisation task is extremely important, especially in the audit of systems under development, because it is the moment when the auditor first comes face to face with user line management, although not necessarily with his colleagues in the DP organisation if he is already experienced in working with them. The auditor must convince the user line management that he is an ally in the development of their system and attempt to explain to them what his future role will be in the development process.

Further to the initial familiarisation, there may be a need to make some adjustments to the objectives and scope of the audit and, in consequence, to the audit programme which has been derived from the scope items. These adjustments must, of course, be agreed with the senior line management, in the area to be audited, otherwise there may be different expectations from the audit and the auditor may find himself being challenged on the ground he is investigating. The final outcome of this stage, which commences with the initial familiarisation, is the derivation of the audit programme.

The last two stages of the generalised audit methodology—steps 9-17—are essentially the same for any audit. At the beginning of the third stage—step 9—, the auditor needs to decide upon the types of tools and techniques that he will use in approaching his task. These tools and techniques, for auditing in the EDP area, are listed in **5.**, below, and specific tools and techniques which have proved valuable in systems development auditing are discussed further in this and the three following chapters.

The next step—step 10—of the methodology is the detailed familiarisation with the area in which the auditor is working. This is accomplished by selecting appropriate persons, from the company organigram, whom the auditor will interview, as well as a study of the company policies, plans, procedures, standards and practices in the area being investigated. The essential difference, at this stage, between systems development auditing and other types of audits is that the familiarisation is a continuing process throughout the audit.

Systems development auditing is less easily divided into discrete time phases than other audits. This is illustrated in **Figures 44** and **45** which show the typical audit time allocation for the audit of a system under development and for a non-development audit.

In an audit with a fixed time frame, the auditor will spend a certain part of his allocated manpower effort on the detailed familiarisation of the business area although his knowledge and understanding will continue to grow throughout the audit. In the audit of a system under development, steps 6-10 of the methodology will be repeated, perhaps many times, during the systems development cycle (SDC). This is because the system concept and documentation evolve over time with the requirement that the auditor must continually update his knowledge and understanding with project progress.

Figure 44 Typical audit time allocation for a non-system development audit

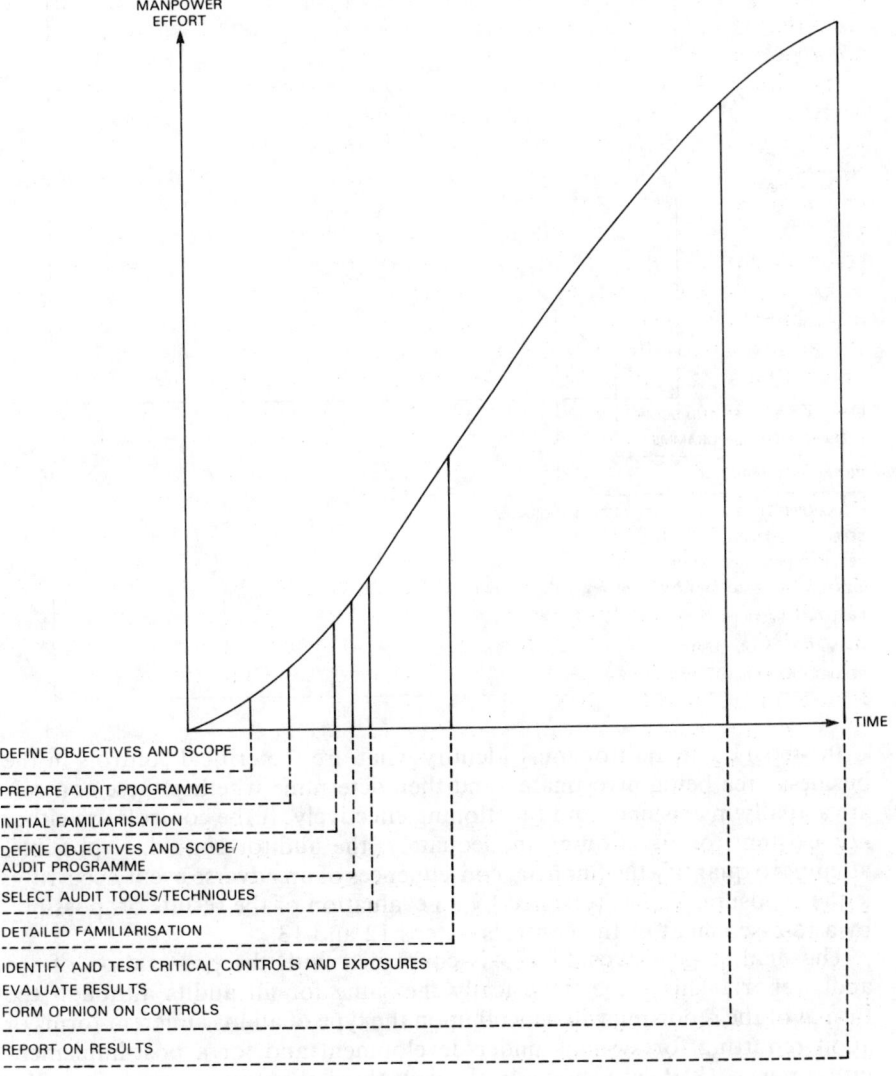

MANPOWER
EFFORT

TIME

DEFINE OBJECTIVES AND SCOPE
PREPARE AUDIT PROGRAMME
INITIAL FAMILIARISATION
DEFINE OBJECTIVES AND SCOPE/
AUDIT PROGRAMME
SELECT AUDIT TOOLS/TECHNIQUES
DETAILED FAMILIARISATION
IDENTIFY AND TEST CRITICAL CONTROLS AND EXPOSURES
EVALUATE RESULTS
FORM OPINION ON CONTROLS
REPORT ON RESULTS

Figure 45   Typical audit time allocation for a system under development

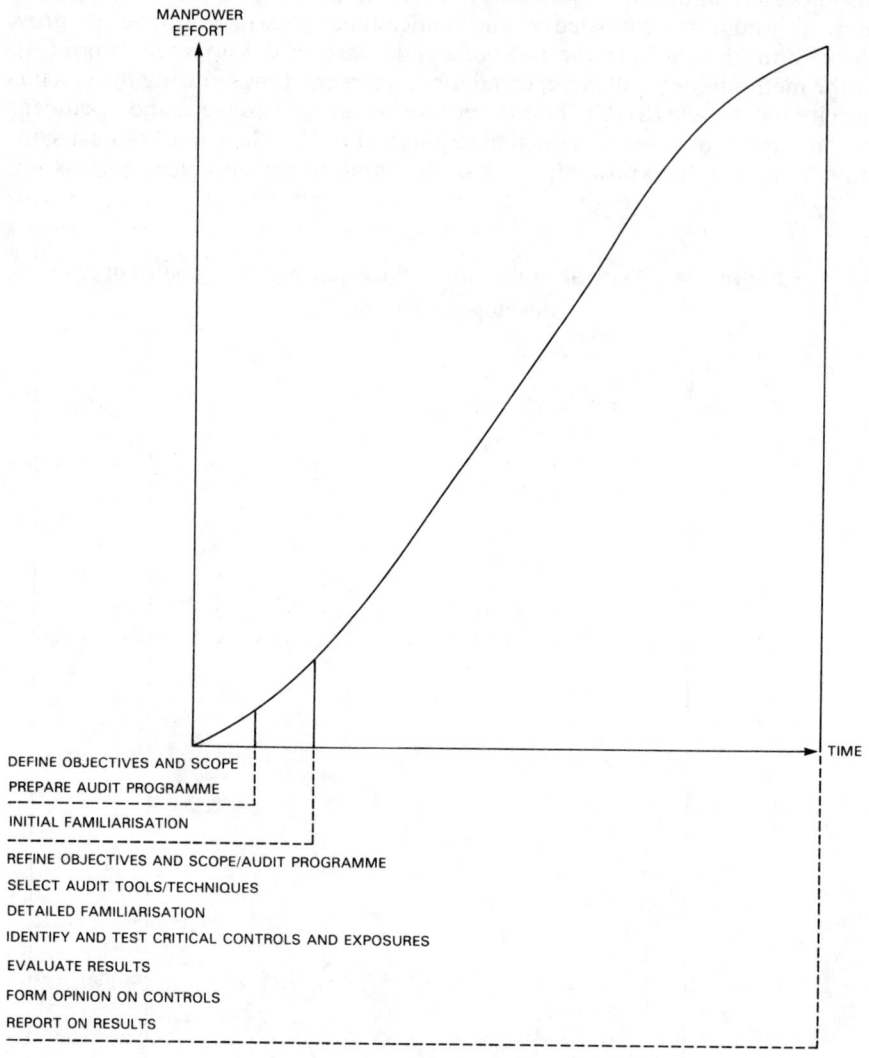

In step 11, the auditor must identify what are the critical controls in the business area being investigated and then determine whether these controls are actually in existence and functioning effectively. If the controls are either non-existent, or functioning inadequately, the auditor should, if possible, attempt to quantify the financial consequences of an adverse event occurring, ie the exposure. This is followed by an evaluation of the results or, possibly, by a re-assessment of the controls—steps 12 and 13.

The final stage—steps 14-17—is concerned with the preparation of the audit report. This stage is basically the same for all audits although the format of the reporting will depend upon the type of audit. Different forms of audit reporting for systems under development and for a post-implementation review (PIR) are shown in the next three chapters.

The application of steps 9-17 in the area of systems development auditing is discussed further in chapters 10 to 12. Chapter 10 discusses the identification, testing and reporting of the development controls framework for a personnel information and computing system. Chapter 11 discusses the identification, testing and reporting of the application controls framework of a logistics system which is neither too simple nor too complicated to hide the essential controls requirements. Finally, chapter 12 discusses the identification, testing and reporting on the controls framework for a materials management system which had recently been implemented. By using diverse examples in the way, the intention is to show how there is a certain commonality in the application controls as well as control essentials which are unique to the particular application system.

3. OBJECTIVES AND SCOPE

An example of a typical audit objectives and scope for the development of a computing system is given in **Table 21.**

Table 21   Standard objectives and scope for the audit of a system under development

Internal audit —/—/—

XYZ Information and computing system

AUDIT OBJECTIVES

To ensure:

(1) the system is developed in accordance with the company policies, procedures, standards and practices;
(2) the system will be managed in accordance with the company policies, procedures, standards and practices;
(3) there will be adequate arrangements for security and privacy for the data held by the system;
(4) that the processing results will be accurate and complete;
(5) that the system will be both effective and efficient.

AUDIT SCOPE

To co-operate with the USER and DP functions in establishing the following.

1   SYSTEM DEVELOPMENT CONTROLS

(1) system development controls—to ensure that the system is developed in accordance with the Company policies, procedures, standards and practices.

Table 21—*continued*

2 APPLICATION SYSTEM CONTROLS

(1) system management controls—to ensure the centralised system hardware and operating system software are being used effectively and efficiently.

(2) Application management controls—to support the operation of the system, in the user area, in accordance with the Company policies, procedures, standards and practices.

(3) Transaction origination controls—governing the origination, approval, and processing of source documents, the preparation of data processing input transactions, and associated error prevention, detection and correction procedures.

(4) Data entry controls—governing both terminal and batch data entry, data validation, transaction or batch proofing and balancing, error identification and reporting, and error correction and re-entry.

(5) Data communications controls (if applicable)—governing the accuracy and completeness of data communications, including message accountability, data protection, hardware and software, security and privacy, error identification and reporting.

(6) Computer processing controls—governing the accuracy, correctness and completeness of transaction processing, including transaction validation against masterfiles, error identification and reporting.

(7) Data storage and retrieval controls—to ensure masterfile data accuracy and completeness, correct transaction/ masterfile cut-off, data security and privacy, error handling, back-up and recovery and retention.

(8) Output processing controls—governing manual balancing and reconciliation of data processing output, control over source documents and output data retention.

It is important that, at the commencement of the audit, there should be a clear understanding, with the user organisation and the DP function, of the objectives and scope for the audit involvement in the project. The nature of the audit involvement should be discussed with, and agreed by, the project manager as well as the type of documentation, if any, that internal audit is expected to produce. If this is not done at the beginning of the project, there can emerge friction, at a later date, if the project manager sees internal audit as an intruder who is constantly looking over his shoulder for signs of trouble.

The author has heard from project managers that this is the way they perceive of internal audit. This is unfortunate because it is a complete misconception of the role that internal audit can, and should, play in the system development process, as well as being counter-productive. Internal audit should be perceived as a committed party to the system development process whose role has been described in chapter 2, **6.**, as:

(1) ensuring that there are adequate controls on the effectiveness and efficiency of the systems development process;

(2) giving reasonable assurance to management that critical systems are implemented with adequate built-in controls for security and privacy

of data, accuracy and completeness of processing and effectiveness and efficiency of operation.

It is, therefore, extremely important that the auditor should clarify the nature of his role with his colleagues at the commencement of the project.

4. AUDIT PROGRAMME

The audit programme is the central pivot around which the discharge of the scope of the work will revolve and care and attention spent at this stage, in drawing up the programme, will be well rewarded during subsequent stages of the audit. The programme should evolve naturally from the scope items that the auditor has initially listed in his objectives and scope, for the audit, and can be used as the basis for drawing up specific questionnaires for each auditee that the auditor needs to interview.

The audit programme shows the essential controls that the auditor will examine, and test for, during the course of the audit and a format for drawing up the audit programme is shown in **Figure 46**.

In auditing an area with an established controls framework, such as an application computing system, the DP organisation, etc, the audit programme will largely be drawn up during step 3 of the generalised audit methodology described in **3.**, above. Some modifications may be made to the programme, during the conduct of the audit, as the auditor's understanding of the subject area of the audit increases during the detailed familiarisation phase.

The audit programme, for a system under development, will be composed of two essential parts which correspond to the auditor's areas of interest, namely:

(1) the system development controls;
(2) the application computing system controls.

The first part of the audit programme will exist in broad outline, based on the system development controls which have been given, as examples, in **Table 9**, at the end of chapter 4, and **Table 20**, at the end of chapter 8. This framework of controls requires to be customised, as the project progresses, depending upon the project development strategy of the project manager and his selection of project tactics. The methodology of developing the system development controls in a customised audit programme forms the basis of chapter 10.

The second part of the programme will be unwritten at the start of the audit, ie the commencement of the project, although the auditor might have a concept sketched out in his mind, based on his experiences with other systems of a similar nature. The controls framework, which forms the basis of this part of the audit programme, will be developed during the analysis, specification and design phases of the systems development cycle and should be represented, eventually, by the 'controls specification' report. The methodology of developing the application system controls framework, and the

Figure 46   A format for an audit programme

Ref:		Page of
AUDIT PROGRAMME:		
SCOPE ITEM:		

REF.	CONTROL DETAIL

application of this framework in a customised audit programme, forms the basis of chapter 11.

Finally, chapter 12, on the post-implementation review (PIR) of a system, gives an example of an audit programme which may be generally applied for this type of audit. A PIR is, in principal, an application controls review undertaken within a relatively short time, eg six months, of the system becoming operational. The essential control objectives of the PIR are to determine whether the stated objectives and functional requirements of the system have been satisfied and to ensure that the system is effective and efficient in meeting the user requirements. The auditor should have assured himself that the other essential control objectives of security, privacy, accuracy and completeness were being achieved by the application controls framework that he has been instrumental in drawing up as described in chapter 11.

5.   AUDIT TOOLS AND TECHNIQUES

There has been a wide range of tools and techniques quoted as being used in different areas of audit. A list of those which have been used in computing audit is shown in **Table 22**.

It is not intended to discuss all these tools and techniques, in this work, except those that are particularly applicable in the area of application systems control design and assessment of systems development controls. If the reader should wish to learn more about the tools and techniques which are used in other areas of computing audit, he is referred to reference 4, at the end of chapter 3, which contains a detailed description of these.

The particular techniques which have been used in assisting in the design of application system controls or in selecting and evaluating system development controls are risk and exposure matrices and control flowcharts. The concept of risk and exposure matrices, for identifying and quantifying potential threats to company resources, has already been introduced in chapter 1. The concept is further expanded upon in chapters 10 and 11 for the selection and evaluation of system development controls and for the design of application system controls.

The other useful aid in designing application system controls, and also for auditing the controls in application computing systems, is the controls flowchart, a blank example of which is shown in **Figure 47**. In using the controls flowchart, each of the principal system processes is mapped onto a separate flowchart and the principal controls for each of these processes highlighted against each event in the process. The use of the controls flowchart, in the development of application system controls, is demonstrated in chapter 11 and, as a means of identifying essential controls in an operational application system, in chapter 12.

6.   DISCHARGE OF THE AUDIT

The discharge of the audit covers steps 4-17 of the generalised audit methodology discussed in **2.**, above. For an audit with a fixed time frame, the auditor will need to identify, in the initial familiarisation task, the auditees he will interview in discharging the audit as well as the type of documentation/ paperwork he should review. Thus, he may decide that it is necessary to review the invoices received for a particular period and covering a specific area of the company business. This he may do on a comprehensive basis or by using some form of statistical sampling technique to reduce the work burden.

Two valuable techniques that may be used to assist in the planning and conduct of interviews are the:

(1) interview matrix,
(2) interview questionnaire.

These are not specific techniques for use in computing auditing and have, therefore, not been listed in **Table 22**.

The interview matrix is built up from the audit programme, as shown in **Figure 48**. The reference numbers of the controls that the auditor has

Table 22   Computing Audit tools and techniques

(A)   AUDIT PLANNING AND MANAGEMENT

    (1)   Audit area selection.
    (2)   Simulation/modelling.
    (3)   Scoring.
    (4)   Multisite audit software.
    (5)   Competency centre.

(B)   PROGRAM CONTROLS

    (6)   Test data method.
    (7)   Base case system evaluation.
    (8)   Parallel operation.
    (9)   Integrated test facility.
    (10)   Parallel simulation.

(C)   SELECTION AND MONITORING OF DATA PROCESSING TRANSACTIONS

    (11)   Transaction selection.
    (12)   Embedded audit data collection.
    (13)   Extended records.

(D)   VERIFICATION

    (14)   Generalised audit software.
    (15)   Terminal audit software.
    (16)   Special purpose audit programmes.

(E)   ANALYSIS OF COMPUTER PROGRAMS

    (17)   Snapshot.
    (18)   Manual tracing and mapping.
    (19)   Computer-aided tracing and mapping.
    (20)   Program flowcharting.

(F)   COMPUTER SERVICE CENTRE

    (21)   Job accounting data analysis.
    (22)   Audit guide.
    (23)   Disaster testing.

(G)   APPLICATION SYSTEM DEVELOPMENT

    (24)   Post-implementation review (PIR).
    (25)   Standards and guidelines.
    (26)   Systems development cycle (SDC).
    (27)   Quality assurance.
    (28)   Code comparison.
    (29)   Risk and exposure matrices.
    (30)   Control flowcharts.

Figure 47   A controls flowchart

System:		Scope no.:
		Prepared date:
Function(s):		Reviewed date:

NARRATIVE	OPERATION	CONTROLS

Figure 48   The format for an interview matrix

AUDIT REF:		INTERVIEW MATRIX	PREPARED BY:	DATE:
AUDIT TITLE:			REVIEWED BY:	DATE:

INTERVIEWEE / AUDIT PROGRAMME REFERENCE															

identified as being relevant to the scope items, that define the coverage of the audit, are set out along the horizontal axis of the matrix. A list of essential interviewees, that the auditor has identified as being relevant to the audit, are set out along the vertical axis. The profile of controls, that fall within the work area of each of the interviewees, is then marked off by inserting a cross against the interviewee name and the relevant control.

This technique is particularly useful if there is a large number of items in the audit programme, as was the situation in the PIR interview matrix, discussed in chapter 12. All the relevant controls from the audit programme, which are applicable to each interviewee, are identified in one operation and can then be assembled together in an audit questionnaire a typical format for which is shown in **Figure 49**.

Figure 49   The format of an audit questionnaire

Ref:		Page of
AUDIT QUESTIONNAIRE:		
SCOPE ITEM:		
AUDITEE:		

REF.	QUESTION	ANSWER

This enables the auditor to cover all the ground he needs to in one, or possibly, two interviews without having to retrace his steps a number of times because he forgot to discuss a particular control. Further, by handing the interviewee a copy of the questionnaire, and explaining its purpose, the author has personally observed that there is immediately established a common ground between the auditor and interviewee which seems to give a considerable measure of comfort to the latter.

The audit questionnaire, for each interviewee, an example of which is shown in chapter 12, is most effectively prepared if the audit programme has been set up on a word-processor. The customised audit questionnaires can then be rapidly produced simply by a process of 'cutting and pasting'.

The audit of a system under development will differ from an audit with a fixed time frame in that the audit programme, as we have seen in **4.**, above, is largely unwritten at the start of the audit. However, once the programme has been developed, the auditor can use a similar approach to that described above, ie construct an interview matrix and draw up an audit questionnaire which can be used as a checklist to test for the controls.

The interviews on the application system controls framework, once this has been defined, will be largely—or entirely—with the project manager and user focal point(s), who have the responsibility for implementing the controls. The interviews on the system development controls framework will also be with the project manager but, in this case, the chairman of the steering committee may also be involved.

Apart from testing and reporting on the controls framework through interviews, the auditor of systems under development will also be involved in other activities which enable him to make a continuous assessment of the controls throughout the system development process. If he is a recognised member of the project group, as we suggested (in chapter 4) that he should be, then he will also attend regular meetings of that group, possibly on a weekly basis. As a recognised member of the project group, he may also be asked to attend, as an observer, meetings of the steering committee. At these meetings, he may be asked to express his own views on various aspects of the project. Indeed, he may feel that he has a right to express his view even if he is not asked.

Throughout the development of the system, the auditor will also receive documents of a variety of different natures. The types of documents which are produced during the development process are listed in the next section under working papers.

The development of large systems may generate a very substantial amount of documentation, the reading of which is considerably demanding on the auditor's time. This fact alone suggests that the auditor should not be simultaneously involved in more that 2-3 major systems in order that he can provide an appropriate level of service and not disappoint the auditees by failing to produce his input at the appropriate time.

7.   WORKING PAPERS

The auditor's working papers are extremely important in any audit, and are the foundation on which the audit report is based. The term 'working papers', in this context, is defined in the broadest sense as meaning all those documents which are generated during the systems development process. The working papers for the development audit will, therefore, include:

(1) steering committee/project group minutes;
(2) management reports;
(3) technical reports;
(4) the 'handover package';
(5) the project development plan;
(6) the project implementation plan;
(7) the audit programme;
(8) audit questionnaires;
(9) project progress reports;
(10) reports of special studies;
(11) quality assurance reviews;
(12) terms of reference for steering committee;
(13) terms of reference for project group;
(14) copies of system inputs/outputs;
(15) copies of system control reports;
(16) audit reports.

The working papers are part of the evidence on which the auditor's conclusions are made on the application system controls and the system development controls. The very considerable range of documentation that the auditor is required to review, during the course of the audit, evidently places a heavy burden on his time. This reinforces the conclusion that the auditor would be unwise to involve himself in more than 2-3 major projects at the same time.

The auditor's working papers should be retained even after system implementation, which may be regarded as the end of the system development audit. They are the natural starting point for a post-implementation review (PIR), as well as an application system operational audit, since all the documentation the auditor may need to review for these types of audit will already have been assembled. This will save the auditor much time and trouble since he is immediately aware of what documentation there is available to support the system. Further, there is probably no other single source existing in the company where all the documentation is available in one place.

The existence of a controls specification within the system documentation is also the natural starting point for an application system operational audit. The controls specification defines the controls which have been agreed with the users during the development of the system. In auditing an operational system, the auditor should be concentrating on whether those controls are working effectively and efficiently in meeting the set objectives, ie:

(1) maintaining security and privacy;
(2) ensuring accuracy and completeness;
(3) ensuring effective and efficient system operation.

8.   REPORTING

The audit report is the final stage of the auditor's involvement in the investigation and is, unquestionably, the most important stage because the audit report is the only visible product which remains when the audit is complete. The reporting stage, which covers Steps 14-17 of the generalised audit methodology, is also the most sensitive stage of any audit because the audit findings are now presented, in writing, perhaps for the first time.

The format of a standard audit report consists of three parts, namely:

(1) PART 1—management summary;
(2) PART 2—background, objectives and scope;
(3) PART 3—findings and recommendations.

This type of format was used in reporting on the PIR discussed in chapter 12. The internal audit committee are generally only circulated with Parts 1 and 2 which provide, in the management summary, an audit opinion on the adequacy of the controls framework. The line management in the area involved are circulated also with part 3 which contains the detailed audit findings and recommendations which it is their responsibility to ensure are implemented. Internal audit expect to be informed on the implementation of all recommendations.

Audit reports tend to be sensitive documents because they ultimately reach the hands of the company top management who sit on the audit committee. In order to keep the report as succinct as possible, there will be the minimum of detail necessary to support the conclusions of the auditor. The consequence is that the recommendations may be seen in a different context by the audit committee members who are not familiar with the detailed background. Auditees are usually very conscious of the wording and the clearing of audit reports can be a very protracted process. Thus, steps 15 and 16 of the generalised audit methodology are iterative and may be repeated a number of times before the final audit report is issued.

An effective way of expediting the agreement on the report, is to provide the auditees with immediate feedback following the conduct of all interviews. This enables the auditee to see how the auditor has interpreted his statements during the course of the interview. The feedback may be given either as a copy of the completed audit questionnaire or as a written description of the processes which have been described in the auditee area. The auditor should also attach a covering note asking the auditee if s/he is in agreement with what has been written. In this way, any errors of fact can, one hopes, be eliminated before the first draft of the audit report is produced. This has a significant advantage since nothing causes more friction, at the reporting stage, than mis-interpretation or misrepresentation of fact.

The audit reporting on systems under development follows broadly the same lines and steps 14-17 are represented in both the methodology for selecting and evaluating system development controls and for designing controls into computing systems. However, the actual format of the audit reports follows a different pattern from that of development audits due to the influence of the time scale.

There are two types of audit reports produced during the development of computing systems, namely:

(1) reports on the application and system development controls to line management;
(2) summary reports to the internal audit committee expressing an audit opinion on the strength of the controls.

The essential difference between reporting on audits with a fixed time frame, and development audits is that, in the latter case, the reporting process must be timely. The process of clearing audit reports with auditees could, we have suggested, be a protracted process which is self-defeating with development audit reports. This is because the project progress is dynamic in marching towards an automated solution to the users' business problems and, if reporting does not keep pace with the project progress, the reports lose their relevance. Thus, development audit reports must be short, relevant and timely produced. There are examples given in chapters 10-12 of both these types of audit reports.

10 Selecting and evaluating system development controls

This chapter discusses the audit role in the selection and evaluation of system development controls. The purpose of the audit involvement is to minimise the potential exposure created by committing resources to a project and the possible consequence either that the outcome will not be the product that was required or that there will be no outcome at all.

The controls framework for a system under development is described, in **2.**, below, as consisting of a number of intersecting sets rather than the concentric layers concept used to describe the application system controls framework. The influence of the project development strategy, upon the system development controls is demonstrated by the use of selected examples of the practical application of the SDC.

The remainder of this chapter is then devoted to the development of an audit methodology—illustrated in flowchart form in **3.**—which may be applied in the selection and evaluation of the systems development controls. The key features of the methodology are the use of the project specific SDC and risk and exposure matrices for the selection and evaluation of the development controls framework.

The final section discusses the way the internal auditor may report his findings and conclusions on the development controls framework to the :

(1) local line management,
(2) internal audit committee.

1. PURPOSE AND BACKGROUND

We have already mentioned in chapter 2, **6.**, above, that the auditor has two roles in the system development process. The first of the roles, of the internal auditor, is to ensure that there are adequate controls on the effectiveness and efficiency of the systems development process. The what and how of the systems development process has already been covered in chapters 5 to 8 and the controls have been covered in chapter 4 under the following key control areas;

(1) systems development cycle;
(2) project management;
(3) data administration;
(4) data base management software (DBMS) selection;
(5) data base administration;

(6) system design and construction;
(7) system implementation and acceptance;
(8) system documentation.

Further, we have discussed in chapter 2, **2.**, the fact that the responsibility for control resides with the line management who have charge of the company resources. A project involves the commitment of company resources and therefore the line management who handle those resources have the responsibility to ensure the exposures to those resources are minimised. This is most effectively achieved by ensuring that the project has a proper framework of control, at the start, instead of retro-fitting controls when the project is some way 'down the road'.

The purpose of the audit involvement, in the system development process, is to minimise the potential exposure created by committing resources to a project and the possible consequence that the outcome will not be the product that was required or that there may be no outcome at all—there are many examples of the situation that is shown in **Figure 50**. We seek to minimise the potential exposure by ensuring that the project starts its life with a properly agreed framework of system development controls. This agreement should be reached between the system sponsor, the project manager and internal audit, and the controls framework should be regularly reviewed as the project progresses through its various stages.

We have already discussed under prototyping, in chapter 8, the fact that there may be a variety of ways by which the development process may fail to meet its objectives. This, however, is no reason to discard the methodology but it is a reason to question the controls framework and why it failed to ensure that the development process was successful. The objective of this chapter is to discuss the controls that the auditor should look for in the system development process. The presence or absence of the controls would be a certain indicator of the likely successful outcome of the project. Further, this chapter also proposes to discuss the methodology of auditing the controls in the system development process.

2.   A SYSTEM DEVELOPMENT CONTROLS FRAMEWORK

The controls framework for a system under development should be regarded as consisting of a number of intersecting sets rather like that shown in **Figure 51** instead of the concentric layers concept that we have used to describe the application system controls. These sets have already been divided into the key control areas discussed in the previous section. The controls which comprise each set will be strongly influenced by the what and how of the system development process and, especially, by the strategy selection of the project manager.

The strategy of the project manager will determine the path that the project will take. Some examples of the application of the SDC and how the development strategy affects the outcome of the development process are shown in **Figures 52a** to **52d**. The first example shows a project where there is still a fair amount of uncertainty at the end of the feasibility study about the scope and direction of the project. A formal checkpoint has been chosen, at

Figure 50 System development without an adequate controls framework

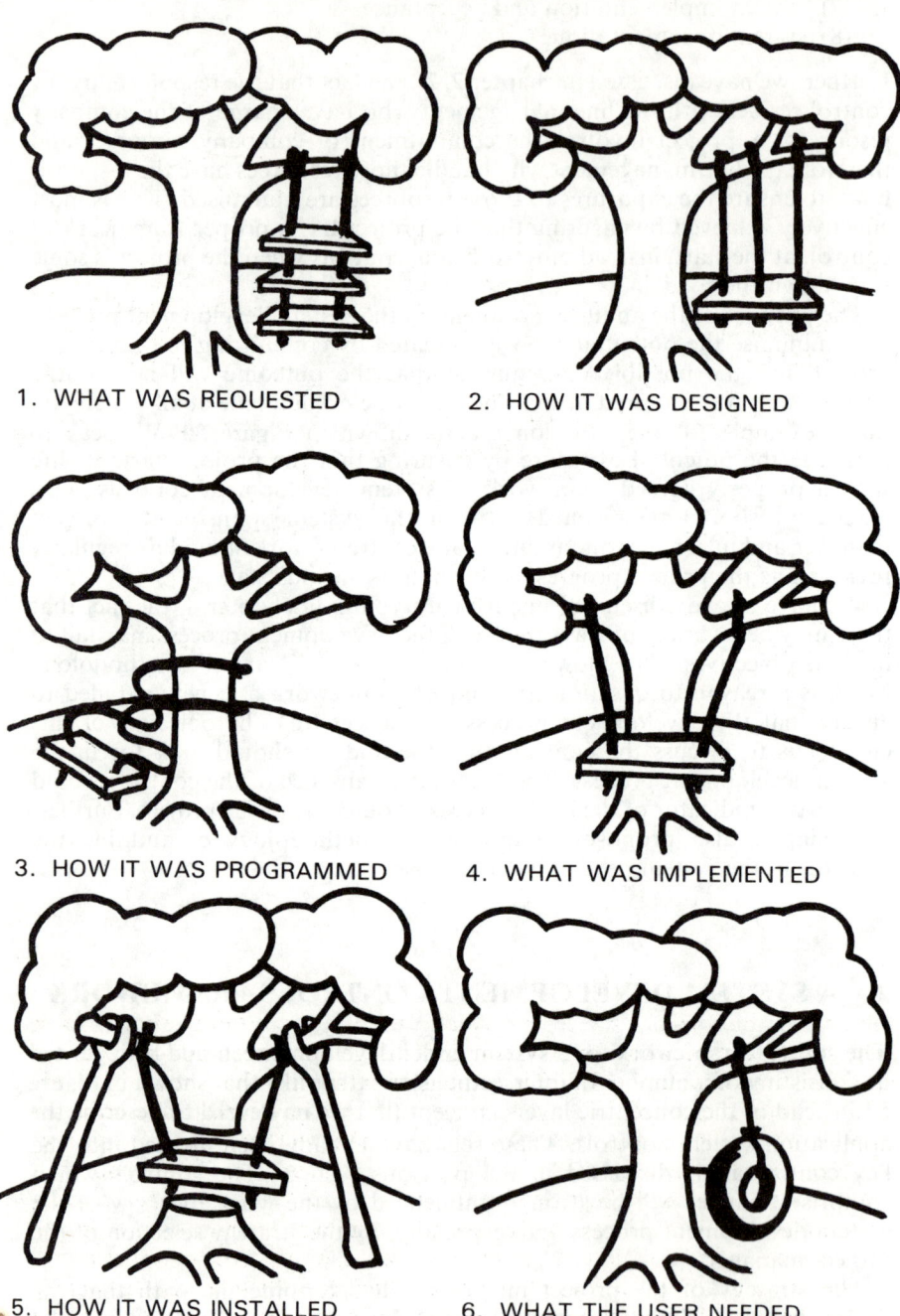

1. WHAT WAS REQUESTED

2. HOW IT WAS DESIGNED

3. HOW IT WAS PROGRAMMED

4. WHAT WAS IMPLEMENTED

5. HOW IT WAS INSTALLED

6. WHAT THE USER NEEDED

Figure 51   A systems development controls framework

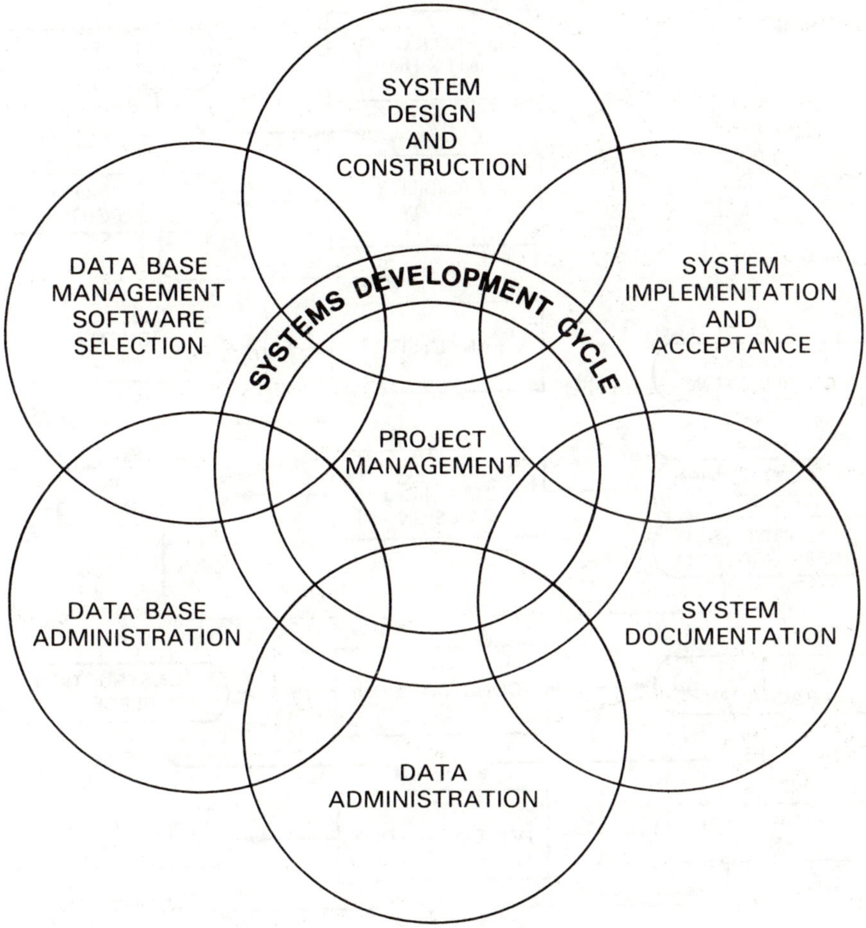

the end of the analysis phase, by which time any uncertainty should have been resolved. Specification and technical design have been merged because an automated development aid is to be used to specify the system.

The second example illustrates a system being developed within an established application and technical environment so that the feasibility and strategy can be settled within the project initiation phase. The detailed requirements and specification are to be signed off before authorising progress to technical design. There are no significant technical problems or uncertainties and so technical design has been merged with construction.

The third example illustrates a project where, following the feasibility study, the detailed requirements and user specification are to be defined by prototyping. The prototype might cover all or part of the user requirements, eg just the conversation structure and screen layouts for data entry or enquiry. No significant problems are anticipated and an estimate for completion of merged analysis, specification and technical design phases can

Figure 52a A project specific development cycle

Example 1

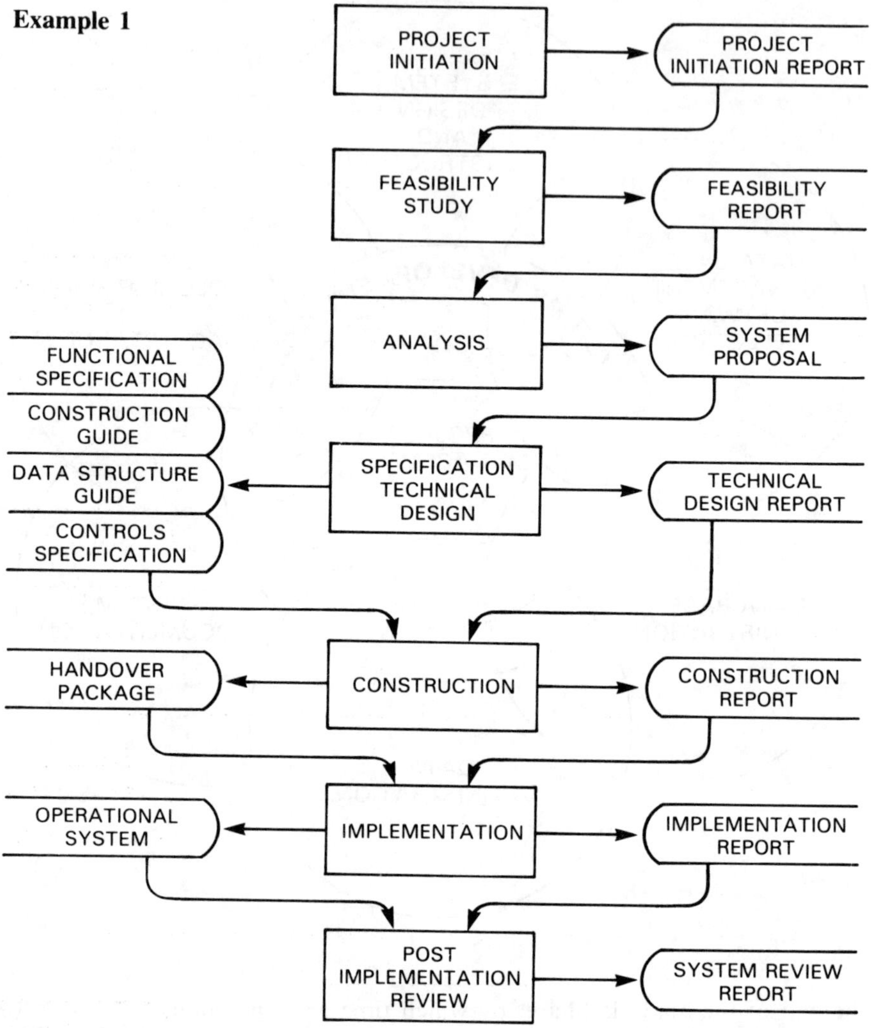

```
PROJECT                          PROJECT
INITIATION          ───►    INITIATION REPORT

FEASIBILITY                     FEASIBILITY
STUDY               ───►          REPORT

                                 SYSTEM
FUNCTIONAL          ANALYSIS ───► PROPOSAL
SPECIFICATION

CONSTRUCTION
GUIDE

DATA STRUCTURE  ◄── SPECIFICATION  ───► TECHNICAL
GUIDE               TECHNICAL          DESIGN REPORT
                    DESIGN
CONTROLS
SPECIFICATION

HANDOVER        ◄── CONSTRUCTION ───► CONSTRUCTION
PACKAGE                                REPORT

OPERATIONAL     ◄── IMPLEMENTATION ───► IMPLEMENTATION
SYSTEM                                   REPORT

                    POST
                    IMPLEMENTATION ───► SYSTEM REVIEW
                    REVIEW              REPORT
```

be made with confidence. At that point, a firm estimate to complete construction is possible. This example, in expanded form, has already been demonstrated in **Figure 40**, to illustrate the prototyping process in more detail.

The fourth example illustrates the minimum requirements of the SDC. This development project is an enhancement to an existing system with specification documents being updated, rather than being produced for the first time. Post-implementation review is not needed.

The controls in each of the different key control areas of the system

Figure 52b   A project specific development cycle

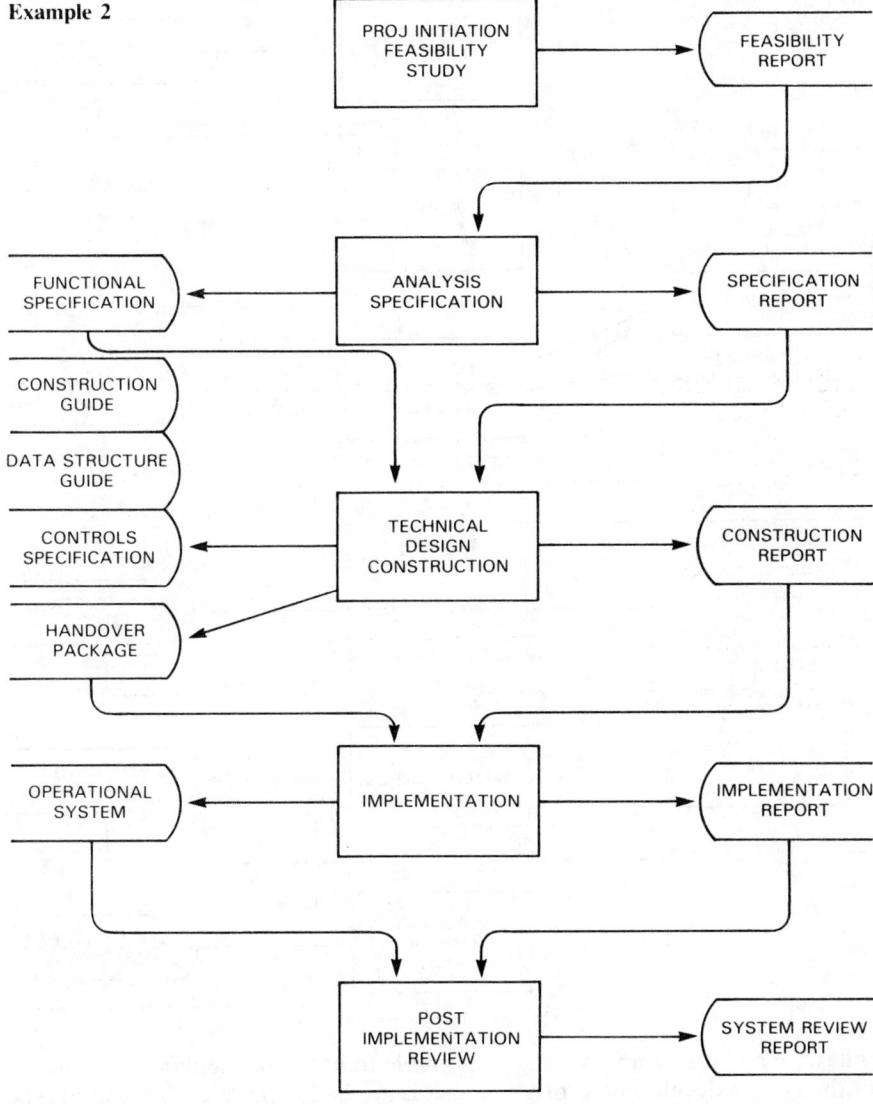

Example 2

development process have been described in chapter 4. The concept of the intersecting sets approach implies that some controls will be equally relevant in several of the key control areas. Thus, the existence of standards and guidelines, which we have listed as control 2.4 under project management, is also recorded under data administration as control 3.5 and under data base administration as control 4.3.

The central hub of the controls framework will be the essential controls on the management of the project and the methodology, ie the SDC, through which the project manager operates, as we have already shown in **Figure 52.** However, the framework of controls should not be seen as fixed and

Figure 52c   A project specific development cycle

Example 3

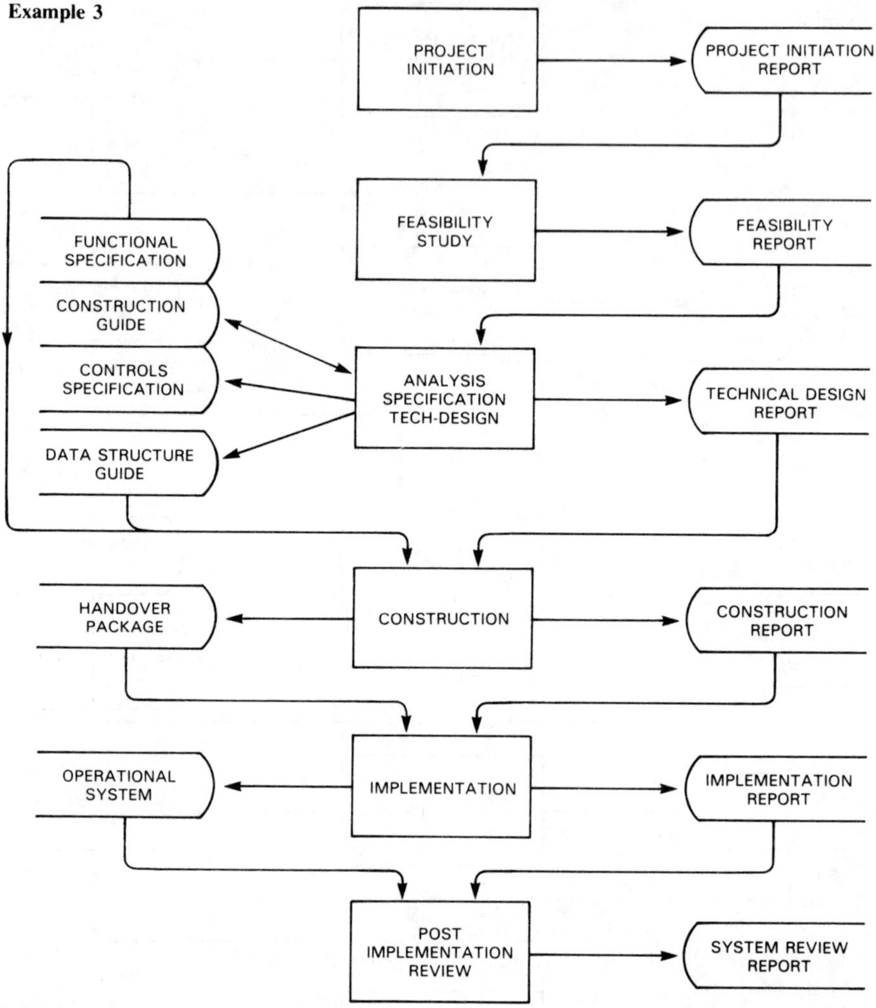

inflexible but something which is adaptable to fit the particular requirements of the system development process, as it is applied in practice. This should be clear, from the examples shown in **Figures 53a** to **53d**, that there will be differing controls requirements depending on how the system development methodology is worked out.

3.   AUDIT METHODOLOGY

There are 17 steps in the audit methodology for the selection and evaluation of systems development controls, as set out below.

Figure 52d   A project specific development cycle

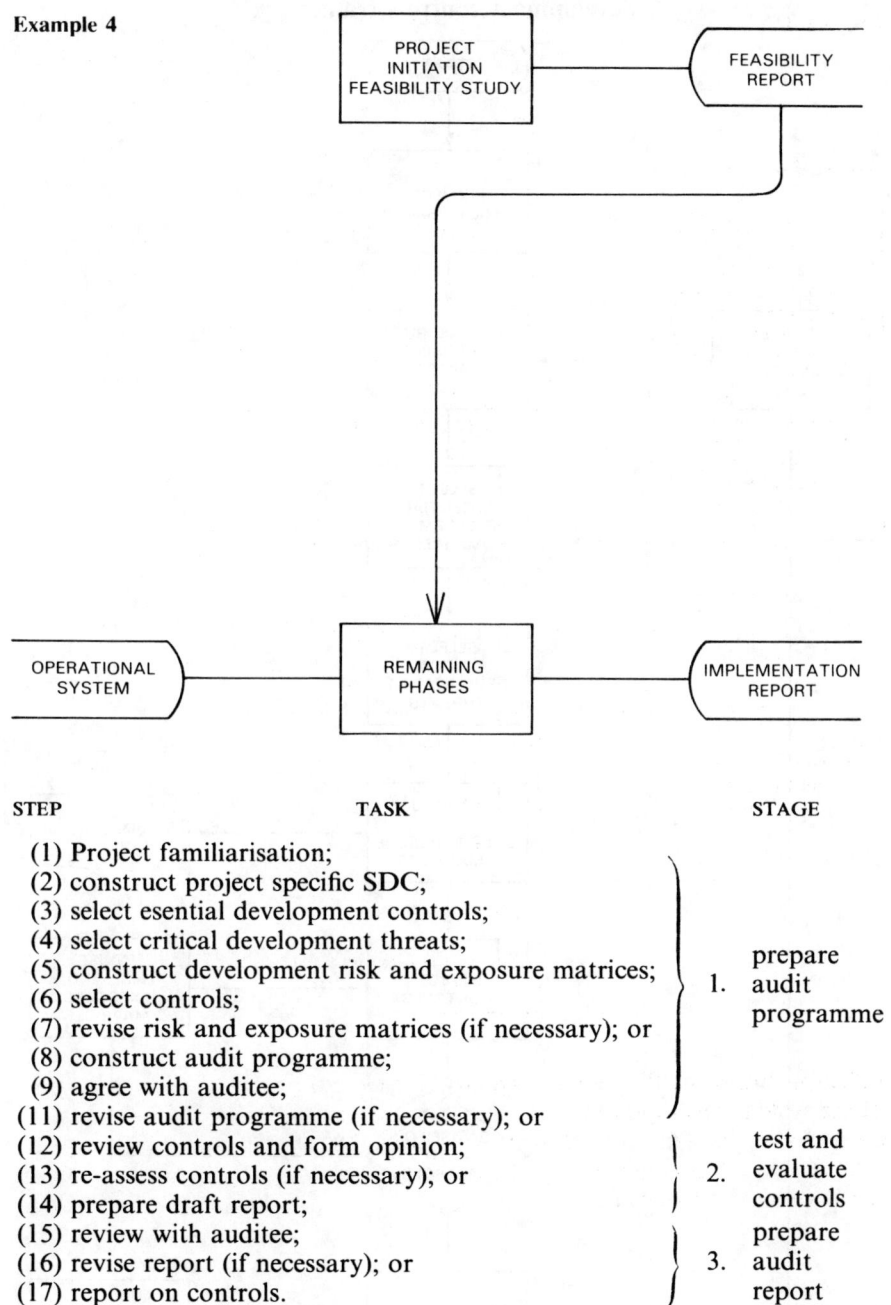

Example 4

STEP   TASK   STAGE

(1) Project familiarisation;
(2) construct project specific SDC;
(3) select esential development controls;
(4) select critical development threats;
(5) construct development risk and exposure matrices;   1. prepare audit programme
(6) select controls;
(7) revise risk and exposure matrices (if necessary); or
(8) construct audit programme;
(9) agree with auditee;
(11) revise audit programme (if necessary); or
(12) review controls and form opinion;   2. test and evaluate controls
(13) re-assess controls (if necessary); or
(14) prepare draft report;
(15) review with auditee;   3. prepare audit report
(16) revise report (if necessary); or
(17) report on controls.

These steps, in the audit methodology, are shown in flowchart form in **Figure 53** and the application of the methodology is discussed further in the remaining sections of this chapter. There are three essential stages in this

Figure 53 Audit methodology for selecting and evaluating a systems development controls framework

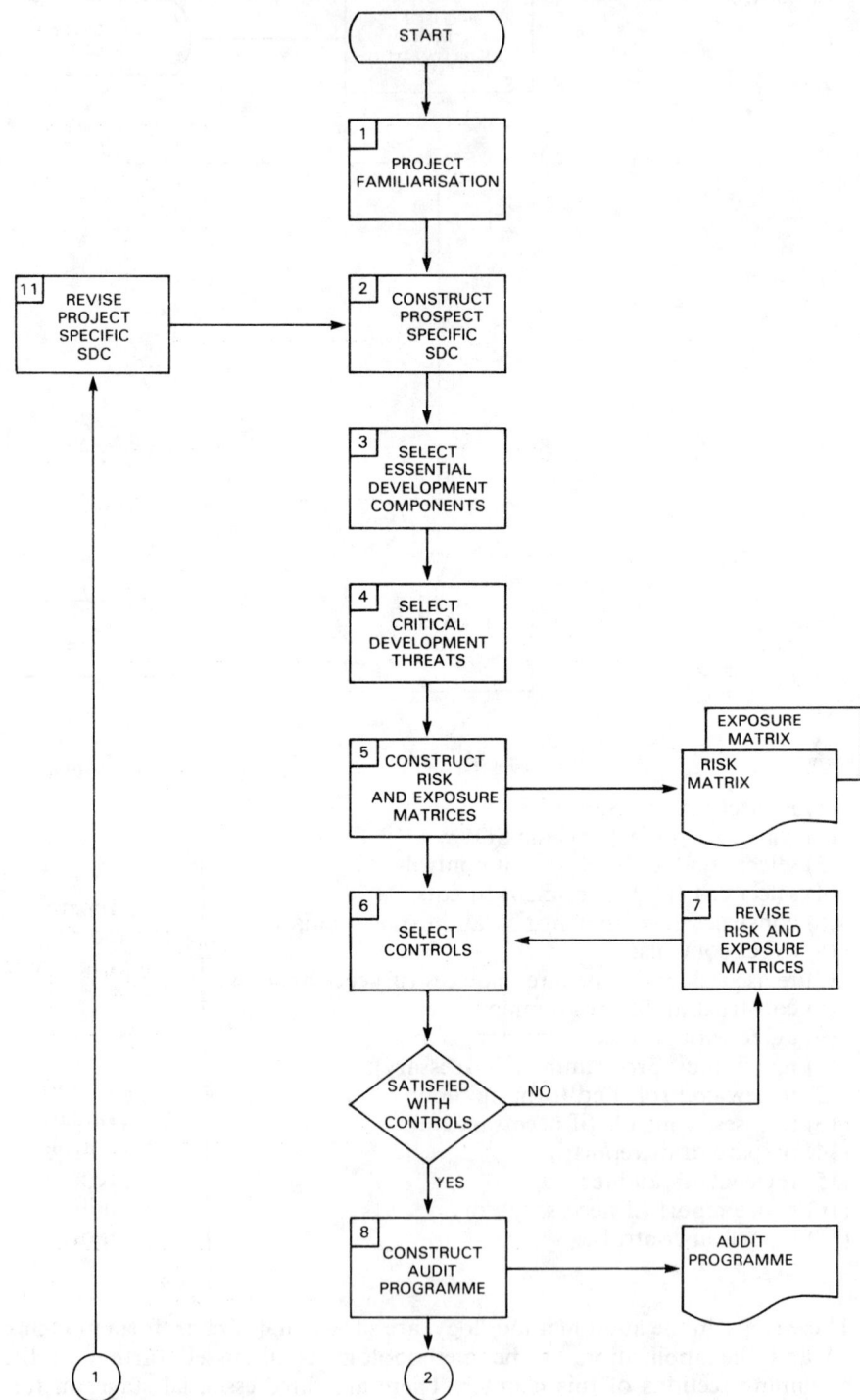

Figure 53 Audit methodology for selecting and evaluating a systems development controls framework—*continued*

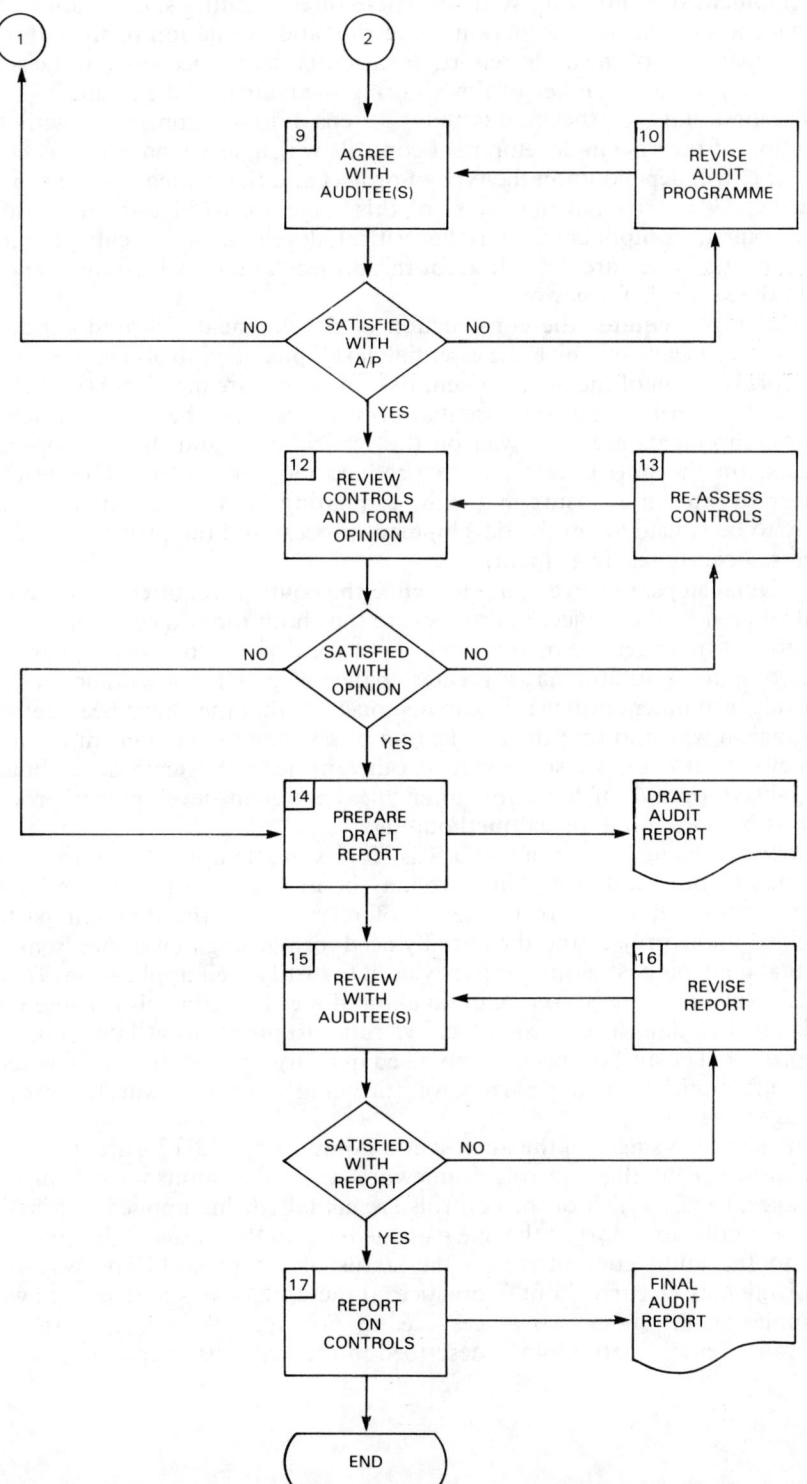

methodology because, as we have discussed in the previous chapter, the objectives and scope may be regarded as a fixed parameter in auditing the development of computing systems. These three essential stages namely the preparation of the audit programme, testing and evaluation of the controls and preparation of the audit report, are also iterative processes and the steps may be repeated a number of times during the course of the audit.

The first stage of the methodology—steps 1-10—is concerned with the selection of the system development controls which, as we have discussed in **2**. above, will depend upon the type of project and the strategy of the project manager. The principal objectives of this stage are to identify the system development components, and the critical development threats to those components, which are important for this project, and for which we intend to build the controls framework.

This stage, requires the construction of development risk and exposure matrices by means of which the essential development controls are identified. The construction of the development risk and exposure matrices is described further in **6**., below, but the essential principle is that, the system development components are displayed on the vertical axis, and the development threats, on the horizontal axis, to produce the risk matrix. This is then converted into an exposure matrix by estimating the value of the resources likely to be consumed in the development process and the probability of an adverse occurrence, ie a threat.

The final steps, in stage 1, are to define the controls required for each key control area of the project and to ensure that both the project sponsor and the project manager are in agreement with the derived controls framework. The computing auditor has a greater chance of gaining acceptance for his controls recommendations if he can demonstrate that they have been derived in a logical way and that the application of a systems development controls framework has proved successful in other projects. Systems development specialists approve of logic for, after all, the system development process itself is based upon a logical methodology.

However, being human, it can be easy for us to attempt to cut corners, for the sake of time and cost. Thus, we may be inclined to say that we know, from experience, what are the terms of reference of the different parties involved in the project and they hardly need formalising in writing. Remember that controls cost money and they need to justify their application. This is indeed true but we need to be careful about discarding controls because they look superficial, as a result of which we run into problems at later stages of the project. The author has been involved in a large project in which, several years after initiation, the parties were arguing over who was the project manager.

The next two stages in the audit methodolgy—steps 12-17—are, firstly, to regularly review the controls framework with the sponsor and project manager, to test which of the controls are actually being applied in practice and, secondly, to report to the line management on the status of the controls, and to the audit committee, on the status of the project. The way that reporting may be carried out in practice, at these two levels, is discussed with examples in **8**. These two stages are, in principle, the same as for the generalised audit methodology described in the previous chapter.

4. SYSTEM DEVELOPMENT COMPONENTS

The examples shown in **Figures 52a** to **52d** of the systems development cycle clearly demonstrate that the development components will not have the same degree of importance for every system. Therefore, the framework of controls will need to be customised for each project. As we have discussed in **3.**, above, the first stage in the audit methodology, is to identify the system development components for which we intend to build our framework of control. This we do by drawing up a project specific systems development cycle for the system we are auditing which defines, at the commencement of the project, the type of strategy the project manager intends to follow. This is illustrated in **Figure 54**.

The project specific development cycle, shown in the illustration, was for the development of a system for which the decision had already been made, at an early stage of the project, that the preferred strategy was to select an available package, which could be customised, rather than to build a system in-house. Thus, an important part of the system development cycle controls was to ensure that there was a methodology available for the evaluation and ranking of commercially available packages. In this case, there was not, and the project manager was required, at an early stage of the project, to construct an evaluation and ranking checklist in order to review the available software. This control, and its application, which is shown in **8.**, below, was considered by audit as a potential source of control weakness, since the construction of the checklist was essentially subjective and based, to a large degree, on the experience of the project manager. However, in actual practice, it worked very successfully.

The other system development components, that were identified as being important for this particular project, were:

(1) project management;
(2) data administration;
(3) system design and construction;
(4) system implementation and acceptance.

Project management was seen as particularly important because of the size of the project, the interest of all functional areas in the data and the involvement of three different locations, in the UK. Data administration was seen as a particularly sensitive issue because of questions of rights of ownership, that we have already discussed in chapter 4, **3.**, above.

System design and construction was regarded as important because customisation of the package was to be carried out by an outside software supplier over whom the company had no control except, in the worst situation, by a cancellation of the contract. Thus it was important to ensure that the outside supplier had sufficient financial viability to continue to operate in the longer term, as well as skilled resources available to make the necessary modifications in the time schedule laid down. It was also important to ensure that, once the scope of work had been agreed with the software supplier on the system design, as well as the charges for the required work, any modifications should be submitted to stringent change control procedures as described in chapter 7, **9.**

System implementation and acceptance was another key control area that

Figure 54   The project specific development cycle

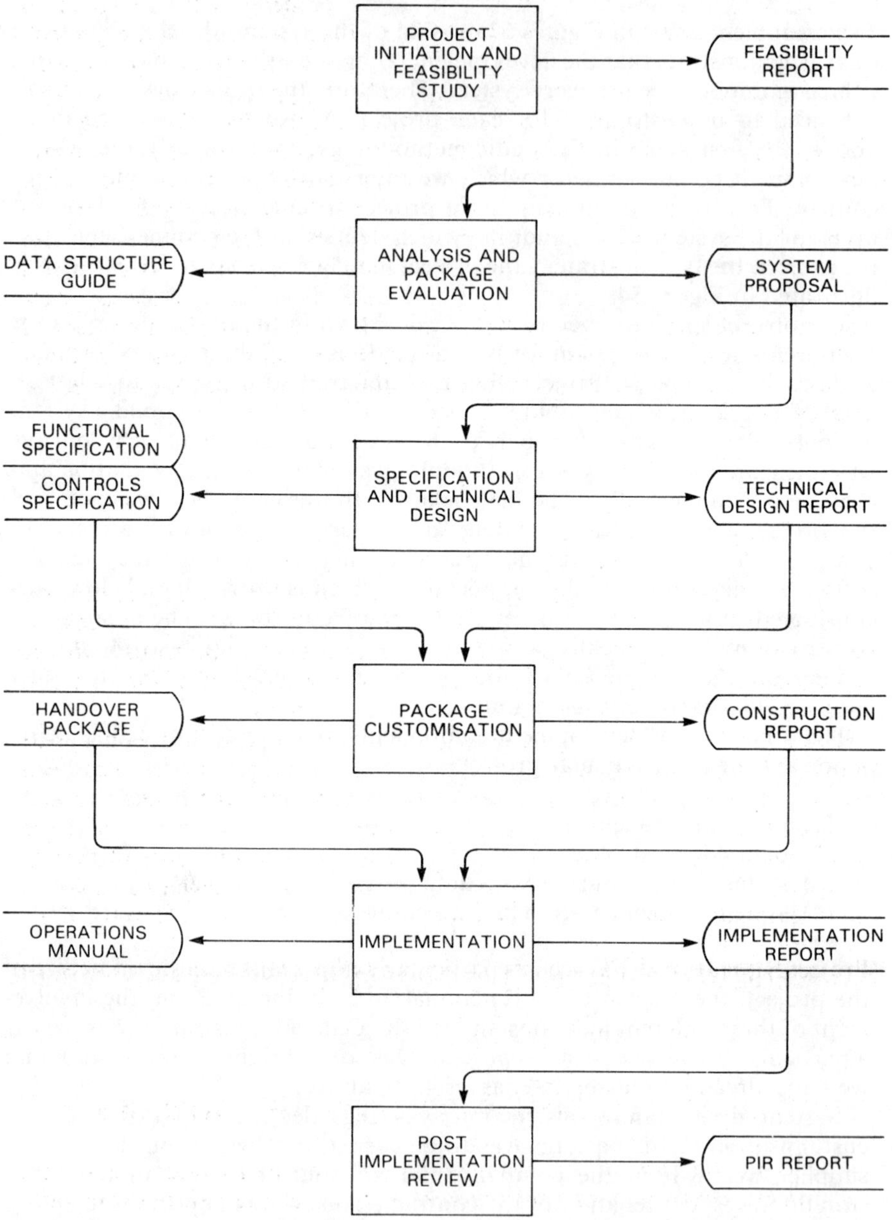

was considered important for this project, because it was to be implemented in three company locations simultaneously, as well as in all functional areas in the company. Thus there were vital issues of security and privacy that had to be determined, prior to implementation, to what data different groups of persons within the company would have access.

Data base management software (DBMS) selection was not considered a vital control area, in itself, because the software package was supplied with its own DBMS and the package evaluation controls were designed to evaluate the effectiveness of the DBMS at an early stage of the project. Further, the package was designed to run on the current range of processors, with which the company already had a number of years of experience, and there was a recognised data base administration specialist. Thus it was not considered that the addition of this system to the company's software portfolio, would change the nature of the data base administration function.

Finally, the system documentation was essentially available, from the supplier, as part of the initial package evaluation exercise. However, there were a number of system development documents required, as shown in **Figure 55**. The most important of these were the system proposal, data structure guide and fuctional specification. The preparation and content of all these documents was described in the company standards and guidelines so this area of the system development controls was not considered to represent a high exposure.

5. THREATS

Threats in the system development process may be regarded as any adverse occurrence which leads to a delay in the timing, an increase in the cost or change in the scope of the project. The assessment of the threats to the project, is an important step in leading to the construction of the risk and exposure matrices, which we describe in the next section.

The implication of the threat to the system component, will depend a great deal on what particular stage of the system development process has been reached. Thus, the absence of an implementation plan, at the analysis and package evaluation phase, in **Figure 54**, would not be as serious as at the implementation phase later in the project. Examples of the types of threats which are relevant to the system development process are listed in **Table 23.** The threat itself is the absence of one or other of the items listed in the table which form part of the specific project development methodology that is being followed.

6. DEVELOPMENT RISK AND EXPOSURE MATRICES

Steps 3-5 in the audit methodology, for selecting and evaluating system development controls, represent the construction of the risk and exposure matrices. The risk matrix is set up with the system components on the vertical axis and the threats along the horizontal axis. The effect of the critical threats may be evaluated against the key control areas under the headings:

$$C = \text{cost increase}$$
$$S = \text{scope change}$$
$$T = \text{time change}$$

The risk matrix, which now appears as in **Figure 55**, gives a coarse measure

Table 23   Threats to the systems development process

1. Terms of reference.

2. Development strategy.

3. Development plan.

4. Implementation plan.

5. Standards and guidelines.

6. Project management.

7. Project plan.

8. Prototyping software.

9. Data administrator.

10. Data base administrator.

11. Internal audit.

12. Package evaluation and selection criteria.

13. Steering committee.

14. Project group.

15. Quality assurance.

16. Project reporting.

17. Training.

18. Critical path analysis.

of the vulnerable areas for the particular project. In practice, the number of vertical columns, which represent the potential threats to each of the system development components, would be much greater than those shown in the illustration. However, if the construction of the matrix and the evaluation of the exposures is carried out using one of the numerous commercially available spreadsheet packages, the exercise is greatly simplified and can be repeated as often as desired, as the project progresses along its development path. In this particular case, the author used an IBM PC/XT combined with the LOTUS 1-2-3 spreadsheet package.

The system development risk matrix may now be converted into an exposure matrix by using an assessment of the value of that component in the system development process and the probability of occurrence of the threat. This has been carried out using a first estimate for the values of the components, and probabilities of the threats, to produce the development exposure matrix shown in **Figure 56**. Both the development risk and development exposure matrices have been illustrated in simplified form in order that the principles should not be obscured by the details of the process. The process may then be repeated, using alternative values for the compo-

Figure 55   A development risk matrix

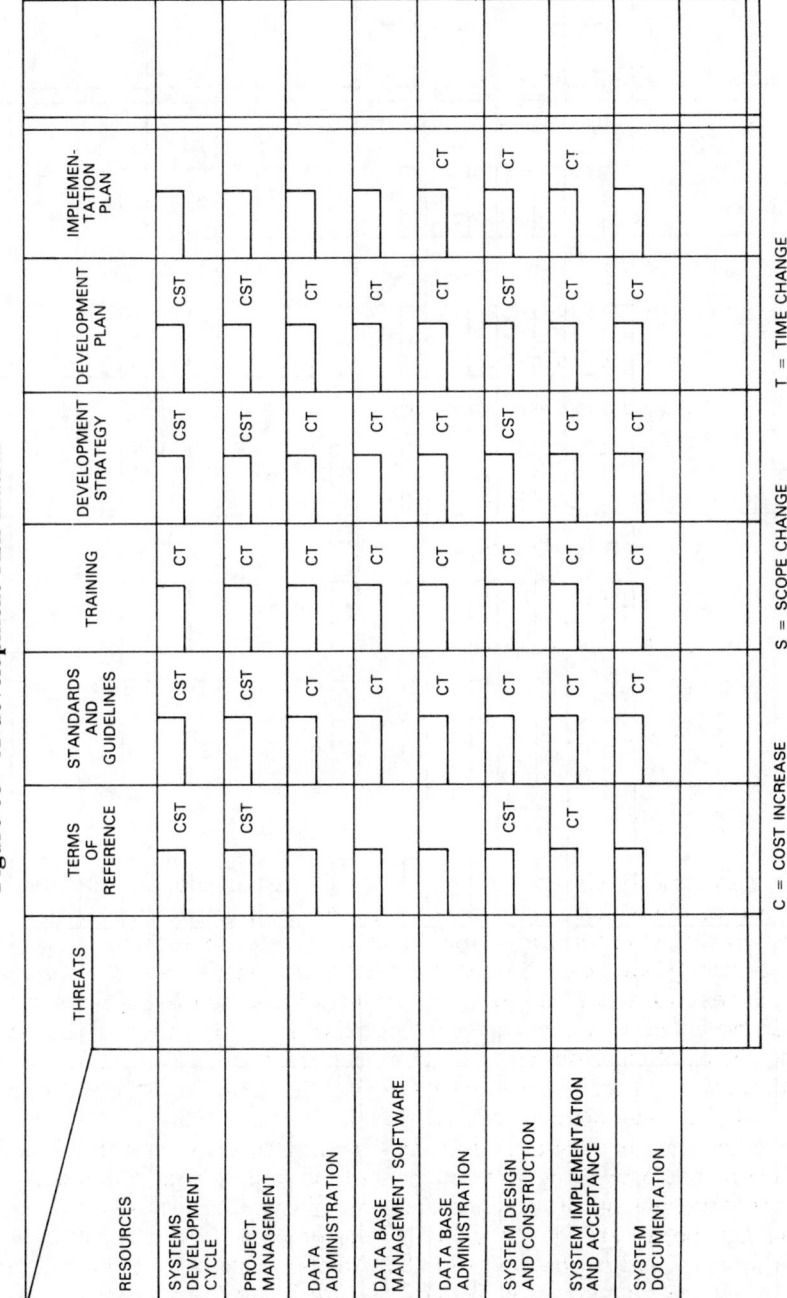

RESOURCES \ THREATS	TERMS OF REFERENCE	STANDARDS AND GUIDELINES	TRAINING	DEVELOPMENT STRATEGY	DEVELOPMENT PLAN	IMPLEMEN- TATION PLAN	
SYSTEMS DEVELOPMENT CYCLE	CST	CST	CT	CST	CST		
PROJECT MANAGEMENT	CST	CST	CT	CST	CST		
DATA ADMINISTRATION		CT	CT	CT	CT		
DATA BASE MANAGEMENT SOFTWARE		CT	CT	CT	CT		
DATA BASE ADMINISTRATION		CT	CT	CT	CT	CT	
SYSTEM DESIGN AND CONSTRUCTION	CST	CT	CT	CST	CST	CT	
SYSTEM IMPLEMENTATION AND ACCEPTANCE	CT	CT	CT	CT	CT	CT	
SYSTEM DOCUMENTATION		CT	CT	CT	CT		

C = COST INCREASE   S = SCOPE CHANGE   T = TIME CHANGE

Figure 56　A development exposure matrix

RESOURCES	VALUE £K	TERMS OF REFERENCE	STANDARDS AND GUIDELINES	TRAINING	DEVELOPMENT STRATEGY	DEVELOPMENT PLAN	IMPLEMENTATION PLAN	TOTAL EXPOSURE £K
SYSTEMS DEVELOPMENT CYCLE	200	.01 CST 2	.01 CST 2	.01 CT 2	.01 CST 2	.01 CST 2		10
PROJECT MANAGEMENT	200	.01 CST 2	.01 CST 2	.01 CT 2	.01 CST 2	.01 CST 2		10
DATA ADMINISTRATION	100		.01 CT 1	.01 CT 1	.01 CT 1	.01 CT 1		4
DATA BASE MANAGEMENT SOFTWARE	100		.01 CT 1	.01 CT 1	.01 CT 1	.01 CT 1		4
DATA BASE ADMINISTRATION	100		.01 CT 1	.01 CT 1	.01 CT 1	.01 CT 1	.01 CT 1	5
SYSTEM DESIGN AND CONSTRUCTION	1000	.01 CST 10	.01 CT 10	.01 CT 10	.01 CST 10	.01 CST 10	.01 CT 10	60
SYSTEM IMPLEMENTATION AND ACCEPTANCE	200	.01 CT 2	.01 CT 2	.01 CT 2	.01 CT 2	.01 CT 2	.01 CT 2	12
SYSTEM DOCUMENTATION	100		.01 CT 1	.01 CT 1	.01 CT 1	.01 CT 1		4
	2000	16	20	20	20	20	13	109

C = COST INCREASE　　S = SCOPE CHANGE　　T = TIME CHANGE

nents and, if desired, for the probabilities, and in this way a feel for the sensitivity of the project in the different component areas is obtained. The process may also be repeated by different members of the project group, and the results compared, so as to obtain a group assessment of the sensitive project component areas.

The author freely admits that the evaluation of the project exposures in this way, is a subjective process and there can be a wide degree of latitude in the assessment of component values and the probabilities of the threats. For example, we may value the systems development cycle as the cost of acquiring the methodology or at the estimated total cost of the project, on the basis that without a development methodology, there is a very high likelihood of failure.

The evaluation of probabilities is also subjective and we must use our best judgement in each case. For example, we may consider that the probability of failure without appropriate terms of reference for the project steering committee and project group is relatively low. The probability of failure without a proper development strategy and development plan we may rate much more highly. Further, our estimates for the probabilities may change, during the course of the SDC, and we have recommended, in chapter 5, that a re-evaluation of risk and exposure should be carried out during each phase of the cycle.

In spite of the subjective nature of the evaluations, experience has shown that the construction of risk and exposure matrices is extremely valuable in focusing attention on the sensitive areas in the systems development process and highlighting the risk and exposures for a specific project. Further, the simplicity of the exercise, when carried out with some appropriate computer hardware and software, which enables the auditor to perform as many iterations as he so desires with comparatively little commitment in time and resources, make the construction of the development risk and exposure matrices a valuable technique in the systems development process. The value of the methodology increases with the skill and experience of the auditor, which develop with his involvement, over time, in different projects and give him a greater sensitivity for the areas of high risk and exposure as well as of the important threats, for which there should be adequate control.

The final outcome of steps 3-5 of the audit methodology, is to produce a clearer indication of the vulnerable areas in the project specific systems development process. The next step is to select the most appropriate controls, which should give us a high assurance of the successful outcome of the project, and to agree these controls, in the form of an audit programme, with the line management in both the user area, and the DP function, responsible for the development of the project.

7. AUDIT PROGRAMME

The development controls which were eventually selected for the audit programme were drawn from **Table 9**, at the end of chapter 4, under the following key component areas:

    (1) systems development cycle;

(2) project management;
(3) data administration;
(4) system design and construction;
(5) system implementation and acceptance.

These were considered to be the minimum necessary controls to provide the greatest assurance of a successful outcome of the project and to reduce the potential project exposure to a minimum. The controls were issued to the line management in both the system sponsor and data processing areas, in the form of a checklist, with the understanding that they would be used as the basis for an audit review and evaluation to access the effectiveness and efficiency of the project development process. The first part of the programme is shown in the following section, on audit reporting, with the audit observation/auditee comments on the controls details.

An important part of the development controls framework was the control developed by the project manager for the evaluation and selection of readily available software packages in the subject area. This control, which is shown in **Table 24**, was divided into ten areas and each of the areas was allotted a score rating and a weighting against which the package features were assessed. A short list of nine packages was selected as being potentially capable of providing the features that were required in the software for the system. The scoring was carried out by the project manager, and a user representative, after a visit to vendors of each of the short-listed packages, and the score ratings summarised in a table. From this exercise, there emerged one clearly favoured candidate which was able to provide all the desired features and so, at an early stage of the project, the selection decision was made.

Table 24   Software package evaluation and selection criteria

(1) BUSINESS FUNCTIONS

—Employee record keeping;
—position/job control;
—absence control/time administration;
—history records;
—population/organisation analysis;
—treatment of mass changes;
—integration with other modules, eg payroll, pensions.

(2) SOFTWARE FEATURES

—On-line/batch features;
—menu driven and/or command driven;
—programming languages;
—use of tables/routines/modules;
—existence of automatic features
  (i)   movement from position to position;
  (ii) reporting 'paths';
—letter generator;
—downloading and bridging to/from other systems;
—ownership of source code;
—end-user customisation;
—programme testing procedures.

Table 24—*continued*

(3) DATABASE ENVIRONMENT

—Data base management system ;
—data base structure and flexibility;
—data dictionary
   (i)   concepts and functions;
   (ii) contents and printouts;
   (iii) user control;
   (iv) data base administration;
—use of tables/code sets;
—data entry and updating mode, concepts and procedures;
—validation rules;
—audit trail/logging;
—compatible with other DBMS's;
—link with EXCELERATOR.

(4) ON-LINE/BATCH QUERY AND RETRIEVAL FACILITIES

—Language used;
—functions available;
—accessible data
   (i)   data files;
   (ii) data dictionary;
   (iii) tables;
   (iv) user and system libraries;
—sub-files;
—batch report generator;
—standard reports (on-line and batch).

(5) SYSTEM SECURITY, ADMINISTRATION AND CONTROL

—System description;
—system flowcharts/diagrams;
—'housekeeping' functions;
—methods/levels of security/confidentiality;
—access/authorisation profiles;
—on-line monitoring by user department;
—backup/restore facility.

(6) USER FRIENDLINESS

(a) Terminal features
   —PF keys;
   —cursor;
   —HELP facilities;
   —visual appearance;
   —validations;
   —screen painting;
   —block mode/character mode screens;
   —error messages;
   —user prompts.

(b) Documentation
   —End user;
   —technical;
   —systems;

Table 24—*continued*

—enhancements/'bug' announcements;
—new system releases.

(c) User training
    —Level of skill required;
    —before, on and after implementation;
    —in-house/on-site;
    —level, eg line focal points, personnel, etc.

(7) INTERFACES

—Availability from same terminal;
—interactive use;
—transfer of data between systems.

(8) IMPLEMENTATION STRATEGY

—Approach;
—plan;
—previous experience.

(9) VENDOR SUPPORT AND MAINTENANCE

—Before installation;
—after installation;
—updates/new releases, hardware and/or software;
—telephone support;
—location of customer support;
—number of support staff and experience;
—response time to call-out;
—customisation.

(10) 'IN-HOUSE' EXPERIENCE/EXPERTISE

—hardware;
—software;
—data base management system;
—query/reporting facilities;
—previous experience with vendor.

8.   AUDIT REVIEW AND REPORTING

The final stage, and not least in importance, of the audit methodology is the review and reporting on the controls which have been selected as being most likely to ensure a successful outcome of the systems development process. This review, as has already been suggested, is carried out at two levels namely:

(1) to the line management directly involved with the project;
(2) to the internal audit committee.

The manner of reporting at both these levels is illustrated in the examples which follow.

(1)   TO THE LINE MANAGEMENT DIRECTLY INVOLVED WITH THE PROJECT.

AUDIT MEMORANDUM

FROM : Auditor   TEL

TO : Messrs Jones,   DATE
         Smith,
         etc.

AUDIT REVIEW NO1

INTERNAL AUDIT   —/—/—

SUBJECT: Personnel System

(1)   Introduction

This is the first of what is intended to be a series of reviews, covering the personnel system development controls which have been agreed between the sponsor, the project manager and internal audit. The controls have been issued as a checklist divided into sections covering the following areas:

(1) systems development cycle;
(2) project management;
(3) data administration;
(4) system design and construction;
(5) system implementation and acceptance.

At each review, it is intended to cover at least one complete section of the controls checklist and all action items that were outstanding from previous reviews. This review has been carried out between the project sponsor, the project manager and internal audit.

(2)   Outstanding actions previous reviews.

This is the first controls review to be made for this project and, therefore, there are no outstanding action items from previous reviews.

(3)   Controls checklist

The current status on controls 1.1-1.13, the system development cycle controls, is shown in the attached tables to this audit memorandum [see p 228–230].

(4)   Control weaknesses

Control ref	Audit observations/recommendations
1.5	There are no written terms of reference in existence for either the project steering committee or the project group.
	We do not consider this a major control weakness, at this stage, but would recommend that appropriate written terms of reference be provided to both the steering committee and the project group.
	ACTION: sponsor/project manager
1.6	All members of the steering committee have not been provided with the standards and guidelines on the role and activities of steering committees.
	We would suggest that, if the steering committee is to function effectively, there should be a proper

understanding of its role and activities and the standards and guidelines should be made available to all its members.

ACTION: sponsor/project manager

1.7   The user representatives on the steering committee have not received any formal training in the application of the systems development cycle and project development work.

We would recommend that all persons without formal training should attend the appropriate company courses on the systems development cycle and project development work.

ACTION: sponsor/project manager

1.8   The user representatives on the project group have had no formal training in the content and application of the systems development cycle or in project development work.

We would recommend that the user representatives should attend the appropriate company course on the systems development cycle and project development work.

ACTION: project manager

1.9   Formal written job descriptions are not available for all members of the project group.

We do not consider this a major control weakness but would recommend that job descriptions be drawn up for the positions of project leader, data administrator and data analyst.

ACTION: project manager

1.13   There are no company standards and guidelines for the evaluation and selection of application software packages.

This is a MAJOR control weakness since the project manager is using his own selection criteria for the evaluation of packages and the judgement is very much subjective. We would recommend that formal standards and guidelines should be drawn up for package evaluation and selection.

ACTION: project manager

(2) TO THE INTERNAL AUDIT COMMITTEE

AUDIT MEMORANDUM

FROM : Auditor   TEL:

TO : Messrs Lyon,   DATE:
Foxe,
etc.

INTERNAL AUDIT $-/-/-$

SUBJECT :   Personnel System

This project is included in the 19— internal audit plan as a system under development. The main objectives for the on-going audit involvement are:

(1) to assess the effectiveness and efficiency of project development controls;
(2) to give reasonable assurance that the system will be implemented with adequate built-in controls for security and privacy of data, accuracy and completeness of processing and effectiveness and efficiency of operation.

As the system has not yet reached the stage of implementation, the controls framework for operating the system has still to be constructed. However, since a system proposal report has been recently issued, we feel this is an appropriate checkpoint to report our view on the effectiveness of the project development controls.

To enable a structured review to be made, we have constructed a development controls checklist concentrating on the following areas:

(1) systems development cycle;
(2) project management;
(3) data administration;
(4) system design and construction;
(5) system implementation and acceptance.

We have now undertaken the first review with the project manager and the system sponsor covering the controls in sections 1—the systems development cycle. As a result of this review, several control weaknesses were identified which have been, or are being, corrected, and consequently we are of the opinion that, at this stage, the project is being soundly managed and controlled.

The remaining sections of the checklist, ie sections 2-5, will be reviewed in a similar fashion, during the second half of the year, the precise timing of each section depending on the project development progress.

Attachment to Audit Memorandum 1

Ref: /   /

AUDIT PROGRAMME: A PERSONNEL INFORMATION AND COMPUTING SYSTEM

SCOPE ITEM 1: SYSTEMS DEVELOPMENT CYCLE

Ref	Control detail	Audit observation/auditee comment
1.1	There is a clear written request from the sponsor of the nature of the work to be performed.	The objectives and scope for the system development are given in a study report which has been approved by the personnel information system coordination group (PISCG).
1.2	There is a written statement of the costs/benefits for the project or other grounds on which the project is being justified.	This system is needed to replace the numerous computer systems currently holding personnel information. It is, therefore, being justified on other than cost/benefit grounds.
1.3	There is a clearly established standard and guideline on the systems methodology which is to be followed.	There is an established, and written, system development methodology—the SDC—and copies of this have been provided to all members of the project group.
1.4	The role of all the following participants in the SBC has been clearly defined and understood: 1. project group 2. end user 3. sponsor 4. steering committee 5. project manager 6. strategic planning 7. operations 8. technical services 9. data administration 10. data base administration 11. internal audit 12. quality assurance 13. application support	The sponsor of the system is the personnel director and the principal end-user is the personnel recruitment and administrtion department. There is now a clearly established project group and a project manager who is recognised by both the sponsor and DP department. Internal audit are represented on the project group and the objectives and scope for the audit involvement have been agreed by sponsor and project manager. The role and responsibilities of the other SDC participants will be clarified further to the issue of the feasibility report. ACTION: Project manager

Attachment to Audit Memorandum 1—*continued*

Ref	Control detail	Audit observation/auditee comment
1.5	The terms of reference of the project steering committee and the project group have been clearly defined in writing.	There are no formal written terms of reference available for either the project steering committee or project group.
		All members of the project steering committee have been provided with the company standards and guidelines on the role and authorities of steering committees.
1.6	The project steering committee members are sufficiently familiar with the nature of their role and responsibilities.	The user representatives on the project steering committee have not received any formal training in the application of the SDC and project development work.
1.7	The user representative(s) on the steering committee have been trained in the application of the systems development methodology.	There are regular progress meetings (informal checkpoints) and there will be a first formal checkpoint upon completion of the data analysis phase when approval will be required from the project steering committee for further development.
		<u>ACTION</u>: steering committee
1.8	The user representative(s) on the project group and the project manager have been trained in the application of the systems development methodology and in project development work.	

Attachment to Audit Memorandum 1—*continued*

Ref: / /

AUDIT PROGRAMME: A PERSONNEL INFORMATION AND COMPUTING SYSTEM

SCOPE ITEM 1: SYSTEMS DEVELOPMENT CYCLE

Ref	Control detail	Audit observation/auditee comment
1.9	The project manager has established a development strategy in terms of: 1. selection of checkpoints, formal and informal, 2. choice of development tactics, 3. choice of project control mechanisms, 4. project organisation.	There are regular progress meetings (informal checkpoints) and there will be a first formal checkpoint upon completion of the data analysis phase when approval will be required from the project steering committee for further development. ACTION: steering committee
1.10	There is an outline implementation plan available covering: 1. phased implementation of the system, 2. the conversion or changeover requirements, 3. lead-times for new equipment, recruitment and training needs, 4. user reorganisation, recruitment and training needs, 5. contingency and fallback arrangements, 6. tasks, responsibilities and outline schedule.	The implementation plan will be drawn up at the end of the data activity and analysis phase when there is a clearer concept of the system design. ACTION: project manager
1.11	There is a development plan available covering: 1. detailed estimates for the next phase, 2. machine resources required for the next phase, 3. outline estimates for remainder of project, phase by phase and for each sub-project, if appropriate.	The development plan will be drawn up at the end of the data activity and analysis phase when there is a clearer concept of the system design. ACTION: project manager
1.12	For package solutions there is: 1. a short list of potential products and vendors, 2. an assessment of the degree of tailoring required, 3. a short list of available machines which can run the package, 4. an assessment of the impact on the current hardware strategy, 5. a package evaluation methodology, 6. a performance appraisal procedure, 7. a reporting procedure on package performance, 8. a user acceptance procedure.	A catalogue of currently available personnel software packages is being used as a basis for shortlisting possible candidates for this system. In addition, discussions are being held with a number of established equipment/software suppliers. There are no existing standards and guidelines, within the company, for the evaluation and selection of application software packages. Thus, a package evaluation methodology and ranking appraisal criteria need to be drawn up. ACTION: project manager

11 Designing controls into computing systems

This chapter explains why controls in computing systems are essential and describes a methodology for designing the system controls framework as well as the objectives to be satisfied by the system controls. The methodology may be used for designing controls into any computing system and is based upon the use of two valuable audit techniques, namely:

(1) risk and exposure matrices;
(2) control flowcharts.

In using risk and exposure matrices in system controls design, the auditor identifies, in the first instance, the essential system components and the potential threats to those components. A component of a computing system is defined as a part over which we seek to maintain control. A list of system components is given, in **4**.

A threat is defined as an adverse occurrence which causes the loss, destruction or corruption, of the system components. A table of potential threats is given, in **5**.

The use of risk and exposure matrices, and control flowcharts, is described in the development of a personnel movements system and the derived controls framework is shown. The derived controls framework forms the basis of an audit programme which is used to monitor the implementation of the system controls.

The practical application of the audit programme in the form of a checklist is demonstrated and the final section discusses the way the internal auditor may report his findings and conclusions on the application system controls to the:

(1) local line management,
(2) internal audit committee.

1. PURPOSE AND BACKGROUND

We have already briefly discussed in chapter 2, **5.**, above, the involvement of the auditor in assisting in the design of a framework of controls in a computing system. Further, we have mentioned in chapter 2, **6.**, above, that one of the responsibilities of the computing auditor is 'to give reasonable assurance to management that critical systems are implemented with adequate built-in controls'. The purpose of this undertaking is to:

(1) avoid the more costly task of retro-fitting controls to systems after they have been implemented;

(2) avoid costly mistakes that may arise from operating systems without an adequate framework of control.

There are many examples recorded of costly mistakes that have occurred by operating a computing system with an inadequate controls framework. Thus, one UK company recently reported the loss of approximately £400,000 due to a fraud carried out by two of their accountants. The fraud was made possible because one of the accountants had, in a previous job, designed the accounts payable system and, therefore, knew its weak points.

The accountants inserted fictitious suppliers into the system because, against procedures, they had somehow acquired knowledge of the unique password required for making entries to the suppliers file. They also knew the passwords for processing invoices. The fictitious suppliers were given supplier codes reserved for freight, or miscellaneous services, and these codes enabled payments to be made without the need for matching invoices. Fictitious vouchers were then fed into the payment system using vouchers which required only the accountant's signature. Since the accountants had free access to the file room, they were able to remove all documentation after the payment process was completed. The payments were generally charged to inventory or suspense accounts. If an item was queried, the accountants handled the matter themselves and prepared further vouchers to move the charges, from one ledger account to another, until the queries stopped.

The control weaknesses that were highlighted as a result of this episode were:

(1) password security for the master file was compromised;

(2) passwords were shared between a number of users;

(3) passwords were not changed frequently enough;

(4) controls over the authorisation of input and review of additions, or changes, to the supplier master file were inadequate;

(5) the use and issue of adjustment vouchers for processing accounts payable transactions were not controlled;

(6) the design of inventory and suspense reports did not highlight outstanding items;

(7) the accountants deliberately discouraged their staff from questioning their actions;

(8) suspense accounts were neither monitored or reviewed by management;

(9) departmental management did not accept Head Office suggestions to improve internal controls and Head Office did not insist that these were implemented.

This is only one example of the kind of exposures that companies face by implementing a computing system with an inadequate controls framework. An extensive study on computer fraud was carried out in the UK, in 1983, by BIS Applied Systems, and reported in March 1984 in the journal 'EDPACS'. The study was based on 95 cases of computer abuse. Some points that were highlighted were:

—those who commit computer fraud tend to hold managerial or supervisory positions;

—firms that were victims of such fraud were usually in the fields of finance or industry;

—many of the frauds succeeded because the victims did not understand the need to provide for a proper segregation of duties;

—the widespread use of small business computers will expose more organisations to the threat of dishonest members within EDP staff;

—there is a need for computer security training;

—some proprietary application system packages provide little or no safeguards against unauthorised access;

—the role of the internal auditor in fighting computer crime is becoming more important;

—a majority of the fraud cases involved losses of $15,000 or less; only one or two cases were in excess of $750,000 and the average loss was about $45,000;

—almost all of those who committed the frauds were fired from their jobs;

—information about how the fraud was uncovered was somewhat sketchy but about 20% were detected by internal audit or other controls;

—some victims were unhappy they could not press charges because they lacked evidence that could be used in Court;

—bad luck, or some other fluke was involved in the detection of 17% of the frauds;

—in 63% of the cases, the fraud was based upon the manipulation of input and source documents;

—the computer was used to cover up the fraud in 12% of cases;

—misuse of computer resources was a factor in 7% of the frauds;

—only 5% of the incidents involved tampering with the software;

—remote terminals played a role in 15% of the reported cases;

—male fraud perpetrators outnumbered their female counterparts 4 : 1;

—about 13% of the cases involved collusion;

—only 26% of the perpetrators were EDP employees;

—auditors lacked the experience needed to build business systems controls which could detect fraud and catch the perpetrators;

—most frauds stem from weaknesses in accounting systems;

—part of the problem is the mutual suspicion that exists between auditors and managers.

A follow-up exercise, carried out three years later, revealed that the average amount stolen in any computer fraud, detected in Britain, had risen eightfold—from £31,000 in 1983 to £262,000 in 1986. The maximum loss had increased from £500,000 to £10 million and the largest losses were due to the growing use of electronic funds transfer (EFT) systems.

The conclusion of the BIS study team, was that astute management control was the only defence against computer fraud. It is clear, therefore, that the role of the computing auditor, in assisting in the design of the system controls, will continue to increase as the potential exposure rises.

2.   AN APPLICATION SYSTEM CONTROLS FRAMEWORK

We have already discussed in chapter 3, **1.**, above, that the controls framework of a computing system consists of several concentric layers, as shown in **Figure 9**. These have been illustrated as consisting of:

(1) extra corporate environmental controls, ie legal and societal controls;
(2) general corporate environmental controls;
(3) functional business environmental controls;
(4) computer operating and processing environmental controls.

These are illustrated again, in **Figure 57**, with the 'black box' opened up to show the operating and processing controls of the computing system.

Further, we have shown in **Table 5** that the objectives in designing the system controls are:

(1) security;
(2) privacy;
(3) accuracy;
(4) completeness;
(5) effectiveness;
(6) efficiency.

What has to be borne in mind, in the design process, is that the implementation of a controls framework must be cost effective in seeking to achieve these objectives. For example, the tighter we attempt to make the security net around our system, in terms of both physical and logical access controls, the greater will be the cost of operating the system as well as the sacrifice in terms of effectiveness and efficiency. If we appoint a security officer, within the company, to police the system security, there is an additional manpower cost

Figure 57   Application system controls framework

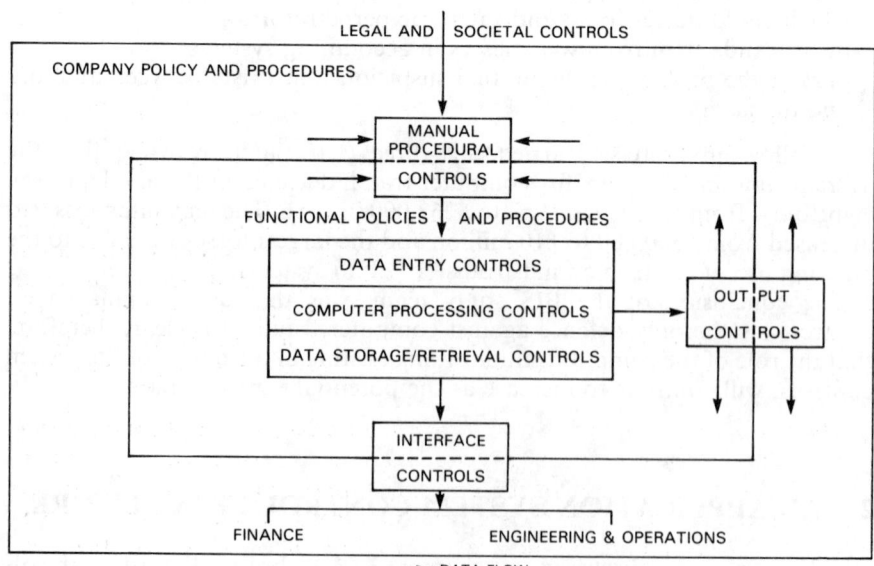

which must be evaluated against the value to the company of the information assets being held and processed by the system. Not every system could justify this type of control.

If we refer back to chapter 2, **1.**, we see that under the objective and scope of the statement of responsibilities of internal auditors the audit objective includes 'promoting effective control at reasonable cost'. This we have to keep firmly in mind, when designing the system controls, to ensure that every recommendation we make, in the controls package, can be justified for the type of system that we have under scrutiny. This is discussed further in **7.**, below, on risk and exposure, for an application system under development.

3. AUDIT METHODOLOGY

The audit methodology for the design of the application system controls consists of 18 steps, as set out below.

STEP	TASK	STAGE
(1) Select essential system components;		
(2) select critical threats;		
(3) construct risk and exposure matrices;		
(4) select controls for system components;		
(5) revise risk and exposure matrices (if necessary); or		
(6) identify computing functions;		prepare
(7) construct controls flowcharts;		1 audit
(8) select processing controls;		programme
(9) revise controls flowcharts (if necessary); or		
(10) prepare audit programme;		
(11) agree with auditee(s);		
(12) revise audit programme (if necessary);		
(13) review controls and form opinion;		test and
(14) re-assess controls (if necessary); or		2 evaluate controls
(15) prepare draft audit report;		prepare
(16) review with auditee(s);		3 audit
(17) revise report (if necessary) or,		report
(18) report on conclusions.		

These steps in the audit methodology are shown, in flowchart form, in **Figure 58** and the application of the methodology is discussed further in the remaining sections of this chapter. The three essential stages in this audit methodology namely, preparation of the audit programme, testing and evaluation of the controls and preparation of the audit report are all iterative processes and the steps may be repeated a number of times during the course of the audit.

The two audit techniques which form the core of the application system controls design methodology are the risk and exposure matrices and the controls flowchart. The use of risk and exposure matrices, for the selection of system development controls, has been described in the previous chapter. The use of the technique, in the selection of application system controls, will be demonstrated in **6.**, below.

Figure 58   An audit methodology for developing and testing an application system controls framework

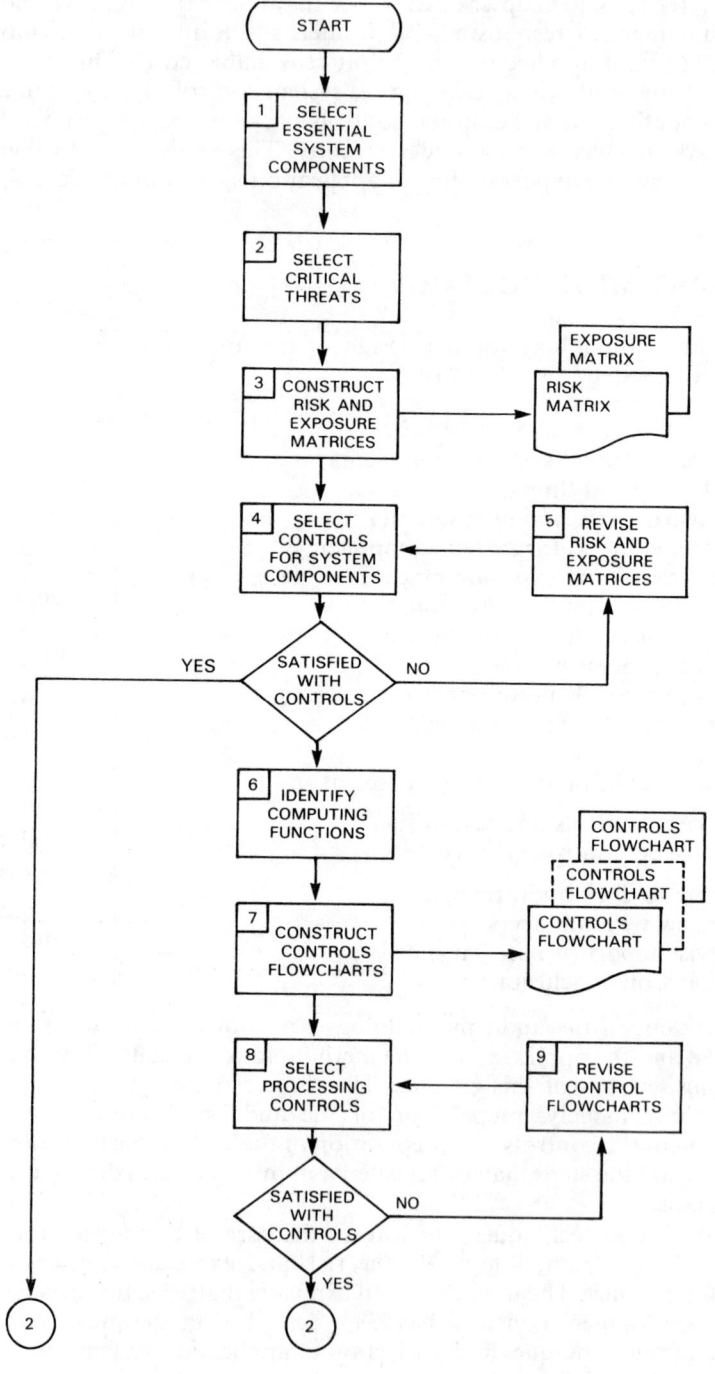

Figure 58   An audit methodology for developing and testing an application system controls framework—*continued*

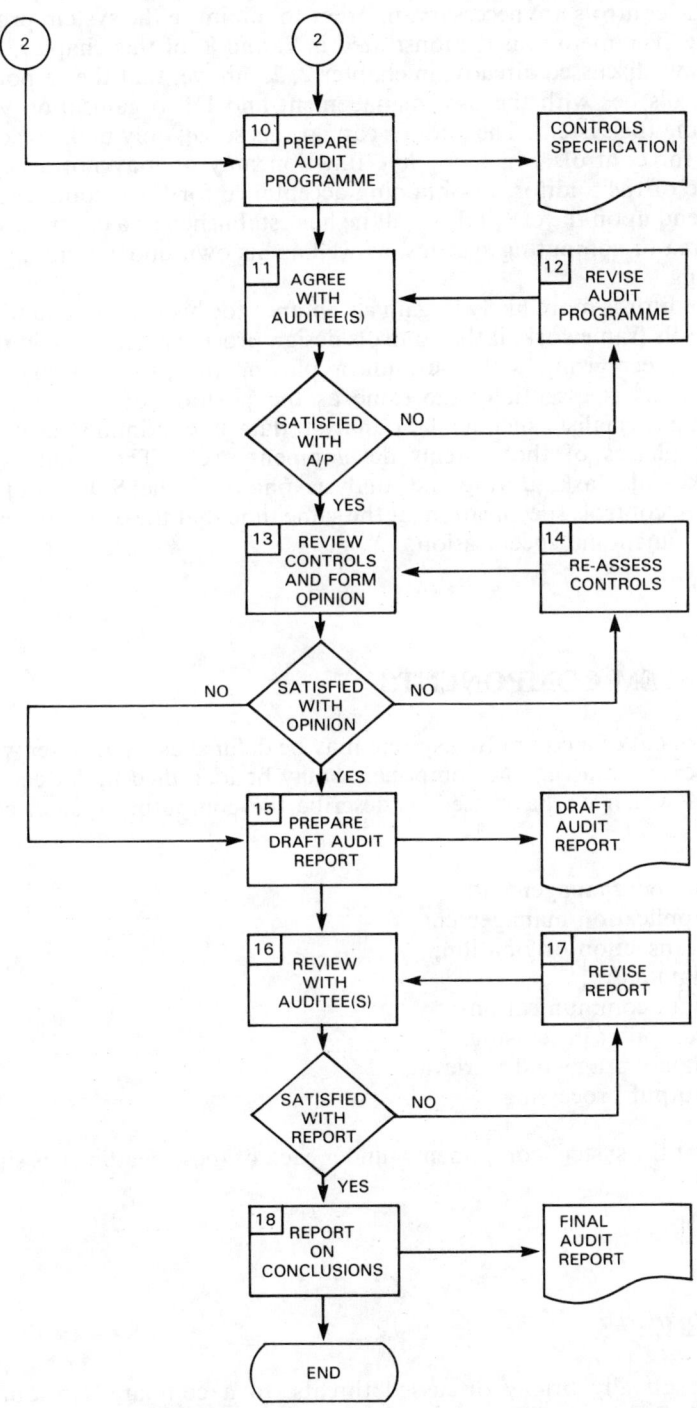

The other valuable audit technique, for the design of controls in computing systems, is the use of the controls flowchart. The purpose of using the controls flowchart is to diagram the computing functions, so as to highlight where the controls are necessary, in order to minimise the system processing exposure. The method is demonstrated in **7.** and **8.** of this chapter, below.

We have discussed already, in chapter 2, **2.**, above, that the responsibility for controls lies with the user management and DP organisation which is developing the system. The auditor can, at this stage, only make recommendations for controls which the line function may or may not accept. The influence of the auditor, in obtaining acceptance for his recommendations, will depend upon the credibility that he has established as a controls 'expert', in the area of computing systems, as well as his own understanding of data processing.

The auditor is more likely to gain acceptance for his recommendations, on the controls framework, if the controls design process is seen as a joint effort by the project group with the auditor playing the principal role, in this activity. This is essentially the same as the position of any of the data processing specialists such as data analyst, data base administrator, during different phases of the systems development cycle. The auditor should undertake this task, during the analysis phase of the SDC, and would produce a 'controls specification' at the same time that the development team issue the functional specification.

4.   SYSTEM COMPONENTS

A component of a computing system may be defined as a part over which we seek to exert control. The components may be identified under each of the headings which we have used to describe the computing system controls, namely:

(1) system management;
(2) application management;
(3) transaction origination;
(4) data entry;
(5) data communications;
(6) computer processing;
(7) data storage and retrieval;
(8) output processing.

A list of the system components, under each of these headings, is shown in **Table 25**.

5.   THREATS

We have already briefly discussed threats, to a company's resources, in chapter 1, **7.**, above. This section concentrates specifically on threats to the

Table 25 The components of an application computing system

(1) SYSTEM MANAGEMENT
1. System manager.
2. System management manual.
3. Operations manual.
4. Data base administrator.

(2) APPLICATION MANAGEMENT.
5. Application manager/group.
6. Data administrator.
7. Functional specification.
8. Construction guide.
9. Data structure guide.
10. User guide.
11. Procedure manuals.

(3) TRANSACTION ORIGINATION
12. Raw input.
13. Input forms.
14. Negotiable instruments.
15. 'Audit' trail.

(4) DATA ENTRY
16. User IDs.
17. Passwords.
18. Access profiles.
19. Input devices.
20. Input personnel.

(5) DATA COMMUNICATIONS
21. Circuits.
22. Equipment.
23. Network.
24. Personnel.

(6) COMPUTER PROCESSING
25. Communications processor.
26. Central processor.
27. System console.
28. Electrical supply.
29. Safety equipment.
30. Air conditioning.
31. Data centre.
32. Operators.
33. Operating system.
34. Application programs.
35. Data base management software.
36. Data base operating standards.
37. Data dictionary.

(7) DATA STORAGE AND RETRIEVAL
38. Storage devices.
39. Data files.
40. Media library.

(8) OUTPUT PROCESSING
41. Output devices.
42. Computer stationary.
43. Output personnel.
44. Interfaces.
45. Hard copy.

components in a computing system and, in this context, a threat may be defined as an adverse occurrence which causes the loss or corruption of, or destruction to, the system components.

A list of the potential threats to the computing system components is given in **Table 26**.

6. RISK AND EXPOSURE MATRICES

The next five sections describe a practical example, of the use of the audit methodology, for building the controls in an application computing system. The system, in this instance, was intended to monitor the movement of personnel working in the offshore North Sea oil industry environment and is referred to as the personnel-on-board (POB) system. The principal objective, of the system was to provide, both onshore and offshore, a continuously available record of personnel on board offshore installations that was accurate and up-to-date. This would assist the company in meeting its legal requirement of maintaining a defined minimum amount of information about all offshore personnel as well as improving on emergency response and security.

The system design is based upon the use of a simple and accurate data capture device, ie a bar code reader attached to a terminal, to record actual arrivals on, and departures from, installations. The transaction entry is carried out by reading a unique bar coded number on the rear side of an offshore identity card which all persons travelling offshore were obliged to carry. This information is transmitted to the shore by the offshore installation microwave link-up and the shore/offshore troposcatter system and is received at the company offices and processed by a dedicated mini-computer.

The main processes, performed by the system, are:

(1) reference information maintenance,
(2) person's arrival/departure recording and reporting,
(3) POB reporting,
(4) arrivals/departures log reporting,
(5) personal details reporting,
(6) exception reporting and entry of corrections.

The first steps—steps 1-5—in the application system controls design are to construct the risk and exposure matrices in order to select the system component controls. The technique of constructing a risk matrix, and from this an exposure matrix, in the selection and evaluation of system develop-

Table 26   Types of threats

(A) ACTS OF GOD
1. Fire.
2. Flood.
3. Act of war.
4. Other catastrophe.

(B) HARDWARE AND PROGRAM FAILURES
5. Computer outage.
6. File unit damages disk track.
7. Tape unit damages part of tape.
8. Disk, or other volume, unreadable.
9. Hardware/software error damages file.
10. Data transmission error not detected.
11. Card (or other input) chewed up by machine.
12. Error in application program damages record.

(C) HUMAN CARELESSNESS
13. Keypunch error.
14. Terminal operator input error.
15. Computer operator error.
16. Wrong volume mounted and updated.
17. Wrong version of program used.
18. Accident during program testing.
19. Mislaid tape or disk.
20. Physical damage to tape or disk.

(D) MALICIOUS DAMAGE
21. Looting.
22. Violent sabotage.
23. Non-violent sabotage (tape erasure).
24. Malicious computer operator.
25. Malicious programmer.
26. Malicious tape librarian.
27. Malicious terminal operator.
28. Malicious user.
29. Playful malignancy.

(E) CRIME
30. Embezzlement.
31. Industrial espionage.
32. Employee selling comercial secrets.
33. Employee selling data for mailing lists.
34. Data bank information used for bribary or extortion.

(F) INVASION OF PRIVACY
35. Casual curiosity.
36. Looking up data of competitor.
37. Obtaining personnel information.
38. Accidental revealing of private information.
39. Malicious invasion of privacy.

ment controls, has been demonstrated in the previous chapter. The process of designing the matrices for the application computing system controls selection is exactly the same. In this case, the system components are shown on the vertical column and the potential threats to those components along the horizontal axis to produce, in the first instance, the risk matrix.

In constructing the risk matrix, a review is made each of the components listed in **4.**, above, to see which are relevant for the particular system under development and these are entered on the vertical axis. The same procedure is followed for the potential threats described in **5.** and a short list is identified which is inserted along the horizontal axis. The risk matrix is then completed by associating each of the individual system components with each of the relevant threats, to those components, under the headings:

$$L = \text{loss},$$
$$D = \text{destruction},$$
$$C = \text{corruption}.$$

The risk matrix should then appear as in **Figure 59**.

The risk matrix is now converted into an exposure matrix. This is achieved in two steps. The first step is to insert, into the column for the component values, an assessment of the value of each component to the enterprise. Following this, a probability value of the threats occurring is inserted into the small boxes, in each component/threat area, and the exposure is evaluated as the product of component value and probability of loss or destruction. The final exposure matrix then appears as in **Figure 60**.

These matrices have been shown in simplified form in order that the principles of the methodology are not obscured by the details of the process. In practice, the matrices should be set up using one of the many spread sheet packages that are available, as we have suggested in the previous chapter. If a blank master format is set up, using the system components and threats that we have described earlier in this chapter, the appropriate values may then be entered, into the blank master, for each particular system with which the auditor is concerned. Iterations may then be performed as often as desired in order to obtain a 'feel' for the criticality of the system and the sensitivity of its components.

The assessment of probabilities is recognised as a subjective process and is, therefore, open to a wide degree of interpretation. However, the whole exercise is an iterative process and made considerably easier by electronic spread sheet capabilities. If the initial matrix is set up as described above, refinements can be made to component values and to probabilities by simply inserting the new assessments and recalculating the entire matrix in one operation. The values, which emerge indicate the major exposures, for the system under development, and to which we should pay particular attention in designing the system controls.

We have already observed that one of the roles of the computing auditor is to ensure that critical systems are built with an adequate controls framework. Further, we have commented that control should be achieved at a reasonable cost, to the enterprise. It is at this stage, therefore, that we need to assess the criticality of the system to decide what controls, we should recommend be incorporated into the final product of the system development process.

The POB system is representative of those types of systems where the value of the data to the enterprise is difficult to evaluate with precision. Thus, the auditor needs to carry out a number of iterations, with different values, in order to obtain a 'feel' for the vulnerability of the system. In **Figure 61**,

Figure 59 An application system risk matrix

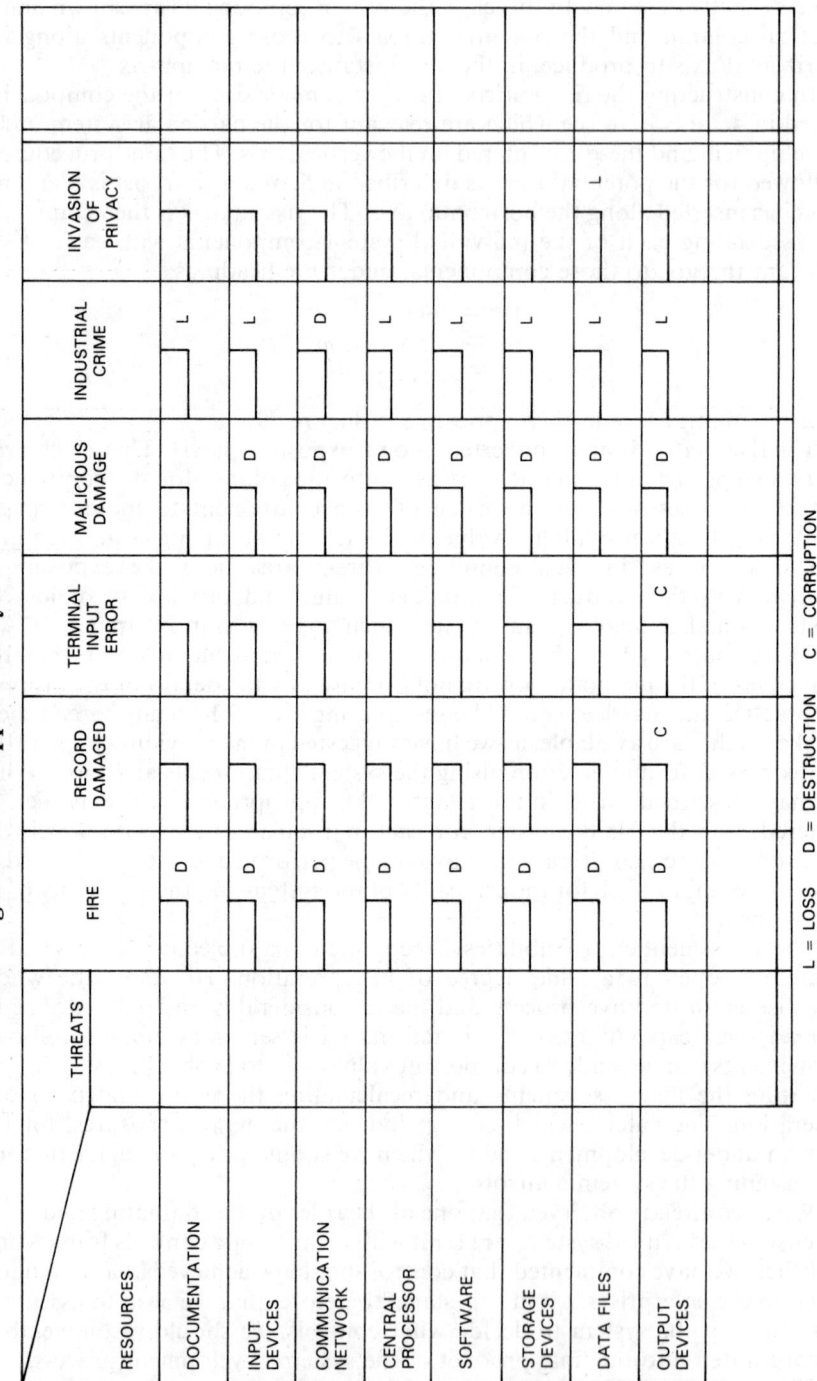

THREATS RESOURCES	FIRE	RECORD DAMAGED	TERMINAL INPUT ERROR	MALICIOUS DAMAGE	INDUSTRIAL CRIME	INVASION OF PRIVACY	
DOCUMENTATION	D				L		
INPUT DEVICES	D			D	L		
COMMUNICATION NETWORK	D			D	D		
CENTRAL PROCESSOR	D			D	L		
SOFTWARE	D			D	L		
STORAGE DEVICES	D			D	L		
DATA FILES	D	C	C	D	L	L	
OUTPUT DEVICES	D			D			

L = LOSS   D = DESTRUCTION   C = CORRUPTION

Figure 60 An application system exposure matrix

RESOURCES	VALUE £K	FIRE	RECORD DAMAGED	TERMINAL INPUT ERROR	MALICIOUS DAMAGE	INDUSTRIAL CRIME	INVASION OF PRIVACY	TOTAL EXPOSURE £K
DOCUMENTATION	100	.001 D <1				.01 L 1		1
INPUT DEVICES	100	.001 D <1			.01 D 1	.01 L 1		2
COMMUNICATION NETWORK	200	.001 D <1			.01 D 2	.01 D 1		4
CENTRAL PROCESSOR	500	.001 D <1			.01 D 5	.01 L 5		10.5
SOFTWARE	200	.001 D <1			.01 D 2	.01 L 2		4
STORAGE DEVICES	100	.001 D <1			.01 D 1	.01 L 1		2
DATA FILES	200	.001 D <1	.01 C 2	.01 C 2	.01 D 2	.01 L 2	.01 L 2	10
OUTPUT DEVICES	100	.001 D <1			.01 D 1	.01 L 1		2
	1500	0.5	2	2	14	15	2	35.5

L = LOSS   D = DESTRUCTION   C = CORRUPTION

below, we have made an assessment of the component value of the data as the annual cost of storing and maintaining that data. However, there are alternative ways in which the value of the data to the enterprise could be evaluated. One such way is to consider the value of the data if the result of its loss or destruction is to prevent the further continuation of the business enterprise. In this way, the value of the data should be assessed as the present day value (PDV) of the discounted stream of earnings that the enterprise could have received had it continued to operate. This may be evaluated as:

$$PDV = \frac{A_1}{(1+i)} + \frac{A_2}{(1+i)^2} + \frac{A_3}{(1+i)^3} \cdots \frac{A_n}{(1+i)^n}$$

where A is an amount received at the end of each future year and i is the rate if interest we consider appropriate in the situation.

We shall assume that the present day value of the future discounted stream of earnings on the assets of the enterprise is £10 million, and insert this new value into the exposure matrix. Further, let us now revise the possibility of the loss of our data, through malicious damage, to a new value of 0.01. The result, of these two changes, is to produce a totally different perspective for the system as the criticality rating becomes much higher.

Thus, in the case of the system illustrated in Figure 60, we should not attempt to produce a rigid and comprehensive framework of control, because the system could not justify the cost of the controls. An example, is a customer service maintenance system which maintains a record of all work performed, and all new parts fitted, to a customer's car. The value of this information to a third party is minimal and so the data is not likely to be lost by theft.

However, the same type of system which is used to maintain historical records of maintenance, service or operational activity, could be much more critical. An example is a system holding the records of an oil company drilling activities, in a particular location, and its assessment of the likelihood of finding crude oil or gas. This information could be of enormous value to another company in making an assessment of what it was prepared to bid in a licensing round, to obtain the rights to drill and exploit nearby concessions. Thus, the loss to the company of the data, through theft, would be a serious matter and, therefore, an effective control on security would be given a high priority in designing the system controls.

Further examples of such critical systems are:

—a system holding maintenance information on aircraft would be vital to the airline flying the aircraft, although this information would not be of much value to a third party, except, perhaps, in the instance of a sale of the aircraft—accuracy and completeness would be given high ratings in designing the system controls.
—a system holding maintenance information in a nuclear power station would be vital for ensuring the safety of the reactors as well as the local residents in the area, although this information would not be of much interest to a third party, except perhaps a government department concerned with monitoring such activity—again, accuracy and completeness would rate highly in designing the system controls.
—a system holding records on the previous treatment of patients in a

hospital would be vital in the event of treatment to patients brought in in an emergency—this information could also be of interest to a third party with malicious intent and security, privacy, accuracy and completeness would be given high ratings in designing the system controls.

We repeat that, it is important that effective control should be achieved at reasonable cost, and in designing the controls framework an assessment must be made of the criticality of the system to the enterprise. Non-critical systems may be operated with a far looser framework of controls than a system judged, by the nature of the data that it holds, to be critical.

7. SYSTEM FUNCTIONS

The next steps in the audit methodology—steps 6-8—are to identify the system functions, construct the controls flowcharts and select the essential processing controls. The system functions, in this particular case, were identified as follows.

(1) PERSONNEL ARRIVALS/DEPARTURES

This function ensures that as a person arrives on, or departs from, an installation, the event is recorded on the data base. A log report will be automatically output on the installation as this event occurs.

(2) AMEND PERSON'S SPONSORING DEPARTMENT REFERENCE INDICATOR(SDRI)

All offshore personnel require to be sponsored by a department which has a bed allocation, in order that the allocation of beds can be controlled. Should the SDRI change, on a subsequent offshore visit, or while that person is currently offshore, the system will need to be updated.

(3) REPORTS SUB-MENU

A number of reports may be produced from the system by the selection of the reports sub-menu. Some of the reports, eg end of flying POB, will be generated routinely by the platform administrator each day, while others will be produced ad hoc.

(4) LOAD CURRENT POB

In the event of a system failure which results in loss of all records for a certain time period, it will be time consuming to reconstitute the installation POB when the system is recovered. The system files will be reconstituted, there-fore, by rereading all the ID cards of persons on the installation(s).

(5) AMEND INSTALLATION CONNECTION

Several of the offshore 'installations' are mobiles which may be moved from one fixed installation to another. The system recognises this mobility by the use of the installation connection indicator.

8. CONTROLS FLOWCHARTS

Step 7, in the audit methodolgy, is the construction of the controls flowcharts for each of the system functions that have been identified in **7.**, above. An example of a controls flowchart for one of the system functions, namely the personnel arrivals/departures function, is shown in **Figure 61**.

The controls flowchart is intended to assist in the identification of the essential controls required, in each of the key control areas that we have identified previously, ie transaction origination, data entry, data communications, computer processing, data storage/retrieval, and output processing.

The flowchart is divided into five main areas, the first two of which identify the system and the particular system function, respectively. The remaining three areas are columns, the central one of which shows, in the most elementary form, a flowchart for that particular system function. A list of the symbols used for control charting is shown in **Figure 62**.

The left hand column of the controls flowchart gives a narrative description of the system function under the headings already discussed, ie transaction origination, etc. Finally, the column on the right hand side shows the essential controls, for that system function, against each of the key control areas.

9.   AUDIT PROGRAMME

The next steps in the audit methodology—steps 8-12—are the selection of the controls, the construction of the audit programme and agreement, of the programme, with the auditees. The basis used for the selection of the application system controls will be the sample lists of controls that have already been given in **Table 6**. These controls must be used intelligently for they do not provide answers for every case. The controls, that we finally selected, for the POB system, are shown in the audit programme, **Table 27.**

This audit programme forms the basis of the 'controls specification' that the auditor should issue at the same time as the functional specification.

There will be some similarities between systems and, therefore, in the types of controls which are selected. This is especially so in the areas of system management controls—which are essentially machine-determined—and data communications controls—which are determined by the company's communications network(s). However, there will also be controls which are specific for a particular system.

In the case of the POB system, the data communications controls were common to all systems operated by this company in the offshore environment and, for a particular system, will be taken as a fixed parameter of the controls framework. This was also true of the system management role since the company already operated a number of mini-computers of the same generic type that was to be used for the POB application, and there existed an established system manager for these machines.

The types of validation controls will be dependent on the sort of information being entered into the system. In a materials system, where requisitions are charged to cost centres, it will be necessary to enter an account code to ensure that a cost centre exists, when the requisition is raised. To ensure that the account code is entered correctly, the code may need to be entered twice and the two entries validated against each other. This method may also be used for the POB system with the bar-coded identity card being read twice and the two entries validated against each other. However, with the high reliability of the bar code equipment, combined with a visual check of the ID against the 'echo back' on the terminal screen of the person's ID details, this double entry was not considered to be necessary.

Figure 61   A POB controls flowchart

SYSTEM	FUNCTION(S):
PERSONNEL ON BOARD (POB)	PERSONNEL ARRIVALS/DEPARTURES

NARRATIVE	OPERATION	CONTROLS
TRANSACTION ORIGINATION For all arrivals/departures, a flight manifest list is prepared providing a X-reference for transactions to be processed. All offshore personnel must be issued with an ID card which can be read by a bar code reader.	Helicopter Manifest List ID Cards	● Retention and storage ● User procedures and manuals ● Special purpose forms ● Authorisation ● Document serial numbers ● Special purpose cards
DATA ENTRY Transactions are entered by bar code reader. **DATA COMMUNICATIONS** Transactions transmitted to central administration through the NODNET system.	HP 150	● Terminal sign - on procedures ● Physical security ● Error display ● Error correction procedures ● Communication circuits
COMPUTER PROCESSING Transactions are validated and an acknowledgement is transmitted to source for printing on terminal printer.	VALIDATE AND STORE	● Control totals ● Anticipation controls ● Field checks
DATA STORAGE/RETRIEVAL The D/Bases are updated on - line for all transactions. For a system failure, a special 'cold - start' recovery procedure is defined.	POB/OPRIS D BASE	● DB focal point ● Operating procedures ● Data dictionary ● Physical and data security ● Back - up and recovery
OUTPUT PROCESSING Output reports will be available at source and at administration. Error listings will be produced for all exceptions for follow - up by management. Transactions are listed by ID number, name, date, time and installation.	Transactions by ID Error Listing	● Output report distribution ● Output report format ● Reconciliation ● Retention period ● Correction procedures ● Responsibility for correction ● Error correction processing

Figure 62 Programming flowchart symbols

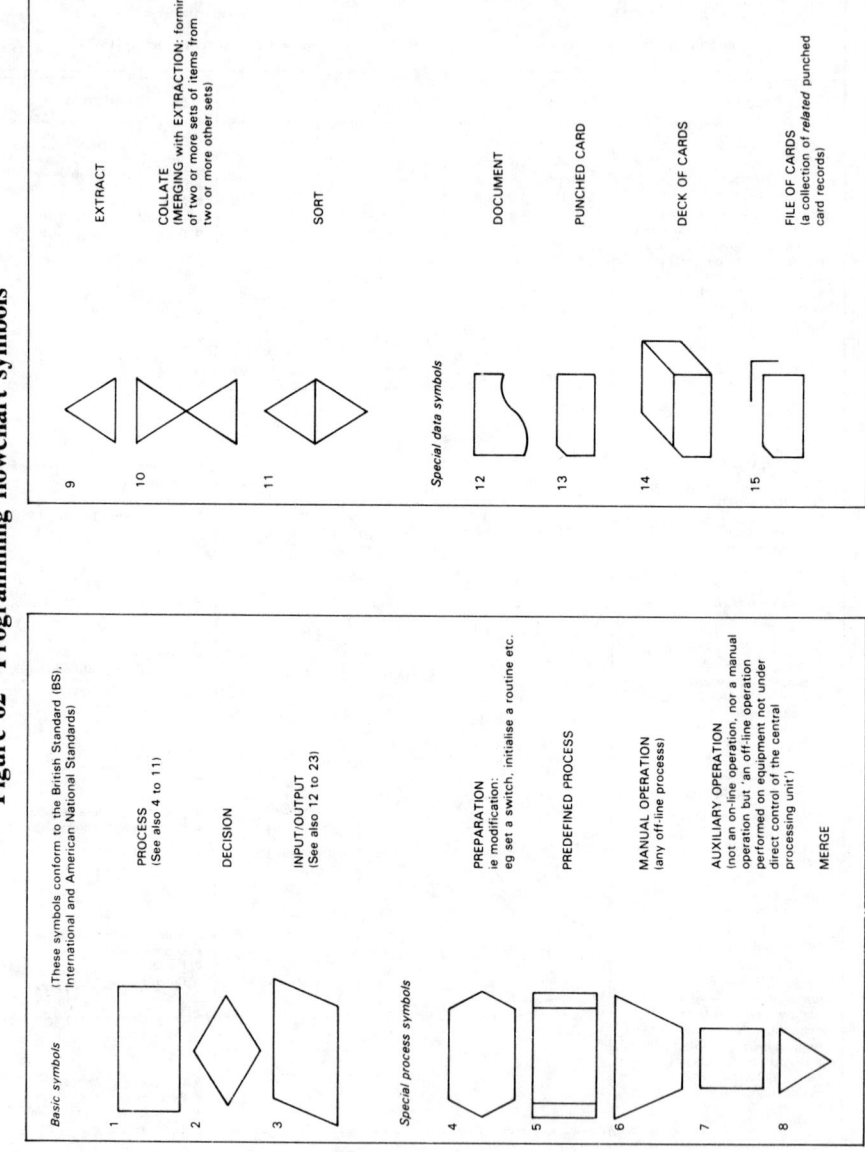

Basic symbols

(These symbols conform to the British Standard (BS), International and American National Standards)

1 PROCESS
  (See also 4 to 11)

2 DECISION

3 INPUT/OUTPUT
  (See also 12 to 23)

Special process symbols

4 PREPARATION
  ie modification:
  eg set a switch, initialise a routine etc.

5 PREDEFINED PROCESS

6 MANUAL OPERATION
  (any off-line process)

7 AUXILIARY OPERATION
  (not an on-line operation, nor a manual operation but 'an off-line operation performed on equipment not under direct control of the central processing unit')

8 MERGE

9 EXTRACT

10 COLLATE
   (MERGING with EXTRACTION: forming of two or more sets of items from two or more other sets)

11 SORT

Special data symbols

12 DOCUMENT

13 PUNCHED CARD

14 DECK OF CARDS

15 FILE OF CARDS
   (a collection of *related* punched card records)

Figure 62 Programming flowchart symbols—*continued*

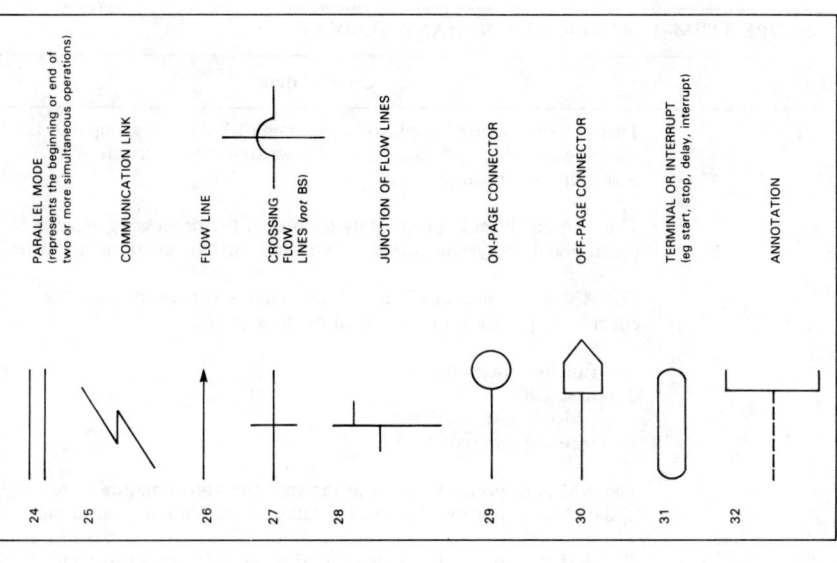

24 PARALLEL MODE (represents the beginning or end of two or more simultaneous operations)

25 COMMUNICATION LINK

26 FLOW LINE

27 CROSSING FLOW LINES (*not* BS)

28 JUNCTION OF FLOW LINES

29 ON-PAGE CONNECTOR

30 OFF-PAGE CONNECTOR

31 TERMINAL OR INTERRUPT (eg start, stop, delay, interrupt)

32 ANNOTATION

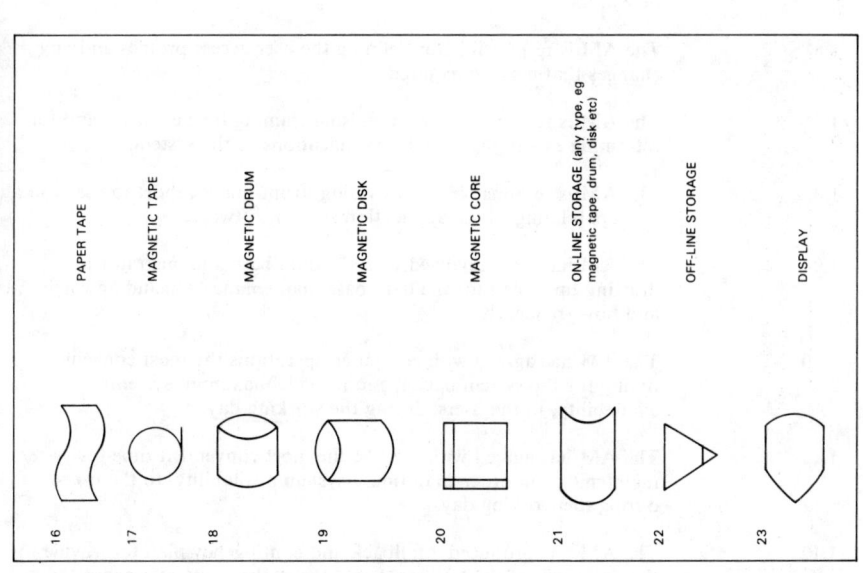

16 PAPER TAPE

17 MAGNETIC TAPE

18 MAGNETIC DRUM

19 MAGNETIC DISK

20 MAGNETIC CORE

21 ON-LINE STORAGE (any type, eg magnetic tape, drum, disk etc)

22 OFF-LINE STORAGE

23 DISPLAY

Table 27   The POB audit programme

AUDIT PROGRAMME: PERSONNEL-ON-BOARD (POB) SYSTEM

SCOPE ITEM 1: APPLICATION MANAGEMENT

Ref	Control detail
1.1	There is a recognised application manager (AM)—or group—in the user organisation and there is (are) a written job description(s) describing the position(s).
1.2	The AM has been appropriately trained in the processing aspects of the application system software and the business functions it satisfies.
1.3	The AM has copies of all the relevant manuals necessary for the effective application management of the system: —functional specification —user guide —procedure manual(s) —training manual(s)
1.4	The AM is responsible for ensuring that the above manuals are updated, are appropriate, and up-dates are circulated to all users.
1.5	The AM is responsible for defining the password structures, eg minimum of six alphanumeric characters and for issuing passwords to new users.
1.6	The AM is responsible for defining the user access profiles and any changes that may be required.
1.7	The AM is responsible for organising training for new users and for retraining existing users with modifications to the system.
1.8	The AM is responsible for providing 'front-line' support to users on all matters relating to the application system software.
1.9	The AM has been involved with the data base administrator in drawing up a plan for the data base maintenance—including when, and how frequently
1.10	The AM has agreed with computer operations the most convenient timing for the system backups to provide maximum system availability, to the users, during the working day.
1.11	The AM has agreed with the SM the most convenient time for system maintenance in order to optimise system availability, to the users, during the working day.
1.12	The AM has produced a fallback and contingency plan to provide for the operation of the business functions in the event of a complete breakdown of the computing system availability.

Table 27   The POB audit programme—*continued*

Ref: /   /

AUDIT PROGRAMME: PERSONNEL-ON-BOARD (POB) SYSTEM

SCOPE ITEM 2: TRANSACTION ORIGINATION

Ref	Control detail
2.1	There will be a user guide provided covering: —preparation of documents, —terminal input procedures, —correction procedures, —documentation flow, —documentation retention, —authorised signatories.
2.2	Source documents should preferably have pre-printed serial numbers to ensure against lost documents.
2.3	The source document number should be included as part of the transaction identification to provide a cross-reference for tracing information.
2.4	All persons who travel offshore must have a valid company identification card.

Table 27   The POB audit programme—*continued*

AUDIT PROGRAMME: PERSONNEL-ON-BOARD (POB) SYSTEM

SCOPE ITEM 3: DATA ENTRY

Ref	Control detail
3.1	Transactions to be entered into the system will have a readily identifiable transaction origin in order to provide an audit trail.
3.2	Procedures for the protection and security of passwords and user IDs will be specified in the user guide.
3.3	There will be adequate physical security at remote sites for terminals, printers and communications equipment.
3.4	There will be adequate recovery facilities and or capabilities for loss, damage, failure or destruction of key pieces of hardware.
3.5	Users will have access only to system menus which are necessary for the performance of their tasks.
3.6	There will be a procedure in the user guide covering the fallback provisions for the entering or recording of data in the event of equipment malfunctioning.
3.7	There will be automated editing of input, for example: —checking for reasonableness of input data with regard to preset criteria, —testing the data for blanks, sign, numeric or alphabetic and comparing with pre-established criteria, —checking for consistency between input fields, —checking for completeness of data.
3.8	The programs will look for duplicate entries of data, eg same ID numbers input on different installations without first a departure being recorded.
3.9	The users will not be able to override computer program edits.
3.10	There will be standing tables, set up before implementation, to validate and verify user IDs and passwords.

Table 27   The POB audit programme—*continued*

AUDIT PROGRAMME: PERSONNEL-ON-BOARD (POB) SYSTEM

SCOPE ITEM 4: DATA COMMUNICATIONS CONTROLS

Ref	Control detail
4.1	There are adequate telecommunications facilities available to all users, especially offshore, to provide a minimum acceptable service level requirement.
4.2	There are suitable backup telecommunications facilities to provide a rapid recovery in the event of telecommunications failure.
4.3	There are appropriate fallback and contingency plans to continue with the business processes in the event of equipment failure.

Table 27   The POB audit programme—*continued*

AUDIT PROGRAMME: PERSONNEL-ON-BOARD (POB) SYSTEM

SCOPE ITEM 5: COMPUTER PROCESSING CONTROLS

Ref	Control detail
5.1	The movement between the opening day POB count and closing day POB count will be reconciled with arrivals/departures during the day.
5.2	A log will be maintained of all unscheduled or unusual interventions with the system.
5.3	There will be a formal procedure established for changing the standing tables of user IDs and passwords.
5.4	There will be a trouble log for reporting on system hardware/software faults.
5.5	The users will be forced directly into the application software, upon logging-on, and will not be able to interact directly with the operating system.
5.6	The system utility commands will be restricted to the use of the SM and some operations staff.
5.7	Procedures will be defined in the user guide for the correction of errors discovered during processing.
5.8	There will be a focal point in the user organisation who has responsibility for checking the exception reports and the correction of all errors discovered.

Table 27   The POB audit programme—*continued*

AUDIT PROGRAMME: PERSONNEL-ON-BOARD (POB) SYSTEM

SCOPE ITEM 6: DATA STORAGE AND RETRIEVAL CONTROLS

Ref	Control detail
6.1	There will be a written statement of who owns the data bases, and the information therein, as well as the authority associated with the rights of ownership.
6.2	There will be a written procedure for the backup and recovery of the data base in the event of total or partial destruction which has been agreed with the application manager.
6.3	The backup and recovery procedures for the data base will be tested before implementation.
6.4	The contents of the data base, definition of entities and attributes and entity interrelationships will be described in the construction and data structure guides.
6.5	The live data base will be maintained separate from any data base used for testing.
6.6	There will be specific software controls to limit users' access capabilities to the data base, such as: —locking out users from parts of the data base that are not authorised, —restricting, changing and updating files to certain users.
6.7	The access of persons to the data base will be determined strictly on a 'need to' basis.
6.8	There will be a user focal point who will be responsible for: —the contents, —the privacy of the data, —the organisation, —the integrity, of the data base.
6.9	There will be a single focal point who has the responsibility for the development and maintenance of the data dictionary.
6.10	All permanent changes that are made to the structure or use of any data item must be recorded in the data dictionary.

Table 27   The POB audit programme—*continued*
Ref: /   /   Page 7 of 7

AUDIT PROGRAMME: PERSONNEL-ON-BOARD (POB) SYSTEM

SCOPE ITEM 7: OUTPUT CONTROLS

Ref	Control detail
7.1	The final daily output control totals, at the end of flying, will be reconciled before printing the 'end-of-day' report.
7.2	System ouput logs will be maintained in order to provide an audit trail.
7.3	There will be a distribution list drawn up for all output reports.
7.4	The retention period for the output reports will be defined.
7.5	The procedure for disposing of expired hard copy reports will be specified.

10.   AUDIT REVIEW AND REPORTING

The final steps in the audit methodology—steps 13-18—are the review of the controls, which have been recognised as desirable, by both the user and project manager, and the reporting of the auditor's opinion on the adequacy of the controls framework. The review process is to ensure that the controls, which have been set out in the controls specification, are actually designed into the system during the system construction and implementation stages of the systems development cycle.

The review process—steps 13 and 14—is most effectively carried out by using the audit programme, as a checklist of controls that the auditor can discuss with the user and the project manager. The format of this checklist is the same as that shown for the audit programme, in chapter 10, and consists of three columns, one containing the control reference, the second the control detail and the third the audit observation, or auditee comment.

The final stage—steps 15-18—is the reporting on the control details. This is carried out at two levels, as we have already described in chapter 9, **8.,** above, namely to:

(1) line management on the application system control details,
(2) internal audit committee on the adequacy of the controls details.

The manner of reporting at both these levels is illustrated in the examples which follow.

(1) TO THE LINE MANAGEMENT DIRECTLY INVOLVED WITH THE PROJECT.

AUDIT MEMORANDUM

FROM : Auditor   TEL

TO : Messrs Jones,   DATE
           Smith,
           etc

AUDIT REVIEW NO.1

INTERNAL AUDIT —/—/—

PERSONNEL-ON-BOARD(POB) SYSTEM

In January, 19—, internal audit issued a POB controls specification which showed the controls considered essential in order to:

(1) ensure the accuracy and completeness of data files and reports;
(2) prevent undetected errors and omissions;
(3) ensure the continuing reliability of data processing results.

This controls specification was produced as a joint effort between the senior user representative, the project manager and internal audit. Further to the issue of the specification, the controls have been translated into an audit checklist for review of progress on implementing the control details.

A review has now been undertaken by internal audit, with the principal user representative and the project manager, on the current status with regard to each of the controls details, previously agreed. The results of this review, are attached to this note [see pp 258–260].

Although a number of action items still remain to be progressed, we are able to report that the essential controls for the system have now been, or are in process of being, established. Before a final report is issued to the internal audit committee, there will be a follow-up review of progress against outstanding actions.

However, at this point we are able to report that the POB system is being implemented with a sound framework of application controls to achieve the system objectives.

ATTACHMENT

(2) TO THE INTERNAL AUDIT COMMITTEE

AUDIT MEMORANDUM

FROM : Auditor   TEL

TO : Messrs Lyon,   DATE
           Foxe,
           etc

INTERNAL AUDIT —/—/—

PERSONNEL-ON-BOARD(POB) SYSTEM

Attachment to Audit Memorandum 1

Ref: / /

AUDIT PROGRAMME: PERSONNEL-ON-BOARD (POB) SYSTEM

SCOPE ITEM 1: APPLICATION MANAGEMENT

Ref	Control detail	Audit observation/auditee comment
1.1	There is a recognised application manager (AM)—or group—in the user organisation and there is (are) a written job description(s) describing the position.	There is a recognised application manager in the user organisation who is a member of the project group. A job description for this position will be completed by the time of system handover. *ACTION = project manager/application manager*
1.2	The AM has been appropriately trained in the processing aspects of the application system software and the business functions it satisfies.	The application manager has been a member of the project group since the beginning of the project and is fully aware of the system functionality and computer processing.
1.3	The AM has copies of all the relevant manuals necessary for the effective application management of the system: — function specification — user guide — procedure manual(s) — training manual(s).	The AM has copies of the functional specification and a user guide, procedures manual and training manual are currently being developed. *ACTION = project manager/application manager*
1.4	The AM is responsible for ensuring that the system manuals are updated, as appropriate, and updates are circulated to all users.	The application manager acknowledges responsibility for the maintenance of the system manuals. *ACTION = application manager*

Attachment to Audit Memorandum 1—*continued*

Ref	Control detail	Audit observation/auditee comment
1.5	The AM is responsible for defining the password structures, eg minimum of six alphanumeric characters and for issuing passwords to new users.	A password application form has been circulated by the application manager and the users have been advised that passwords of less than six alphanumeric characters will not be accepted. *ACTION = application manager*
1.6	The AM is responsible for defining the user access profiles and any changes that may be required.	The access profiles that will be granted to different classes of users are currently being set up in the system.
1.7	The AM is responsible for organising training for new users and for retraining existing users with modifications to the system.	Training is being planned by the AM and will be carried out in the working environment using the training manual as a reference guide. *ACTION = application manager*
1.8	The AM is responsible for providing 'front-line' support to users on all matters relating to the application system software.	The users will be advised that all faults should, in the first instance, be reported to the AM who will decide the most appropriate course of action. *ACTION = application manager*
1.9	The AM has been involved with the data base administrator in drawing up a plan for the data base maintenance—including when, and how frequently.	The schedule of data base maintenance will be planned, further to a period of practical operating experience, when there is a clearer appreciation of the volume of transactions to be handled by the system. *ACTION = application manager*

Attachment to Audit Memorandum 1—*continued*

Ref: /   /

AUDIT PROGRAMME: PERSONNEL-ON-BOARD (POB) SYSTEM

SCOPE ITEM 1: SYSTEM MANAGEMENT AND SUPERVISION CONTROLS

Ref	Control detail	Audit observation/auditee comment
1.10	The AM has agreed with computer operations the most convenient timing for the system backups to provide maximum system availability during the working day.	The system backup has been planned for 5.30 am which is before the current daily offshore flying begins and after the previous days flying has ended.
1.11	The AM has agreed with the SM the most convenient time for system maintenance in order to optimise system availability, to the users, during the working day.	The data base will be transferred to the back-up machine, when maintenance is required on the POB processor, so that the system will be available 7 days/week to the users.
1.12	The AM has produced a fallback and contingency plan to provide for the operation of the business functions in the event of a complete breakdown of the computing system availability.	In the event of a system 'crash' the record of personnel arrivals/departures will be maintained manually until the system returns to operational use. The procedures for dealing with this situation will be described in the procedure manual. *ACTION = application manager*

Internal audit's involvement in the development and implementation if the POB system is an on-going one with the objective of providing reasonable assurance to management that the system will be implemented with adequate built-in controls.

In January 19—, we issued a 'controls specification'. This specification was intended to form the basis for designing the system controls, at the pre-implementation stage of the project.

Further to the successful completion of a pilot trial, we reviewed the current status with regard to each of the controls details previously agreed. The results of this review were issued to both the members of the steering committee and the project group, as a separate audit note.

Although several action items still remain to be progressed, we are able to report that the essential controls, for the system have been, or are in process of being, established. Thus, we are currently of the opinion that the POB system is being implemented with a sound framework of application controls to achieve the system objectives.

References

1 'EDPACS' March 1984.
2 Martin J *Security, Accuracy, and Privacy in Computer Systems* (1973) Prentice-Hall Inc.
3 Wong K K, Farquhar W *Computer Related Fraud Casebook* (1983 and 1986) BIS Applied Systems.

12   Post-implementation review of a computing system

This chapter describes the conduct of a post-implementation review (PIR) which was carried out some six months after the implementation of a major materials management system. The objective of the following sections of the chapter is to set out the controls which were incorporated into the audit programme for the PIR, and to give some examples of the types of control weaknesses that the auditors discovered during their investigations. This should serve to alert the internal auditor, who is required to undertake this type of work to the control areas upon which he should focus his attention.

The purpose of the PIR is to determine whether the stated objectives and functional requirements of the system have been satisfied and whether the system is being operated effectively and efficiently. In this case, it was agreed that the audit would examine eight control areas, namely:

(1) business objectives and functional requirements;
(2) operational performance;
(3) maintenance;
(4) security;
(5) back-up/recovery and fallback;
(6) system interfaces;
(7) developments/enhancements;
(8) user satisfaction.

The PIR may be carried out either by the quality assurance function or by internal audit. However, there is a preference for internal audit since the review cannot then be seen as an 'in-house' appraisal by the DP function.

An audit methodology is described for the conduct of a PIR and this is illustrated in flowchart form in 2., below. The use of the interview matrix is demonstrated as well as the derivation of the interviewee-specific audit questionnaire from the interview matrix.

The remaining sections of this chapter are devoted to the different parts of the audit programme that was constructed for this audit and the particular controls that the auditors examined in each of the control areas. Although the controls are illustrated against the background of the materials system, described in 1., they should be regarded as equally appropriate for other application computing systems.

The final section discusses the way the internal auditor may report his findings, and conclusions, on the application system controls framework to the:

(1) local line management,
(2) internal audit committee.

1. PURPOSE AND BACKGROUND

The purpose of the post-implementation review (PIR) is to determine whether the stated objectives and functional requirements of the system have been satisfied and whether the system is being operated effectively and efficiently. The PIR will usually be carried out between six months to one year after the system has been installed, so that some operational experience has been acquired, and the users have had the chance to become familiar with, practical operation of the system.

The objectives and scope for the PIR will be agreed with both the user group and the project group or application support group. Where necessary a detailed examination of specific areas may be recommended.

It is sometimes suggested that the PIR should also include an assessment of the development methods, including quality of the schedule planning and control, effectiveness of project organisation, procedures and techniques used. However, this is better accomplished as part of the audit involvement, in selecting and evaluating the project development controls, as discussed in chapter 10. Further, the elapsed period, of six months to one year, means that many of the lessons which have been learned for systems development may have been lost or forgotten.

It is possible to undertake a PIR of the system development process immediately following implementation of the system. This has the advantage that the project group will still be in existence and, therefore, the team members should be still available for discussion. However, it has the disadvantage that any review undertaken, so soon after implementation, will lack any clear perspective of the success, or quality, of the system in operation.

The PIR may be carried out either by the quality assurance function or by internal audit. However, there is a preference for internal audit since the review cannot then be seen as an 'in-house' appraisal, by the DP function, and the findings and recommendations will have more force when brought to the attention of the internal audit committee. If internal audit do carry out the PIR, it is better that it should be undertaken by an auditor(s) other than those who were involved in the pre-implementation stage of the project. It is difficult to be totally objective in reviewing and evaluating one's own work.

In describing the methodolgy of a typical PIR in the following chapter an example is used, drawn from practical experience, of the implementation of a major materials control system in a large corporate environment. The new on-line, interactive system was designed to replace an older generation system, based essentially on monthly batch processing, and was developed by the company central materials purchasing office—which also provided a materials consultancy service—for use by other affiliated companies.

It had become clear in the mid-1970s that the current generation of materials systems would not be able to support the materials business requirements into the eighties and beyond. There was always a substantial lag between the occurrence of events and the reporting of those events in the monthly batch processing system. It was felt that a more immediate availability of current information was required, to support the decision making processes in the materials business, and an on-line, real time, data base system was seen as providing the answer.

In broad terms, the centrally developed system comprised an on-line data entry, up-dating and enquiry capability, combined with batch processing, which together supported the following business functions:

(1) requisition administration,
(2) purchasing,
(3) warehouse management,
(4) finance,
(5) standards administration.

There was also a number of local developments, which included four interfaces with other systems:

(1) a maintenance information system link—for transferring information on materials codes and materials ordered and consumed for maintenance on the equipment on the installations,
(2) a standards link—to ensure that a common standard existed across the UK locations for materials codes and buying descriptions,
(3) an accounts payable link—to transfer invoice header information to the materials system to enable invoices to be matched and monitored until final payment,
(4) a finance link—to transfer weekly account codes to the materials system against which requisitions/purchases had to be recorded and a monthly transfer of information to the general ledger on end-of-month stock values.

The system supported a business function handling over £150 million of materials required both on- and offshore to sustain operations. There were four materials warehouses on-shore—shown in **Figure 63**—which were linked directly to the offices dealing with central administration and these together supported nine fixed platforms offshore. Some of these maintained 'satellite' stores of materials that were needed upon immediate demand. The business processes that were supported, at each of the locations, are shown in **Table 28**.

The application was to be run on a mini-computer, with 8 Mb of main memory, which supported the following equipment:

6	*	404 Mb disc drives,
1	*	120 Mb disc drive (spool only),
1	*	6250 bpi tape drive (shared),
1	*	1600 bpi tape drive,
1	*	laser printer,
1	*	matrix printer,
2	*	system consoles,
14	*	remote spooled printers,
98	*	connected VDUs.

The local users ie locations B, C, D, and E, were all linked up by T-boxes—an intelligent, and programmable, communications device—to the local area network (LAN) at location A, where the 'materials' processor was maintained and operated. Similarly, all local users at location A, were linked to the processor through a T-box, attached to the LAN, so that the configuration, shown on the left in **Figure 64**, was equally applicable to all onshore users. The LAN, at location A, was also connected, by high speed data links,

Figure 63   The company locations

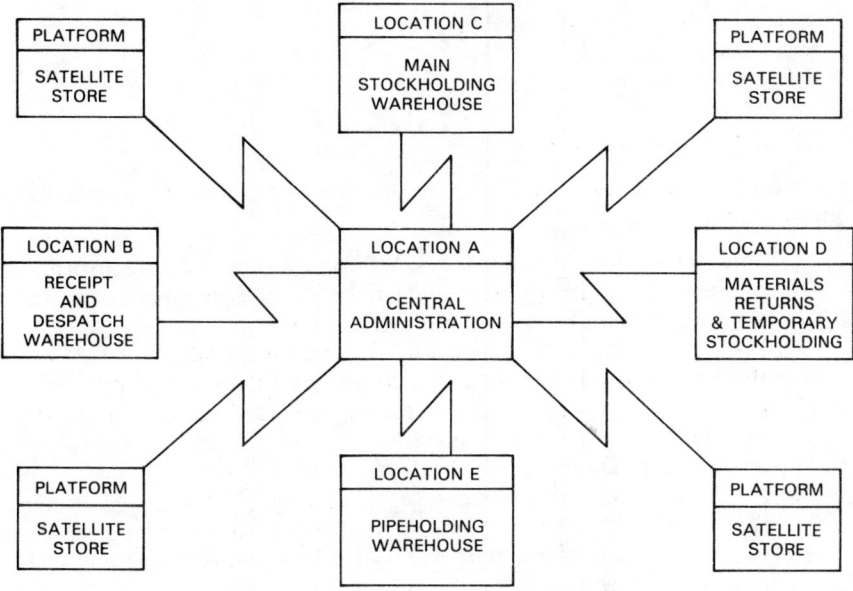

NB THERE ARE 9 FIXED PLATFORMS IN THE NORTH SEA

to other company LAN's in the UK so that data eg materials amounting information, could be transferred from one location to another.

The address, in hexadecimal, which was programmed into the T-box—each could be programmed with two addresses designated as O and I—identifies a specific 'gateway' through which messages could pass and return. Since all messages sent by the terminal device were preceded by the 'gateway' address, they would always be identified by the processor as originating from a device in a specific location. Further, since all messages destined for a specific 'gateway' would only be preceded by the unique address of that 'gateway', they would only be received by the terminal device, residing at that particular location. In exactly the same way, a letter with a unique address would—one hopes—only be delivered to a unique number, in a unique street, in a unique town, etc.

The remote users, ie the offshore users, were linked to the LAN, at location A, by the offshore microwave communication links and a shore to offshore troposcatter link. These links—shown as the zig-zag line in **Figure 64**—connecting MODEM A and MODEM B are totally transparent to the users. The medium of communication simply acts as a carrier for the data transmission and the choice of medium depends upon what is most expedient in the situation.

The offshore terminal devices—VDU's, printers, plotters—were linked to a 16-channel, time-division multiplexor (T-MUX) which, in turn, was linked to a 9·6 Kbits/sec modulator/demodulator device (MODEM) which transmits and receives the data sent over the carrier medium between shore and offshore.

Table 28 The business processes by location

	Call-Off	Requisition/ EDP Supplement	"Sendit"	Purchasing	Receipt	Inspection	Invoicing	Storage	Issue	Despatch
Location A	*	*	—	*	(*)	—	*	(*)	(*)	—
Location C	*	—	—	—	*	*	—	*	*	*
Location B	*	—	—	—	*	*	—	(*)	*	*
Location D	*	—	—	—	*	*	—	*	*	*
Location E	*	—	—	—	*	*	—	*	*	*
Platforms	*	*	*	—	*	—	—	*	*	(*)

NB: (*) not a main function

Figure 64 The communications network

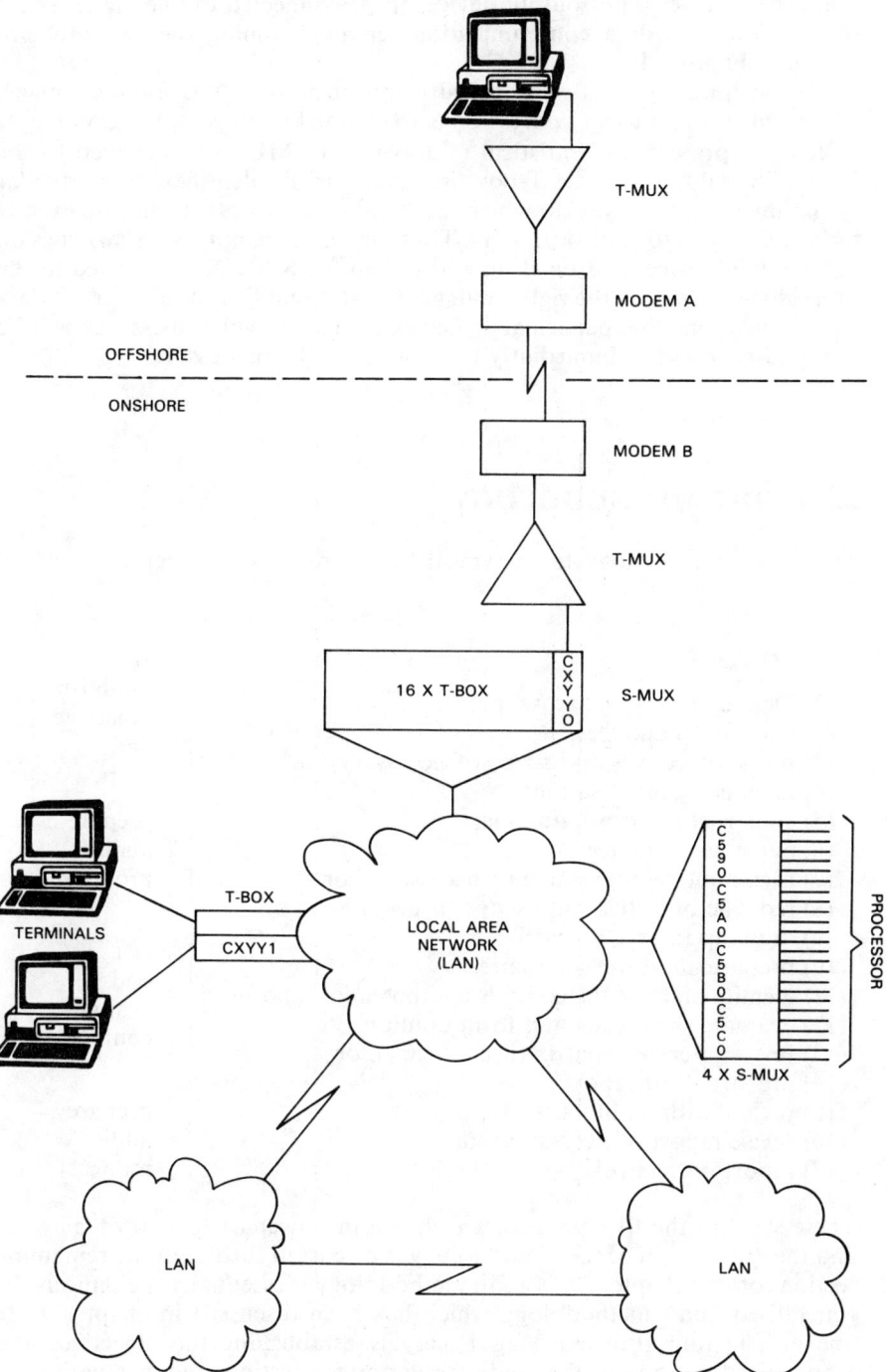

This arrangement, repeated for all the offshore installations, enables a number of slower input/output devices to be connected to one higher speed offshore/onshore data communications channel joining the two modems shown in **Figure 64**.

The onshore modems were linked to an onshore T-MUX (16 channels) which fed through to an address on a 16 channel intelligent, programmable T-Box—in principle, a statistical multiplexor (S-MUX)—connected to the LAN. The address on the T-box, in hexadecimal, identifies the particular communication 'gateway' to which the terminal device is attached; in exactly the same way as for the local users. Thus, when the remote users switches on his terminal device, and types an address on the S-MUXs connected to the processor—shown on the right in **Figure 64**—to establish contact for the data communications, his particular 'gateway', through which messages will be sent and returned, is immediatly recognised by the processor.

2. AUDIT METHODOLOGY

The audit methodology for a typical PIR consists of 17 steps, as set out below.

STEP TASK	STAGE
(1) Define objectives and scope;	establish objectives and scope
(2) agree with auditees;	1
(3) revise objectives and scope (if necessary); or	
(4) detailed familiarisation;	
(5) construct audit programme;	prepare audit programme
(6) agree with auditee(s);	2
(7) revise audit programme (if necessary); or	
(8) redefine objectives and scope (if necessary); or	
(9) draw up interview matrix;	test and evaluate controls
(10) prepare audit questionnaires;	3
(11) identify and test the controls and potential exposures;	
(12) evaluate the results and form opinion;	
(13) revise interview matrix (if necessary); or	
(14) prepare draft report;	prepare audit report
(15) review with auditees;	4
(16) revise report (if necessary); or	
(17) report on controls.	

These steps in the PIR process, are shown in flowchart form, in **Figure 65**, and the application of the methodology is discussed further in the remaining sections of this chapter. This audit methodology is essentially the same as the generalised audit methodology which has been discussed in chapter 9, **2.**, above. The four principal stages, namely establishing the objectives and scope, preparation of the audit programme, testing and evaluation of controls and preparation of the audit report, are all iterative processes, which may be repeated a number of times during the course of the audit.

Figure 65 An audit methodology for a post-implemented review (PIR)

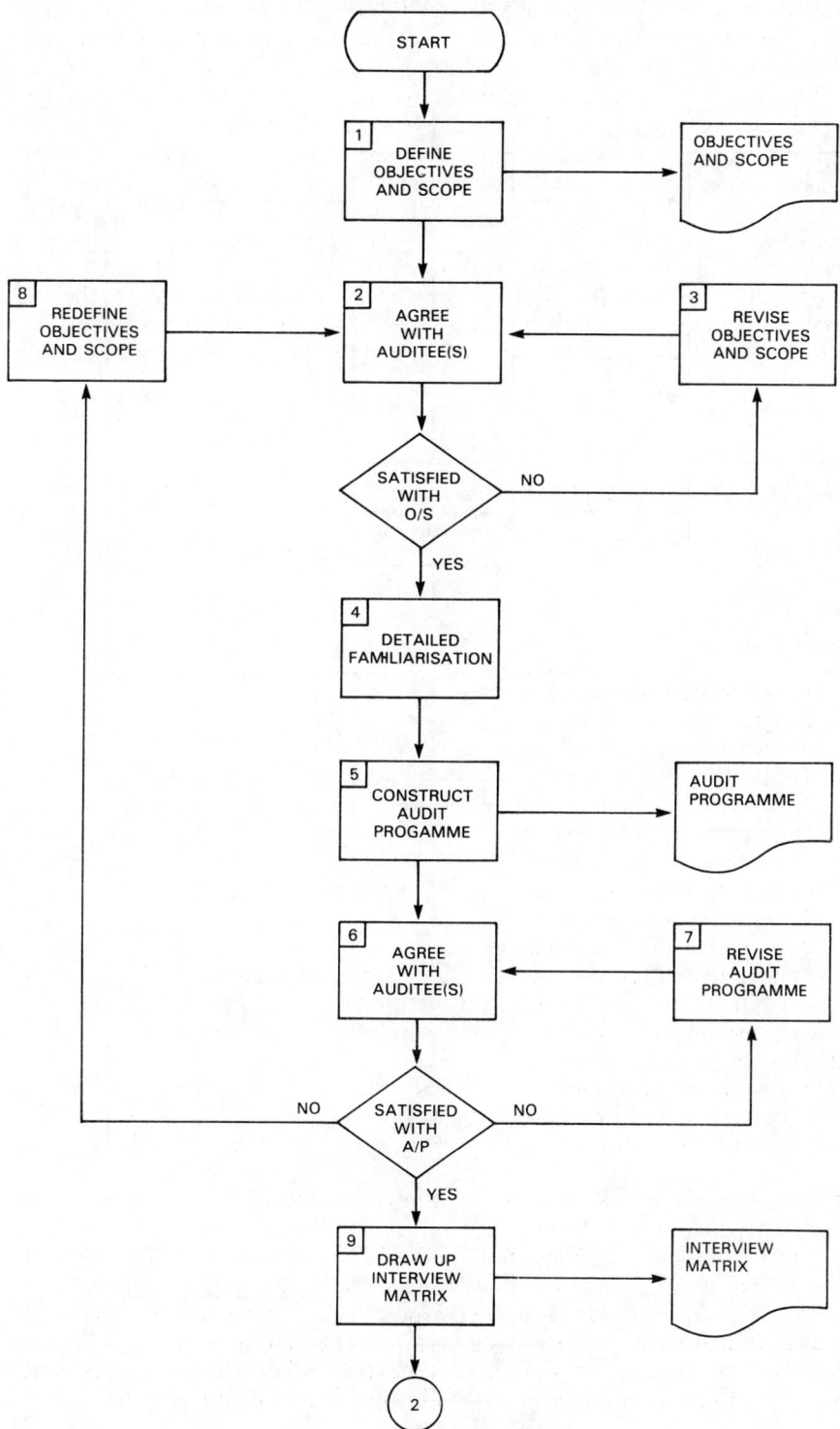

Figure 65   An audit methodology for a post-implementation review (PIR)—*continued*

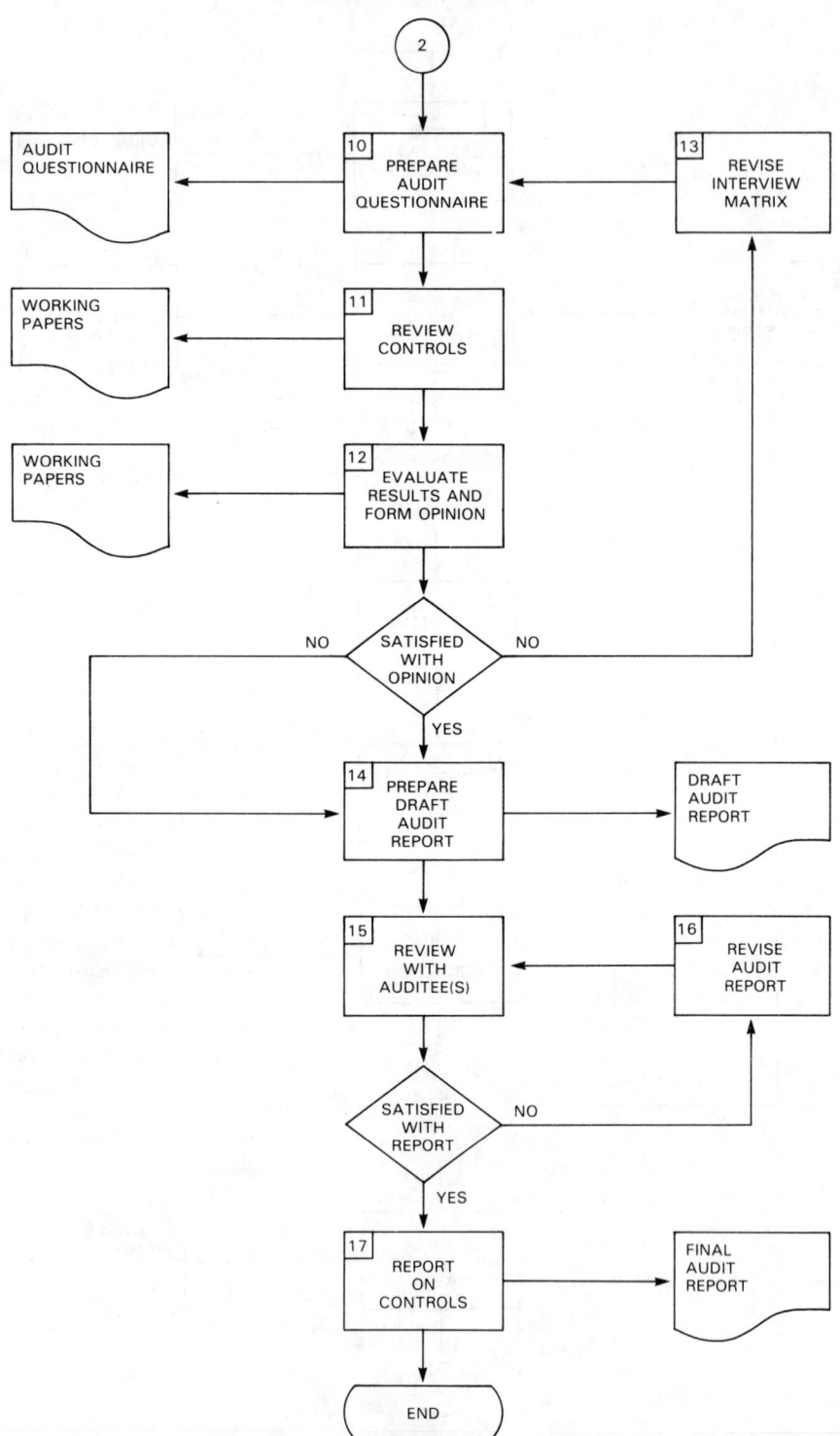

The size of the system, with the large number of geographically dispersed users, required that a considerable amount of familiarisation was necessary before the objectives and scope could be refined into the audit programme. The audit programme, was then used to develop the interview matrix shown in **Figure 66**.

The construction of an interview matrix linked to the audit programme was, in this case, essential because of the large number of different user groups, eg purchasing, warehousing, invoicing, manifesting, expediting, etc who were widely geographically dispersed, as shown previously in **Figure 63**. The interview matrix was then used to draw up audit questionnaires, in the format that we have already demonstrated in **Figure 49**, in chapter 9, and shown again in **Table 29**.

There were 64 interviews carried out in total, with different parties involved in some way with the system, which included the users, computer operations, communications, application support, system management, finance, etc It was estimated that there were more than 150 persons who were involved either directly, as users of the system or supporting the system or, indirectly, as recipients of information from the system.

The interviewees enabled the auditors not only to obtain factual information on the system performance, but also to form an opinion as to whether the system, at management level, was producing the right sort of information for the materials business to be properly managed and controlled.

3. OBJECTIVES AND SCOPE

The objectives and scope for a PIR should be defined as clearly as possible, before the work actually commences, although they may be refined after the initial fieldwork and familiarisation has begun. The purpose of the review, which has already been discussed in **1.**, above, is to assess to what extent the system has been successful in satisfying the business objectives for which it was implemented, and to evaluate its effectiveness and the efficiency of operation. Thus, the objectives for the audit should contain a clear reference to both of these principal aims. The scope items should include operational performance, user satisfaction, and any other areas considered important for the specific system being reviewed.

The objectives and scope, for the PIR, must be clearly understood, and also agreed, by the user organisation and the DP department, who may be both operating and supporting the system. This ensures that at a later stage of the study, there is no disagreement on what was, and what was not, included in the audit. This is especially important at reporting time, when the audit report should give a statement of opinion on the audit objectives.

The objectives and scope which were drawn up for the PIR of the materials control system are given in summarised form in the final audit report for this audit, which is shown in **12.**, below. However, they are repeated again in more detail in **Table 30**.

Figure 66 Part of the interview matrix for a PIR of a materials system

AUDIT REF --/--/--	INTERVIEW MATRIX										PREPARED BY:		DATE: --/--/--	
AUDIT TITLE: POST-IMPLEMENTATION REVIEW OF A MATERIALS SYSTEM											REVIEWED BY:		DATE: --/--/--	

INTERVIEWER \ AUDIT PROGRAMME REFERENCE	1.1	1.2		2.1	2.2	2.3	2.4	2.5	2.6	2.7	2.8	2.9	2.10	2.11	2.12
HEAD OF SUPPLY	X	X													
SENIOR BUYER						X				X	X				
STOCK ANALYST						X				X	X				
EXPEDITER						X				X	X				
SYSTEMS AND METHODS	X	X		X	X		X	X	X	X	X	X	X		X
WAREHOUSE FOREMAN															
MATERIALS RECEIVER						X				X	X				
MATERIALS DISPATCHER						X				X	X				
STOCK CHECKER															
INVOICE CHECKER						X				X	X				
SENIOR ACCOUNTANT															
SYSTEM MANAGER							X	X	X	X					
COMPUTER OPERATIONS														X	
TECHNICAL SUPPORT					X	X		X	X	X	X	X	X		X
COMMUNICATIONS ENGINEER					X	X									

Table 29   An audit questionnaire

Ref: /   /   Page 1 of 1

AUDIT QUESTIONNAIRE: POST-IMPLEMENTATION REVIEW OF A MATER-
IALS SYSTEM

SCOPE ITEM 1: BUSINESS OBJECTIVES AND FUNCTIONAL
REQUIREMENTS

AUDITEE: HEAD OF TRANSPORT AND SUPPLY

Ref	Question	Answer
1.1	There is a clear written description available, in the system documentation, of the users' business objectives to be satisfied by the system.	There is a statement of the business objectives in the feasibility study.
1.2	There is a clear written statement available, in the system documentation, of the users' functional requirements to be satisfied by the system.	There is a statement of the functional requirements in the feasibility study.
1.3	The functional requirements include a statement of the minimum performance expectations to be satisfied.	The performance requirements for the system have been clearly defined in the feasibility study.
1.4	The business objectives and functional requirements have been approved and accepted by the line management.	There is a memo from the steering committee to the project manager approving and accepting the business objectives and functional requirements.

Table 30   Objectives and scope for a post-implementation review

INTERNAL AUDIT —/—/—

POST-IMPLEMENTATION REVIEW OF A MATERIALS SYSTEM

Objectives and scope

(1)   OBJECTIVES
To ensure:

    (1)   the business objectives originally set by the company to justify the installation of the system have been fully achieved;
    (2)   the system is being managed in accordance with the company policies, objectives, standards, procedures and practices;
    (3)   the system is both effective and efficient.

(2) SCOPE

The audit will review the business and system controls in the following main areas:

(1) Business objectives and functional requirements—a review of the original stated objectives set by the company, for the replacement of the batch processing system, by an on-line real-time interactive system, against the practical achievement of those objectives.

(2) Operational performance—a review of practical operations performance, including both hardware and software performance, to ensure the system is being operated in accordance with the company standards, procedures and practices.

(3) Maintenance—a review of practical operating experience within both the user and DP areas to determine whether system maintenance practices are in accordance with the company standards.

(4) Security—to ensure that the system security procedures and practices are in accordance with the company policies and standards.

(5) Back-up/recovery and fallback—to ensure that the back-up/recovery and fallback procedures and practices are in accordance with the stated user requirements and meet the company objectives and standards.

(6) Interfaces—to ensure there are appropriate procedures and practices for the accurate and timely transfer of data across system boundaries and there are clearly defined responsibilities within both the users and DP areas.

(7) Developments/enhancements—to ensure there are appropriate procedures in both the DP and user areas for handling requests for further developments/ enhancements.

(8) User satisfaction—a review of the practical operating experience of system performance within the user area to evaluate the system effectiveness and efficiency in order to ensure that the system adequately supports the materials business requirements of the company.

4.   BUSINESS OBJECTIVES AND FUNCTIONAL REQUIREMENTS

The business objectives and functional requirements are a statement of what the system is designed to achieve for the users in their functional area. This is extremely important because it immediately establishes a list of the criteria by which the performance characteristics of the system may be evaluated.

The essential control that the auditor would be concerned with is that there is, somewhere, a clear written statement of the business objectives and and functional requirements for the system. The audit programme, for this part of the audit, is shown in **Table 31**. The statement of business objectives and functional requirements may be found in the feasibility study, functional specification, specification report, steering committee or project group minutes. The auditor should review all of these as well as minutes of meetings with the end-users, to establish whether there has been any clear statement by the users of their functional requirements.

In this case, the business objectives and functional requirements were described in the feasibility study and are shown, in **Table 32**, as a typical example of the format and content for this type of information.

The auditors were able to report that they were satisfied that there was a clear written statement of the users' business objectives and functional requirements for the system. Further they were able to declare that, in their opinion, these business objectives and functional requirements had been satisfied by the development and implementation teams.

5. OPERATIONAL PERFORMANCE

The operational performance of the system was reviewed under the following headings:

(1) logon;
(2) response times;
(3) system availability/downtime;
(4) hardware performance;
(5) software performance.

The audit programme, showing the controls that were examined, in each of these areas, is shown in **Table 33**.

The audit conclusion was that the operational performance had been very satisfactory during the six months following the implementation although there had been some initial dissatisfaction with the system.

Logging-on to the system had sometimes been a protracted process but this was traced to too few addresses being available on the local area network (LAN) rather than any characteristics of the system hardware/software. There had, during the course of the audit, been additional dedicated addresses added to the LAN and performance had significantly improved.

System response times, especially at peak periods, had been a cause of some annoyance to the user community. However, this was improved by an increase in main memory capacity and there were other ways in which the technical support group were working to improve this feature of the system.

The system availability had been optimised to suit onshore users and had, generally, been highly satisfactory. The offshore user community had not been treated so favourably and the daily backups were made at a time that was considered by them to be most convenient for working. However, audit

Table 31   Audit programme for a post-implementation review

Ref: /   /   Page 1 of 10

	AUDIT PROGRAMME: POST-IMPLEMENTATION REVIEW OF A MATERIALS SYSTEM
	SCOPE ITEM 1: BUSINESS OBJECTIVES AND FUNCTIONAL REQUIREMENTS

Ref	Control detail
1.1	There is a clear written description, available in the system documentation, of the users' business objectives to be satisfied by the system.
1.2	There is a clear written statement, available in the system documentation, of the users' functional requirements to be satisfied by the system.
1.3	The functional requirements include a statement of the minimum performance expectations to be satisfied.
1.4	The business objectives and functional requirements have been approved and accepted by line management.

Table 32   Statement of business objectives and functional requirements

(1) BUSINESS OBJECTIVE

(1) To replace the existing materials management system with a real-time, on-line interactive system without any reduction in system functionality.
(2) To ensure that the target date for the replacement system is no later than end-19—.
(3) To ensure that the cost of replacement should not exceed, without good reason, a total sum of £Kxxx.
(4) To ensure that the operating costs for the replacement system should be no higher than that of the current system.
(5) To ensure that the replacement system should have an expected lifetime of, at least, eight years before obsolescence.

(2) FUNCTIONAL REQUIREMENTS

(1) Terminal access to user data for:
  —on-line enquiry,
  —on-line data capture/validation,
  —on-line data input/validation/update.
(2) Communications capability to meet the requirements of both local and remote users.
(3) Central and communications software to support on-line activities.
(4) Acceptable communications response times, ie 2–3 secs.
(5) Suitable file structures to meet these requirements.
(6) Hard copy images of screen displayed information.
(7) Minimise paper output.
(8) Capability of hierarchical access to information.
(9) Acceptable security of information.
(10) Maximise the control and access a user has over his data by providing:
  —transaction origination validation criteria.
  —ad hoc report production.
  —flexible report/enquiry formats.
  —user created/formatted enquiries.
  —varied sequence options for reports.
(11) Conventional batch processing/reporting facilities.
(12) An on-line interactive data dictionary.
(13) Possible need to interface text processing and telex services.
(14) Requirement to interface directly with other systems.

---

made several recommendations by which this situation could be improved and these were implemented.

The system downtime, excluding time when the system was unavailable due to the month end batch processing, had been only 28 hours, over a six month period, and only 15 hours had been unscheduled downtime—the majority of which had been due to communications problems. This, the auditors concluded was a satisfactory performance for the processor, and faults reported for peripherals had averaged no more than one per week.

The standard available software, such as the operating system, data base management system (DBMS), had proved highly reliable in the post-implementation period although some faults had been detected in the application system software. These had all been of a relatively minor nature and so the auditors were able to conclude that the basic software design was reliable and soundly based.

Table 33   Audit programme for a post-implementation review

Ref: /   /

AUDIT PROGRAMME: POST-IMPLEMENTATION REVIEW OF
A MATERIALS SYSTEM

SCOPE ITEM 2: OPERATIONAL PERFORMANCE

Ref	Control detail
2.1	There is an acceptable ratio, established from practical experience, of available ports on the processor to registered users.
2.2	There is an acceptable ratio, established from practical experience, of available ports on the local area network (LAN) to registered users.
2.3	The users are not being unduly frustrated in their attempts to log-on to the system.
2.4	There is an automatic cut-off for users who do not make use of the system for a certain time period.
2.5	There are performance statistics available showing response times: —at different times during the working day, —on different days during the working week.
2.6	There is a long term monitoring, by the user/technical support group, of the system response times to ensure no deterioration in performance.
2.7	The system response times that are considered acceptable to all user groups have been appropriately defined.
2.8	The users are satisfied that the system response times are satisfactory at all times of the working day.
2.9	The user/technical support groups have considered, if appropriate, the possibility of improving response times by: —staggering access to the system by type of user, —printing reports during off-peak periods.
2.10	There is a written statement with regard to the users' requirements for system availability.
2.11	There are performance statistics available on system availability/downtime relating to: —daily backups, —batch processing, —other scheduled downtime, —unscheduled downtime.
2.12	There is a regular monitoring of system availability by the user/technical support groups to ensure that the system availability meets users' requirements.

AUDIT PROGRAMME: POST-IMPLEMENTATION REVIEW OF
A MATERIALS SYSTEM

SCOPE ITEM 2: OPERATIONAL PERFORMANCE (cont)

Ref	Control detail
2.13	The daily backups are carried out at a time of minimum inconvenience to the users.
2.14	The system maintenance is carried out at a time of minimum inconvenience to the users.
2.15	There is an established procedure in the user and DP functions by which all faults, both hardware and software, are reported.
2.16	There is a fault report log in which all hardware faults, and the causes thereof, are registered: —tape units, —disc drives, —communications equipment, —printers, —VDUs.
2.17	There is a regular monitoring of the hardware fault report log to determine if any trends can be identified.
2.18	There is a fault report log in which all software faults, and the causes thereof, are registered: —operating system, —application programmes, —data dictionary, —query languages, —report generators.
2.19	There is a regular performance monitoring of the software fault report log to determine if any trends can be identified.

6. MAINTENANCE

The maintenance arrangements with the equipment supplier(s) for the processor and the peripherals were reviewed under four headings, namely;

    (1) current maintenance terms;
    (2) procedures;
    (3) processor servicing;
    (4) peripherals servicing;
    (5) data base maintenance.

The audit programme, showing the controls that the auditors examined, in each of these areas, is given in **Table 34**.

The maintenance terms were set out in a contract between the company and the equipment supplier. The procedures were defined in the operations manual and provided for a six monthly servicing of the processor to be carried out on a sunday in order to minimise inconvenience to the users. There was no provision for regular servicing of the peripherals, ie VDU's, remote spooled printers, etc and these were replaced from a pool of spares and repaired by a visiting site engineer from the supplier.

When the application system software had been delivered the data base maintenance programs had not been fully tested and made available to the data base administration group. Although the auditors were not unduly alarmed at the time of the audit, they were concerned that the absence of proven maintenance software would, eventually, lead to a deterioration of system performance.

The auditors' conclusions on the equipment maintenance were that the support arrangements with the supplier were adequate to ensure a high level of system availability to the users and that there are adequate and well understood procedures for the servicing and support of all the company's data processing equipment.

7. SECURITY

The system security was reviewed under four headings, namely:

    (1) passwords,
    (2) access profiles,
    (3) change procedures,
    (4) security breaches.

The audit programme, showing the controls that the auditors examined in each of these areas, is given in **Table 35**.

The user ID and password is the lock and key by which access to the system is obtained. It is extremely important that passwords should be made as difficult to guess as possible and should be changed frequently. However, these objectives must balanced against user inconvenience. Longer passwords are more difficult to guess but they are also easier to forget. In this case, the auditors were satisfied that the passwords should be no less than six alphanumeric characters.

Table 34   Audit programme for a post-implementation review

AUDIT PROGRAMME: POST-IMPLEMENTATION REVIEW OF A
MATERIALS SYSTEM

SCOPE ITEM 3: MAINTENANCE

Ref	Control detail
3.1	There is a written and signed maintenance agreement with the hardware supplier(s) covering all the company's computing equipment.
3.2	The maintenance procedures are clearly understood and being followed by all staff who are involved in the maintenance of the company's hardware: —system manager; —operations personnel; —user support; —technical support; —users.
3.3	There are procedures in the system operations guide covering the maintenance requirements of all the company's computing equipment.
3.4	The equipment has been serviced in accordance with the terms of the maintenance agreement(s).
3.5	There is a maintenance log recording all servicing which has been carried out on the company's computing equipment indicating the date of service and the type of work carried out.
3.6	The servicing on the processor is scheduled so as to cause the minimum of inconvenience to the users.
3.7	There is a pool of spare peripheral equipment so that items can be replaced and serviced without unnecessary inconvenience to the users.
3.8	There are tested and approved 'housekeeping' programs available for the maintenance of the data base.
3.9	There are procedures for the maintenance of the data base in the system operations manual.
3.10	The data base 'housekeeping' is scheduled so as to cause the minimum of inconvenience to the users.

Table 35   Audit programme for a post-implementation review

AUDIT PROGRAMME: POST-IMPLEMENTATION REVIEW OF A
MATERIALS SYSTEM

SCOPE ITEM 4: SECURITY

Ref	Control detail
4.1	There are user IDs and passwords established for all individual users of the system.
4.2	The passwords must be a minimum of six alphanumeric characters.
4.3	There are instructions for the selection and preservation of passwords detailed in the user guide.
4.4	The passwords are 'forced' changed on a regular basis which is determined as a system parameter by the system manager.
4.5	There is an appointed security officer in the user area.
4.6	There is no hard copy listing being maintained of the user passwords either in the form of a machine listing, if this is possible, or on an application form.
4.7	There is no individual, including the system manager, who is able to view the user passwords.
4.8	There is an established procedure for ensuring that all requests for system access are authorised at the appropriate level and are checked by the security officer.
4.9	The user IDs are linked to the system access facilities that are granted to each individual user and a user is granted no more capabilities than required for his function.
4.10	The user IDs are changed when staff move to other jobs.
4.11	The users are not able to gain access to the operating system but are forced directly into the application system upon logging-on.
4.12	The terminals and printers are preferably maintained in a physically secure place and confidential hard copy output is not produced on publicly accessible devices.
4.13	There should be an automatic screen cut-off if terminals are left unattended for a certain time and the user is required to re-enter a password to continue working.
4.14	The console log is regularly reviewed by the operations personnel to determine if there have been any attempted breaches of system security.

By using a mixture of characters and digits, the total number of possible combinations with six alphanumeric characters is two billion. This is reduced to 300 million by the use of alpha characters only. However, most users restrict the number of possibilities still further because they tend to stick to meaningful names.

The access profiles are extremely important because, apart from their implications for security, they also determine how effectively and efficiently the system is used. They are the facilities that the users are given to create, read, update or delete records from the system. If the user profiles are wider than necessary they enable the users to make use of facilities that were not intended for them and, if they are too narrow, they prevent the users from making optimum use of the system.

The conclusion of the audit team on security was that there were some major security weaknesses which should be attended to at the earliest opportunity. Thus, the users were holding a hard copy listing of all the system IDs and passwords as well as a paper file of all password application forms. These, the auditors recommended, should be destroyed. Further, there were a number of ways by which the system security could be breached by the use of certain proprietary software packages available to some users. It was recommended that there should be a separate investigation into this area because it covered all the company's mini-computers.

8.   BACK-UP/RECOVERY AND FALLBACK

The back-up/recovery and fallback arrangements were reviewed under the following headings:

(1) back-up and recovery
   —hardware,
   —database,
   —software,
   —communications.
(2) fallback.

The audit programme, showing the controls that the auditors examined, in each of these areas, is given in **Table 36**.

Back-up and fallback are terms which are frequently confused with each other and for which some explanation is required. Back-up is the availability of another machine on the same site, and data files and software either available on the same site, or at another site but close to hand, so that the system may be rapidly restored to active use, ie recovered, in the event of a critical failure. Fallback is the availability of an alternative site to which all processing can be transferred in the event of a disaster destroying all on-site processing facilities. The greatest problem here for on-line systems is that such a disaster would probably destroy the communications links by which the fallback facilities would be accessed and thus abnegate the fallback arrangements.

The back-up and recovery strategy for this system depended on three essentials:

Table 36 Audit programme for a post-implementation review
Ref: /   /   Page 6 of 10

AUDIT PROGRAMME: POST-IMPLEMENTATION REVIEW OF A
MATERIALS SYSTEM

SCOPE ITEM 5: BACK-UP/RECOVERY AND FALLBACK

Ref	Control detail
5.1	There is an established and written company policy on backup/recovery and fallback arrangements.
5.2	The backup/recovery and fallback arrangements are described in the operations manual.
5.3	The data files and operating system are backed up on a daily basis at a time of minimum inconvenience to users.
5.4	The application system software is backed up on a weekly basis.
5.5	There is an established tape cycle for both the daily and weekly backups and the tapes are clearly labelled and readily identifiable.
5.6	The current generation of backup tapes are maintained on-site in order to enable a rapid recovery to be made in the event of a system crash.
5.7	The on-site tapes are stored in special fire proof steel cabinets which are protected by a HALON system.
5.8	The other generations of tapes are maintained off-site in order to provide for a recovery in the event of a disaster occurring to the operations room.
5.9	The rotation of on-site and off-site backup tapes is carried out according to an established procedure which is clearly described in the operations guide.
5.10	There is a written contingency plan providing for continuation of operations until fallback arrangements can be put into effect.
5.11	There are suitable backup telecommunications facilities to provide a rapid recovery in the event of a telecommunications failure.
5.12	There are appropriate fallback and contingency plans to continue with the business in the event of a system failure.

(1) spare equipment;
(2) maintenance arrangements with the hardware suppliers;
(3) copies of the data base and software.

The company ran a number of mini-computers which were linked together through the local area network (LAN). One of these machines was used as a development machine and another as a back-up machine. There were, in effect, two non-production machines which could be used as back-up machines. In the event of collapse of the normal production machine for the materials system, the company could switch to either machine although this would, generally, be to the recognised back-up machine. A copy of the materials data base and the operating system and application system software would then be required to recover the application on the back-up machine. To access this machine, the users would then require an alternative address on the LAN to the multiplexors which were connected to the back-up machine.

In addition to the back-up equipment, there was a maintenance agreement with the supplier which provided for a twice yearly servicing on the processors and seven-day/weekly call-out in the event of unscheduled downtime. The customer support engineer from the supplier of the hardware, was expected to be at the customer's premises in no more than four hours from receipt of a call, which would ensure that all but the most unlikely faults would be corrected within one day. This was considered to be within the downtime tolerance of the system but, in the event, the operations staff could have recovered on the back-up machine had this been considered desirable.

The back-up and recovery procedures for the data base were described in the system operations manual and were the same for all processors, in the same series, being operated by the comany—apart from timing. They had recently been reviewed and revised and the auditors were satisfied that they were understood by the operations staff and being duly complied with. These are illustrated, in **Figure 67**, which shows the types of files which are saved.

There was a daily save of the application account which produced a back-up of the data files, the operating system, the directory, the account structure and the system configuration. In addition, there was a weekly dump, on a Friday, which produced a back-up of all the above files as well as the application software. Finally, there was a four weekly dump—five weeks if four weeks coincided with the month end batch processing—of all files on the entire machine which included the standard installed software such as data base management system (DBMS), data dictionary, query language, etc.

There was a weekly cycle of back-up tapes maintained for the daily back-up, each week being clearly distinguished by a separate colour code, namely red, green, yellow and blue and each tape had a unique serial number. The daily back-up required ten tapes in total and each day's back-up was retained in a fire proof storage cabinet—protected by a HALON system—until the whole week's series was complete. Following each back-up, the serial numbers for the tapes, which had been used, were entered in a log with the date and the type of save which had been made.

The weekly back-up, which took place on Friday evening, required 13 tapes in total but was, in principle, no different from that on any other day except requiring rather longer because of the dump of the application software. These Friday tapes formed part of the normal four weekly colour

Figure 67 The system backup procedures

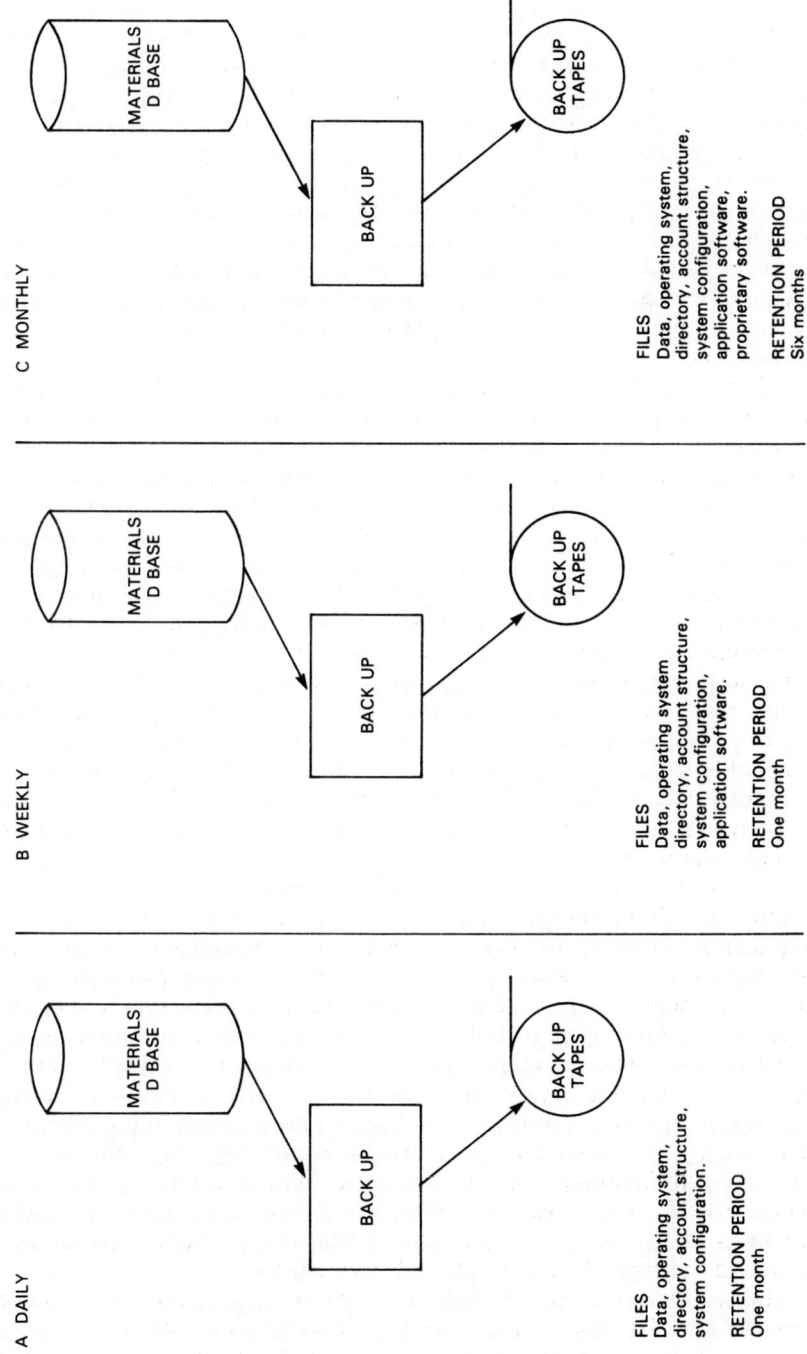

A DAILY

FILES
Data, operating system,
directory, account structure,
system configuration.

RETENTION PERIOD
One month

B WEEKLY

FILES
Data, operating system
directory, account structure,
system configuration,
application software.

RETENTION PERIOD
One month

C MONTHLY

FILES
Data, operating system,
directory, account structure,
system configuration,
application software,
proprietary software.

RETENTION PERIOD
Six months

coded cycle. The monthly back-up was carried out using a separate series of tapes which were retained according to a six monthly cycle.

Each Friday, the storage tapes for the next week's back-up were returned from off-site and on Monday morning the following week, the tapes from the previous week's back-up were sent offsite. Thus, there was a maximum of one whole week, an average of two-and-half days, of back-up saves being held onsite at any one time. This is the degree of risk that the materials business faces in the event of a disaster resulting in the destruction of the onsite backups. This was considered to be an acceptable risk.

The procedures for the recovery of the data base were described in the system operations manual. The re-load procedures were designed to restore initially the operating system, the directory, the account structure and the system configuration from the latest daily system dump that was available. This was followed by a reloading of the application software from the latest weekly dump that was available and the proprietary software from a weekly save that was carried out on a separate machine on which this software was maintained. Finally, the data base was updated from the system log-file and so, in principle, only those user transactions in progress when the system crashed are lost and require re-keying.

The communications links were extremely important to a company working in this type of environment for they not only enabled persons working on offshore installations to both input and retrieve information from data bases maintained onshore, but they also provided the vital contact links with onshore persons through telex and telephone. Data was transmitted and received through the Northern Operations Data Network (NOD-NET) whose central pivot was the shore/offshore link-up by troposcatter with the British Telecom transmitting and receiving station at Scousborough in the Shetland Islands. There was, from there, a land link-up with the company head office at the location A shown in **Figure 64**. Although there were many miles between the end-users offshore and the central database at Location A, so effective were the communications links that the system response times were within seconds and the large distances were completely transparent to the users.

In addition to the provision of back-up circuits, there were also spares of equipment maintained at strategic locations offshore, such as modems and multi-plexors. There were also resident telecom engineers on some of the installations so that repairs could be effected in the shortest possible time.

All data communications with the central administration at Location A were routed via the local area network (Localnet) to which the processor controlling the central data base was attached. The LAN consists of a broadband cable to which a series of devices are connected, eg T-boxes, S-muxes, etc—as shown previously in **Figure 64**—the most important of which is a device called the re-modulator. The broadband cable was strung between the company buildings at Location A and should this become accidentally severed there was a back-up cable already in situ which could be used to re-establish the network. This back-up cable, within the buildings, was laid counter-clockwise to the other cable in order to minimise the risk of an incident severing both cables. The re-modulator was located in the communications centre but there was a back-up located in another building which could be attached to the LAN within a few minutes in the event of a breakdown.

The fallback arrangements provide for the opportunity to restore processing capability following a destruction of the on-site operations centre by fire, flood, explosion, malicious damage, etc. The provision of fallback arrangements inevitably involves a cost which is dependent upon the degree of service that is required. In deciding upon fallback arrangements, an assessment needs to be made of the criticality of the system, the cost of recovery within the period of tolerance and the probability of a disaster occurring.

The company had the opportunity to recover the materials data base on the same type of processor, at another location, which sustained a data base for another system that was considered less critical. However, the likely destruction of the communications links in the event of a disaster would mean that the data base would have to be initially maintained by batch processing. The advantage of on-line, real time processing would be lost.

However, in this particular case it was considered possible to continue with the business operation without the computing system although there would be a considerable inconvenience factor in so doing. The users would, however, need to have a detailed contingency plan that was workable, and understood, by the parties who would be required to implement it.

The audit team's overall conclusions on the back-up and recovery and fallback arrangements—hardware, software, data base and communications—were that they are adequate to provide suitable protection for the most efficient and effective use of the system. They form part of the standard company practices and procedures and are detailed in the various operations manuals.

9.   INTERFACES

The four interfaces between the materials system and other systems, which have been mentioned in **1.**, above, were:

(1) a maintenance information system;
(2) a common materials standards system;
(3) an accounts payable system;
(4) a general ledger system.

The audit programme, showing the controls that the auditors examined, for each of these interfaces, is given in **Table 37**.

The auditors, in addition, constructed a controls flowchart for each of the system interfaces in order to identify the specific processing controls that were being used for each of the interfaces. The control flowchart that was constructed in order to identify the interface controls for the maintenance information system links is shown in **Figure 68**.

The conclusions of the audit team were that there were adequate controls for all of the four system interfaces. The processing arrangements for the interfaces, especially the finance link, were reviewed in detail and the auditors were satisfied that the operational procedures were adequately documented in the operations procedures manual(s)/user guide(s) and that they were well understood and being complied with.

Further, the controls on the transfer of data between systems had been

Table 37   Audit programme for a post-implementation review

AUDIT PROGRAMME: POST-IMPLEMENTATION REVIEW OF A MATERIALS SYSTEM

SCOPE ITEM 6: INTERFACES

Ref	Control detail
6.1	There is a description of the functional requirements for each system interface in the functional specification.
6.2	There is a construction guide/data structure guide available for each system interface.
6.3	There is a description of the computer operations procedures, for each system interface, in the respective system operations manuals.
6.4	There is a description of the user operations procedures for each system interface in the user guides or user procedures manuals.
6.5	The data transfers are all appropriately scheduled so that anticipation checks can be used.
6.6	The data transfers are all appropriately scheduled so that staff are not being retained on-duty unnecessarily—especially at weekends.
6.7	The transfer tapes are all labelled with tape volume number, date of preparation and header and trailer records.
6.8	There are standards lists produced after all tape production runs showing number of records processed, number of records rejected and number of records transferred.
6.9	There are control reports produced to ensure the accuracy and completeness of the data transfer between systems.
6.10	The control reports are all appropriately numbered, dated and headed so that they can be readily identified.
6.11	Production jobs which depend upon the transfer of data between systems are not being run until the operations personnel—or users—are satisfied with the reconciliation reports.
6.12	There are sound procedures to ensure that there is adequate security on the transfer of data between system interfaces.
6.13	The data transfers are not tying-up the company data communications link for excessive periods of time.
6.14	The data transfers over the company communications links are not being carried out at times of high system activity.

Figure 68   A controls flowchart

System:	Scope No.:
A MATERIALS SYSTEM	6

	Prepared Date :
Function(s):	--/--/19--
THE MATERIALS/MAINTENANCE INFORMATION SYSTEM LINKS	Reviewed Date :
	--/--/19--

NARRATIVE	OPERATION	CONTROLS

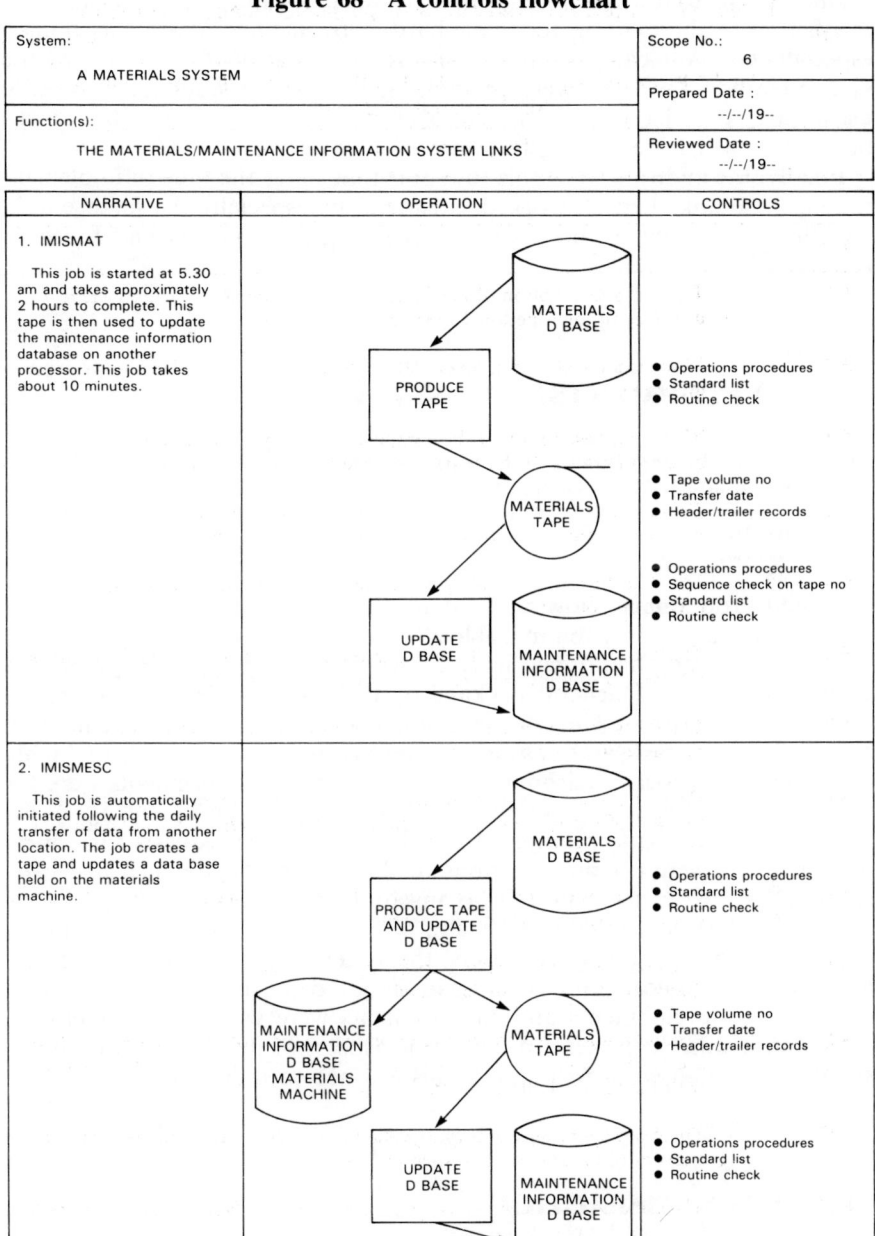

1. IMISMAT

This job is started at 5.30 am and takes approximately 2 hours to complete. This tape is then used to update the maintenance information database on another processor. This job takes about 10 minutes.

MATERIALS D BASE

PRODUCE TAPE

- Operations procedures
- Standard list
- Routine check

MATERIALS TAPE

- Tape volume no
- Transfer date
- Header/trailer records

UPDATE D BASE

MAINTENANCE INFORMATION D BASE

- Operations procedures
- Sequence check on tape no
- Standard list
- Routine check

2. IMISMESC

This job is automatically initiated following the daily transfer of data from another location. The job creates a tape and updates a data base held on the materials machine.

MATERIALS D BASE

PRODUCE TAPE AND UPDATE D BASE

- Operations procedures
- Standard list
- Routine check

MAINTENANCE INFORMATION D BASE MATERIALS MACHINE

MATERIALS TAPE

- Tape volume no
- Transfer date
- Header/trailer records

UPDATE D BASE

MAINTENANCE INFORMATION D BASE

- Operations procedures
- Standard list
- Routine check

examined—with the aid of controls flowcharts—and the auditors were satisfied that there were adequate hard copy listings at critical points, especially communications links, to ensure the integrity of data crossing the system boundaries. There were, in addition, adequate in-built controls being used, such as header and trailer records on files and sequence number checks on the files which were being transferred.

Finally, the auditors were able to report that, since the time of implementation, these links had all worked satisfactorily, especially the finance link, and there had been no occasions when the control reports had failed to reconcile.

10.   DEVELOPMENTS/ENHANCEMENTS

The review of procedures for handling requests for developments/ enhancements was made under two headings:

(1) local,
(2) central.

The audit programme, showing the controls that the auditors examined, in each of these areas, is given in **Table 38**.

We have already mentioned in **1.**, above, that this particular system had been developed as a general package by the principal central purchasing office of the company. The package, supplied centrally, had been enhanced by locally developed 'add-ons' which were considered essential, or highly desirable, to the local environment. Thus, the local enhancements were for modifications to the local 'add-ons' to the centrally developed package or for additional locally written reports from the system. The requests for central developments were for modifications to the core package which had been supplied by the central materials organisation of the company.

The conclusion of the audit team, was that the procedural channels established between the system users, the system support group in the user area and the technical support group in the DP department for dealing with requests for developments and enhancements were working satisfactorily. However, it was recommended that some aspects of the current procedures should be formalised in writing and this was accepted and implemented.

11.   USER SATISFACTION

The user satisfaction with the system was reviewed under the following headings, namely:

(1) User friendliness:
  —ease of use;
  —system generated documentation;
  —new facilities.
(2) Training.

Table 38 Audit programme for a post-implementation review

AUDIT PROGRAMME: POST-IMPLEMENTATION REVIEW OF A
MATERIALS SYSTEM

SCOPE ITEM 7: DEVELOPMENTS/ENHANCEMENTS

Ref	Control detail
7.1	There are written procedures in both the user and DP areas for dealing with user requests for further developments or enhancements to the system.
7.2	The users are aware of the procedural channels that must be followed to record requests for developments/enhancements to the system.
7.3	There is a user support group with whom considered developments/enhancements can be discussed before the formal request procedure is initiated.
7.4	There are standard request forms provided on which users may state their requirements for further developments or enhancements to the system.
7.5	There is a procedure for prioritising user requests.
7.6	The users are informed of the anticipated cost, and likely date, for the implementation of their requests.
7.7	There is an established procedural channel for transmitting requests, for developments/enhancements to the centrally supplied core package, to the central purchasing office.
7.8	There is an active audit involvement in new developments/enhancements to ensure there is an adequate framework of control.

    (3) Documentation:
        —functional specification;
        —user guide;
        —procedures manual;
        —operations manual.
    (4) Output reports.
    (5) User requests (enhancements).
    (6) Equipment requirements.
    (7) System support.
    (8) Statistics requirements.

The audit programme, showing the controls that the auditors examined in each of these areas, is given in **Table 39**.

    The auditors were able to report that there was, generally, a high level of user satisfaction with the system notwithstanding some initial problem areas such as log on/response times/system availability/training. There had been improvements in all these areas which were clearly noticeable to the users. The users had been impressed with the 'friendliness' of the system and, in particular, with the system-generated documentation such as purchase orders and materials receipt sheets which had successfully reduced administrative effort and the associated cost. Further, the users were entirely satisfied with the quality and timeliness of hard copy reports from the system—both from the laser printer and from the remote spooled printers.

    There was a number of areas where the users had made requests for additional features to make the system more effective and efficient in their work. These were currently receiving attention by the support group in the user area and the technical support group in the DP department. The users, in some areas, also made requests for additional equipment, essentially VDUs, which were initially frustrated because of a shortage of available ports on the LAN. However, these requests were fulfilled after additional dedicated addresses were added.

    There was, even a considerable period after implementation, some confusion amongst the users on how to obtain assistance in the event of system failure/downtime. However, audit were able to report that this had now been resolved and the user support group were actively educating the system users in the correct channels to follow.

12. REPORTING

The final audit reporting of the PIR on the system was made to the internal audit committee, using the format shown previously in chapter 9, **8.**, above. This style of audit reporting is illustrated below.

FROM : Auditor   TEL:

TO : Messrs Lyon,   DATE:
       Foxe,
       etc.

INTERNAL AUDIT —/—/—

POST-IMPLEMENTATION REVIEW OF A MATERIALS SYSTEM

PART I

MANAGEMENT SUMMARY

Our conclusions on the objectives for this audit are that we were:

(1) satisfied that the business objectives and functional requirements, as described in the feasibility study, have been essentially achieved by the new materials system;
(2) generally satisfied that the system is being managed in accordance with the company policies, standards, procedures and practices, although we feel that some improvements can be made in system security and have made certain recommendations to this effect;
(3) also satisfied that the system is generally effective and efficient, although we have made a number of recommendations where we feel improvements can be made.

Our recommendations are reported in detail in Part III of this report, but a brief summary of some more significant items is given below:

(1) Response times—response times have degraded somewhat since implementation and this should be attended to by an upgrade in the processor.
(2) Password change procedure—there is no forced password change procedure so extra vigilance should be exercised by the security controller to ensure that all personnel movements are noted and the consequences considered for system access requirements.
(3) Security breaches—we have noted a number of ways in which system security may be breached and a study has now been planned to investigate this area.
(4) Data base maintenance—there are no established data base maintenance procedures in force at the present time, and, while there is no immediate cause for concern, this should be kept under scrutiny.
(5) Fallback—there are no formal fallback arrangements providing for the recovery of computer operations in the event of a disaster and the users should produce a contingency plan based upon manual operation.

PART II

BACKGROUND, OBJECTIVES AND SCOPE

(1) Background

The business processes which ensure that the correct materials are purchased and ultimately delivered to the locations, either directly or indirectly (stock items) occur in the transport and supply department. This department is dispersed geographically, both on and off-shore, to ensure that the business processes are carried out with the optimum efficiency.

The T and S department operates the materials computing system. This has an on-line data entry, updating and enquiry capability, combined with batch processing, which together support the following functions:

(1) requisition administration;

Table 39   Audit programme for a post-implementation review

AUDIT PROGRAMME: POST-IMPLEMENTATION REVIEW OF A
MATERIALS SYSTEM

SCOPE ITEM 8: USER SATISFACTION

Ref	Control detail
8.1	The users find the VDUs are easy to work with and the special function keys provide no difficulties.
8.2	The screen menus are easy to understand and the users are guided step-by-step to the input/retrieval menus they require.
8.3	There is an expert mode capability available so users can directly access the screen menus they require.
8.4	The cursor moves automatically between the input fields so as to minimise the amount of input keying that is required.
8.5	The system generated documents are clear to read and easy to produce.
8.6	The required number of copies of the documents are automatically printed at the requested location.
8.7	There is an adequate explanation provided to users of all new system features which are introduced.
8.8	The introduction of new features is always preceded by an update to the user guide.
8.9	There is a continuing programme of training so that new users are taught how to use the system and previous users updated when new facilities are added.
8.10	The training courses are essentially job-oriented rather than general purpose in nature.
8.11	There is a training manual, in looseleaf form, which can be easily updated when new features are added.
8.12	There is a functional specification, in looseleaf form, which is clearly written in user understandable language and which can be easily updated when changes are made.
8.13	There is an easy-to-read user guide(s), in looseleaf form, which is customised to the requirements of different user groups and the users aware of its existence.
8.14	There is a procedures manual, in looseleaf form, available in all main user areas and the users are aware of its existence.

Table 39 **Audit programme for a post-implementation review**—*continued*
Ref: /   /

AUDIT PROGRAMME: POST-IMPLEMENTATION REVIEW OF A
MATERIALS SYSTEM

SCOPE ITEM 8: USER SATISFACTION

Ref	Control detail
8.15	There is an up-to-date system operations manual available to the computer operations personnel and they understand and are following its instructions.
8.16	The hard copy output from both laser printer and remote spooled printers is dated, has a report identifier and contains appropriate header information.
8.17	The hard copy output is clear to read and quickly produced.
8.18	There are established procedures for the collection of hard copy output, produced on the laser printer in the operations room, from the input/output control section.
9.19	There have been no occurrences of missing reports or pages from reports.
8.20	The users are aware of, and understand, the procedures for dealing with requests for developments/enhancements.
8.21	The users are satisfied that these procedures are functioning effectively and their requests are being timely processed.
8.22	The users are satisfied with the established method of allocating priorities to requests.
8.23	There is an appropriate log being maintained of all requests for developments/enhancements with status information on each request.
8.24	There is an established procedure for dealing with requirements for new/replacement equipment, eg VDUs, printers, etc.
8.25	The users are aware of the established procedure and are satisfied that it is working effectively.
8.26	There is an established support group in the user area to provide immediate assistance on any problems relating to the application software.
8.27	There is an established support group in the DP department for handling problems relating to malfunctioning and processor/communications failures.
8.28	There is a clearly established procedure for dealing with user requests for assistance.

Internal Audit No 86/09/C11
Part III—Findings and recommendations

Item	Findings	Significance	Recommendations	Auditee response
2.	*Operational performance*			
2.1	*Logon* Users of the system generally stay logged on to the system for as long as possible, by the use of the 'Secure Screen' facility, even when they are not intending to use the system for a considerable time period.	The number of ports available for other users is reduced thereby increasing log-on time.	Users who do not anticipate making use of the system for substantial periods should be encouraged to log-off in order to free ports for other potential users. If there were sufficient discipline shown by all users, then we are confident that overall accessibility could be improved. If the above recommendation cannot be effectively implemented, then some form of forced log-off should be considered from the processor if the terminal remains idle for more than a certain period of time.	*DP department* For some programs there is a forced transfer to the 'secure screen' option after 10 minutes. There is an automatic log-off from the 'secure screen' after approximately 30 minutes. We intend to shorten the automatic log-off to 15 minutes.

Item	Findings	Significance	Recommendations	Auditee response
	Users sometimes become impatient with the log-on delay (up to 8 seconds) whilst the Local Area Network (LAN) is being scanned for free addresses, and press carriage return again.	Scanning will abort and return to the first address displaying the message 'NO SESSIONS AVAILABLE ON LOCAL PORT'.	Users should be informed to wait at least 8 seconds after typing the call-up code (C590) to determine whether they have successfully established a call. In no circumstances shold they press carriage return again.	*Materials department* We have already distributed a circular to the users explaining how to make the most effective use of the LAN.
	The appearance of the message 'UNABLE TO OPEN SESSION - NO RESPONSE FROM UNIT' indicates that there has been an address failure on the LAN, and logging-on may prove impossible unless an alternative address can be called by the user.	Log-on aborts at the failed address.	If after, or during, this period, the terminal responds with the message that all ports are occupied, they should be told to type a different call-up code such as C5AO or C5CO.	*Materials department* Users have now been given alternative numbers to call.

(2) purchasing;
(3) warehouse management;
(4) finance;
(5) standards administration.

The materials system is designed to control and provide for the optimum availability of bought-in materials, both in stock and on-order, to sustain the engineering and support activities required by the company.

(2)   Objectives and scope

   (2.1)   Objectives

To ensure:

   (1) the business objectives originally set by the company to justify the installation of the system, and the functional requirements from the system, have been fully achieved:
   (2) the system is being managed in accordance with the company policies, objectives, standards, procedures and practices;
   (3) the system is both effective and efficient.

   (2.2)   Scope

The audit will review the business and system controls in the following areas:

   (1) business objectives and functional requirements;
   (2) operational performance;
   (3) maintenance;
   (4) security;
   (5) back-up/recovery and fallback;
   (6) interfaces;
   (7) developments/enhancements;
   (8) user satisfaction.

PART III

FINDINGS AND RECOMMENDATIONS

The findings and recommendations are presented in the attached table (pp 296–297).
N.B.   This represents only a small part of the final report in order to illustrate the format for presentation.

References

1   Held G, Sarah R *Data Communications: A Comprehensive Approach* (1983) McGraw-Hill Publications Company.

Index